Occupational
Ethics Series

Norman Bowie   Business Ethics
Peter A. French   Ethics in Government
Tom L. Beauchamp & Laurence B. McCullough   Medical Ethics

Elizabeth Beardsley and John Atwell,
Series Editors

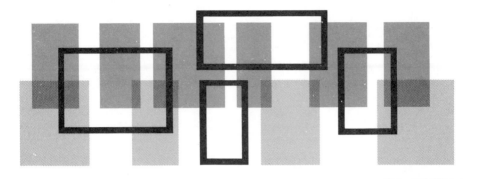

Ethics in the Practice of Psychology

MARY ANN CARROLL
HENRY G. SCHNEIDER
GEORGE R. WESLEY

Appalachian State University

PRENTICE-HALL, INC., Englewood Cliffs, New Jersey 07632

Library of Congress Cataloging in Publication Data

CARROLL, MARY ANN
  Ethics in the practice of psychology.

  Bibliography: p.
  Includes index.
  1. Psychology—Practice—Moral and ethical aspects.
  2. Psychology—Practice—Moral and ethical aspects—Case
  studies. I. Schneider, Henry G. II. Wesley, George
  Randolph,   . III. Title.
  BF75.C37 1985   174'.2   84-6983
  ISBN 0-13-290610-4

Editorial/production supervision:
  Cyndy Lyle Rymer
Manufacturing buyer: Harry P. Baisley

Printed in the United States of America

10 9 8 7 6 5 4 3 2 1

ISBN 0-13-290610-4 {PBK.}

PRENTICE-HALL INTERNATIONAL, INC., *London*
PRENTICE-HALL OF AUSTRALIA PTY. LIMITED, *Sydney*
EDITORA PRENTICE-HALL DO BRASIL, LTDA., *Rio de Janeiro*
PRENTICE-HALL CANADA INC., *Toronto*
PRENTICE-HALL OF INDIA PRIVATE LIMITED, *New Delhi*
PRENTICE-HALL OF JAPAN, INC., *Tokyo*
PRENTICE-HALL OF SOUTHEAST ASIA PTE. LTD., *Singapore*
WHITEHALL BOOKS LIMITED, Wellington, New Zealand

For Charlie, and in memory of Frank
M.A.C.

In memory of my father
H.G.S.

To those of my colleagues who have supported my writing
G.R.W.

Contents

Prentice-Hall Series in
Occupational Ethics

An increasing number of philosophers are coming to appreciate the value of making our discipline constructively available to those whose lives are chiefly focused on some form of practical activity. It is natural that philosophers specializing in ethics should be in the forefront of this movement toward "applied philosophy." In both writing and teaching many leading ethical theorists are currently dealing with concrete issues in individual and social life.

While this change has been taking place within the philosophic community, practitioners in various fields have (for several complex reasons) turned their attention to the ethical dimensions of their own activities. Whether they work in areas traditionally called "professions" or in other occupations, they wish to consider their job-related decisions in relation to ethical principles and social goals. They rightly recognize that many, if not most, ethical problems facing all of us arise in our occupational lives: we are often expected to conduct ourselves "at work" in ways which appear to conflict with the ethical principles believed valid in other social relationships; in our occupations themselves certain normally accepted practices sometimes seem to contradict each other; in short, ethical dilemmas of enormous proportion face the morally conscientious person. Whether philosophical ethics can help resolve these acute problems is an inescapable question.

A third recent development is the growing tendency of students to think of themselves as persons who do or will have certain occupational roles. This tendency is noticeable at several stages of life—in choosing an occupation, in preparing for one already chosen, and in pursuing one that has been entered some time ago.

The convergence of these three contemporary developments has created a need for appropriate teaching materials. The *Occupational Ethics* Series is designed to meet this need. Each volume has been written by a philosopher, with the advice or collaboration of a practitioner in a particular occupation. The volumes are suitable for liberal arts courses in ethics and for programs of preprofessional study, as well as for the general reader who seeks a better understanding of a world that most human beings inhabit, the world of work.

John E. Atwell and Elizabeth L. Beardsley, Editors

Preface

The interaction between psychology and philosophy has strong historical precedents. In recent years the focus of this interaction has been on ethics. Psychologists are concerned with ethical issues in all areas of professional practice, and philosophers have become more involved in applied ethics. Both professions have been changing rapidly over the past few years because of the recent recognition on the part of psychologists of the relevance of ethics to most aspects of professional practice. Many philosophers believe that they should put their skills to practical use and can assist psychologists and other professionals in dealing systematically with ethical problems that arise in their practice.

When philosophers interact with other professionals in the area of ethics, the latter will need a theoretical basis for discussing the ethical issues, while philosophers will need to know specifics about the practice of the profession. The purpose of this book is to encourage this dialogue between psychologists and philosophers. It considers both theory and application and includes examples within the text to illustrate ethical theories and principles and their practical applications. Throughout the book case studies are presented to illustrate problems being discussed in the particular chapter. Some of the ethical issues are obvious, some quite subtle. The issues are not spelled out in order to encourage readers to think them through and to provide a basis for discussion.

Technical language from both disciplines has been avoided so that the book can be read by both philosophers and psychologists, as well as anyone who simply has an interest in the topic. The book is not directed just to philosophers and psychologists but also to such groups as consumers of psychological services, ministers, psychiatrists, researchers in the social sciences, professionals in personnel work, and practitioners in special education. It is also increasingly clear to graduate psychology faculty that graduate students need training in ethics.

This book is not a cookbook for solving ethical problems in the practice of psychology, and we have not attempted to provide solutions to all the problems we raise. We do, however, point out relevant aspects of the problems that require consideration; ethical problems are solved in terms of specifics rather than generalities.

Because legal issues sometimes overlap or conflict with moral issues, we have integrated some discussion of relevant legal considerations and court cases.

We often make reference to the *Ethical Principles of Psychologists* (APA, 1981), which are included in the Appendix so that the reader has ready access to them. In referring to the *Ethical Principles*, we cite only the principle number and some part of the principle. Wherever there is the reference "Principle X," it is to be assumed that it refers to the *Ethical Principles of Psychologists* and can be found in the Appendix.

A table of random numbers was used to generate male and female references in particular examples to avoid sexism and sexist language. In making a general point we have simply used "he or she" or a plural pronoun.

We owe our gratitude to John Atwell, Elizabeth Beardsley, Monroe Beardsley, Allen Dyer, Jim Long, Michael Perlin, Kathleen C. Robinson, Ray Ruble, Frans van der Bogert, and to all the other people who gave us input and support.

M.A.C.

H.G.S.

G.R.W.

Chapter 1

Ethical Problems
and Ethical Theories

Psychologists, like anyone in a profession or occupation, often must deal with ethical problems in the course of their work. Those in the profession may engage in more than one activity—some may do research as well as teach. Others may confine themselves to one activity such as therapy or research. But when discussing the profession as a whole, it is necessary to examine the various activities in which psychologists may engage. Because of the diversity of activities, there will also be a diversity of ethical issues in the field.

Any ethical decision will be based, explicitly or implicitly, on some ethical theory that justifies the decision. We will examine three common ethical theories upon which ethical decisions are based. Since different ethical theories can dictate incompatible decisions, it is important for psychologists to be aware of which theory they endorse and which theory takes precedence when there is a conflict. For example, one cannot maintain that recommended judgments be consistent with society's standards and then go on to affirm an individual's right to choose a particular life style even though it conflicts with accepted norms. This is precisely the kind of problem that psychologists often face in therapy, the problem of the client's autonomy versus society's standards. Unless psychologists are aware of which ethical model they use to resolve conflicts, not only will it be difficult to make consistent decisions but it also will be difficult to provide rational justification.

Before we discuss the theoretical justifications for moral decision making, we first need to distinguish between ethical and other types of problems. *Ethical* questions can be distinguished from questions of *etiquette* and from *practical* problems. Ethics generally involves behavior of individuals that positively or negatively affects other human beings and, in some instances, animals. (We will avoid the question of whether ethical questions arise in cases of behavior which affect only one's self.) Although technically "ethics" refers to the study of what counts as moral behavior and "morality" refers to the practice of ethics, we shall use the terms "ethical" and "moral" interchangeably.

A code of etiquette, unlike a code of ethics, evaluates behavior in terms of being mannerly or polite. If a professional does not abide by the code of professional etiquette in his or her field, we say that person is acting unprofessionally. While we also say this of a professional who acts unethically, merely to say that a person has acted unprofessionally does not necessarily imply un-

1

ethical conduct. While all professions have normative codes or standards, not all professional standards are ethical standards. For example, professional standards may prescribe a particular way of dressing when engaged in certain professional activities. There would be nothing unethical *per se* about a psychologist's wearing dirty blue jeans and appearing unkempt when she has a conference with a child's parents, but such appearance is usually considered inappropriate and unprofessional. To cite another example, it is considered unprofessional to try to convince a person already in therapy with another to begin therapy under oneself. This is not unethical *per se* and would be morally correct if it were in the client's best interest to do so. But it is considered a violation of professional standards regarding one's relationship with colleagues. Etiquette involves adhering to certain socially accepted norms, and professional etiquette concerns the socially accepted behaviors and customs as defined by the profession. But as we shall discuss later in this chapter, behavior in accordance with such norms is not always behavior that is subject to moral evaluation. Hence ethical questions are not to be confused with questions of etiquette.

Ethical problems should not be confused with mere practical problems either. Practical problems are those where one simply has to find the means to achieve some practical end. The consideration is primarily technical and will involve selecting the most efficient means. There is no evaluation of goals, nor may any evaluation be necessary. Moral problems, on the other hand, involve an evaluation of the ends themselves as well as the means to achieve the end (though evaluation of the means is not merely a matter of efficiency). For example, a psychologist may have to find ways to ensure that adequate services are provided for a child he evaluated, a problem of a practical nature. The child's primary problem is emotional disturbance, yet he also has serious learning problems. Deciding on the appropriate diagnostic label can have practical implications, such as which diagnostic label will result in more effective treatment for the child. But if diagnosis determines service availability, then additional problems arise. It would seem that the psychologist must present a completely objective diagnosis (which may harm or fail to help the child through lack of services). But biasing the diagnosis based on availability or quality of services may be required by the duty of beneficence, which we shall discuss later in this chapter. In this case the psychologist must evaluate the ends of his action; that is, what ought to be the aim of the psychologist. The means to achieve the end, to help the child, also must be evaluated but it can be seen that this is not just a technical matter or merely a matter of efficiency, for one must ask not just whether the means to achieve the end are efficient but whether they are morally acceptable according to some standard.

Issues that are moral arise when a person's welfare can be affected by another. This is not to say that all moral issues are moral *problems*; a moral issue becomes a problematic one when there is a real question about what ought to be done. This of course implies that there is a choice to be made. If there is no choice to be made, there is no problem to solve, since what one *ought* to do depends in part on what one *can* do. For example, since psychologists are typically not physicians, they will not have to make a decision to use drug therapy on a client since that is not a possible course of action. However, this is not to say that because there is no choice, there are no difficult problems. A psychologist may see that a hyperactive child needs drug therapy and thus faces the problem of finding a way for the child to get the needed treatment. But the psychologist does not have the choice of whether or not to prescribe a drug and in that sense does not have *that* problem to solve.

Because psychologists' activities directly involve the well-being of others, moral issues abound in the profession. There are rules governing psychologists' behavior which the American Psychological Association (APA) has attempted to explicate in the *Ethical Principles of Psychologists* (1981). These principles deal with psychologists' activities as they affect others and hence focus on moral issues. Exceptions to the rules raise moral problems.

While the *Ethical Principles* clearly focus on important moral issues, they fail to provide all the answers. The *Principles* are intentionally general (to cover broad topics) but this means that they are subject to interpretation. Parts of the *Principles* reflect or suggest the ethical theories that we will discuss, but they do not give a cookbook answer to what should be done in a given situation. As with all sets of rules, they are never completely comprehensive, so the exceptions also raise moral problems. The *Ethical Principles* are designed for all types of psychologists and there are more specific guidelines available for most of the practicing specialties. These specialty guidelines deal with standards of practice likely to be encountered in practicing within a given specialty.

A couple of obvious moral issues are those involving consent and confidentiality, since the client's or subject's welfare can be affected by the psychologist. Consent concerns an acknowledgement of autonomy; confidentiality has to do with trust. However, a moral problem arises in these areas, not over whether to maintain confidentiality, but rather over whether in some cases consent is not necessary or whether a confidence may be justifiably broken. Such problems are obviously moral problems because these actions are contrary to some general moral rule of the profession.

Ethical problems can arise when a person's values conflict. However, not all values are subject to moral evaluation. Some values are mere preferences. For example, a psychology teacher in an introductory psychology course may value teaching the history of psychology and physiological psychology along with other general topics, but time may not permit a detailed discussion of both if the other areas of psychology are to be covered. So a choice must be made. This is a conflict of values which may reduce merely to a conflict of preferences. This particular conflict of values does not raise an ethical problem but merely a practical problem, an evaluation of the best means to accomplish the objective of this particular course. There are, however, conflicts of values where ethical problems do arise. This can be seen in the fact that psychologists value honesty but also value increasing knowledge of human behavior. These values will conflict when a research experiment requires deceiving a subject. This raises an ethical question because the conflict of values involves a conflict of obligations—on the one hand, the obligation to be honest and, on the other, the obligation to increase knowledge of human behavior.

Some moral problems are subtle and may easily be overlooked because they may simply appear to be questions of technique. The question of whether a psychologist should label a client in writing a report or give advice in therapy are good examples. Labeling a client may enable him or her to get special services but a certain label also may have harmful long-term consequences for the client. Giving advice in therapy may be of immediate benefit to the client but doing so may not promote client autonomy in the long run. In both cases, there is a conflict of obligations—to provide immediate help to the client but also to be concerned with the long-term welfare of the client. In each case the psychologist has, and must make, a choice.

We are now in a position to see what are some common bases for the moral choices that psychologists must make. The ethical theories we have chosen to present are ones that commonly enter into discussions of moral problems and ones to which most people appeal, depending on the situation. These theories are: (1) ethical relativism, the view that right and wrong actions are determined either by what is approved of by society or by the individual; (2) utilitarianism, which is based on the ethical principle that one ought to do that act which promotes the greatest happiness for the most people; and (3) a theory derived from Kant's moral philosophy which requires that one's moral decision be universalizable and that one must always treat persons with respect and dignity, as individuals of intrinsic worth who must never be used as objects to be manipulated. All three theories are reflected in the *Ethical Principles*.

Our discussion of these three theories will be brief and will highlight some of the objections commonly raised against them.

ETHICAL RELATIVISM

Because of the wide diversity of moral beliefs it may be thought that there are no absolute moral principles. Since people disagree on what is moral or ethically correct, it is argued that either society or the individual must be the ultimate judge of which acts are right and wrong. This suggests that we can have an empirical criterion for the correctness of a moral decision simply by determining what is approved of by most people in the society (cultural or social relativism) or by consulting one's own feelings on the matter (personal or individual relativism).

Cultural Relativism

Human beings in a given society share a body of customs and beliefs, and this is necessary if they are to live together peacefully. These customs and beliefs regulate the behavior of the members of the society and determine which actions are acceptable and which are not. Socially unacceptable behavior is condemned as wrong; socially acceptable behavior is said to be right, or at least not wrong. Thus the rightness and wrongness of behavior is determined by the society or culture in which a person lives. Since customs and beliefs vary from culture to culture, so will the standards of right and wrong. Cross-cultural research has documented many examples of variations in expected behavior.

There are many problems with this ethical model. It tends to confuse *moral* standards of behavior with the *mores* of the culture, but not all customs or mores are a matter of morality. For example, personal advertising by psychologists is unacceptable according to professional standards, but that is not a moral matter unless a psychologist were to make unrealistic claims, such as "mental health guaranteed in one session." This example involves matters of professional etiquette rather than professional ethics. Not all behavior is subject to moral evaluation but only behavior which may have an effect on another individual. Thus moral questions do not necessarily arise in all cases that concern customary or habitual behavior.

To make no distinction between morality and mores obscures the possibility that all people may in fact share common moral beliefs which are expressed in various ways. For example, it is a custom among Eskimos for a husband to offer his wife as a sex partner to a male visitor. While some Americans engage in similar exchanges, most Americans would condemn this practice as immoral. But the reason for the custom is no doubt based on the moral principle to be considerate of others. Apparently Eskimos believe that this kind of behavior makes the guest feel at home and best demonstrates the considerateness of the host and hostess. Objections to this practice are not a disagreement over the moral principle to be considerate of others but rather a disagreement over how to express this consideration. Disagreements over moral questions may be reduced to disagreement about which behavior best exemplifies acting in accord with a moral principle. Here we have a factual disagreement rather than a disagreement over a basic moral principle.

The cultural relativist position dictates that one must behave in a manner consistent with what is approved of by one's culture. But what needs to be specified is how to define or identify an individual's culture. A given individual shares many social reference groups, each of which possesses the potential for being defined as a cultural group (Stace, 1937). There are cultures within cultures whose standards for socially acceptable behavior diverge. For example, a prisoner might compare her behavior to other prisoners' values or to society's values. What is in accordance with one set of values may be at odds with others. A dyssocial individual (e.g., a drug addict) who is typical of his subculture would not be normal compared to the predominant culture. Conflicting actions could be endorsed depending on which culture or subculture is used as the reference group. This problem obviously has unhappy consequences for this ethical theory, since almost any action could be viewed as moral so long as some reference group (no matter how deviant) approves.

Another variant of this problem is whether when in Rome one should do as the Romans do or whether one should abide by one's own cultural standards. This is a problem when cultures differ dramatically in expectations. To do the former is to be guilty of acting immorally by one's own culture's standards; to do the latter is to be guilty of acting immorally by Roman standards. There can be no appeal to any further principle to decide which culture is right for that presupposes an independent criterion of "right" which the relativist cannot endorse. Consequently, it would appear that one and the same act may be both right and wrong at the same time or even in the same place, depending on which standards of which culture one employs. (It should be pointed out, that though on the surface an act may appear to be the same in two cultures but judged differently, there may be factors about the two cultures, e.g. differences in beliefs, that would prohibit one from saying that the act was the same. For example, the people of one culture may describe a particular act of killing as murder because they believe it to be the unjustified killing of an innocent person, whereas a killing under the same circumstances in another culture would not be described as murder because the people of that culture believe the killing is justified. They might, for instance, believe they are avenging the death of one of their members. And even though the person they killed for revenge was not responsible for their member's death, they may believe that they have a duty to kill another to restore some sort of balance. What this points to is that people of different cultures may differ in their moral beliefs because they have different factual beliefs, as we indicated earlier. This would provide grounds for denying that the act was the same in both cultures.)

We said earlier that the relativist position suggests that there is an empirical criterion for determining whether an act is right or wrong. The criterion in this case is based solely on social approval or disapproval. It then follows that ethical matters are reducible to empirical matters regarding people's preferences about which there can be knowledge. But is it knowledge of the moral rightness or wrongness of behavior or is it rather knowledge of what types of behavior are socially acceptable or unacceptable? It cannot be knowledge of the former since what is true cannot be qualified or modified on a cultural basis. What is true is not culturally relative, only what people consider to be true.

At this point a relativist may interject that this is no argument against relativism but rather simply a denial of the position—it has simply been denied that approval of a practice makes the practice right. For what the relativist claims is that what *is* right in a culture is the same as what people in that culture *think* is right. But what the relativist has done is simply to stipulate a definition of "right." The fact that we can question whether an act is right while at the same time agreeing that people in a given culture approve of it should be sufficient to show that the stipulated definition of "right" is unacceptable. For example, it is not uncommon in mental hospitals (a culture of sorts) for staff members to judge assertive behavior from patients, especially toward the staff, as unhealthy. But just because this judgment is accepted does not mean it is morally correct.

A paradoxical result of cultural relativism as an alleged ethical theory is that it actually eliminates the need for ethics. Ethics is concerned with what counts as responsible behavior—what types of behavior ought to be approved of—and with justification for moral judgments. But cultural relativism reduces merely to factual considerations.

Now it may be true that most people in fact approve of those acts which are right and disapprove of those that are wrong. Our society approves of psychologists' maintaining confidentiality and disapproves of experimentation on people without their consent. But social approval is not the reason *why* an act has moral worth nor is the moral worth of an act (its rightness) determined by its social acceptability. Rather an act's social acceptability ought to be *determined by* its moral worth and its moral worth ought to be the reason why it is approved of by the society. Thus we need an independent criterion for "right" in order to determine whether some behavior ought to be accepted in a society and in order to morally evaluate social values.

Though a relativist may again claim that that is not an argument against relativism but simply a denial of the relativist's claim that there is no independent criterion of right, one need only look at some of the consequences of that theory to show that it is unacceptable. We have already pointed out that a cultural relativist cannot make judgments about the morality of behavior in other cultures. While a relativist may not, and cannot, find this objectionable, relativism offends against the way we are accustomed to thinking about morality. For not only are we willing to say that one culture's moral standards are better or worse that another's (we would not hesitate to claim that a culture which condones human sacrifice surely engages in practices which are morally inferior to one which guarantees human rights), we also want to talk in terms of moral progress (Stace, 1937, 1965). For example, we want to say that moral progress has been made in the area of research in psychology, moving from a time when informed and voluntary consent was not an issue of much concern to the present when that is a major concern of researchers. But according to relativism, morality is relative not only to culture but also to time, and we cannot talk in terms of progress, for "progress" implies some objective standard by which to judge.

Despite the numerous problems with cultural relativism, this theory may emerge in goal selection in therapy. Many clients come to therapy requesting treatment for socially deviant behavior to avoid sanctions and criticisms for being different. A homosexual may want to change her sexual orientation, not because she sees it as unhealthy, but because of social pressure. The therapist's acceptance or rejection of this goal may be influenced by the immediate culture. A therapist in a conservative small town may support this goal whereas a therapist in a more liberal metropolitan area may engage the client in an evaluation of the motivation for selecting this goal. The different responses of the therapists suggests the operation of cultural relativism considerations (which may of course be reasonable). This is not to say, however, that social norms can be identified with moral norms.

Personal Relativism

A personal relativist agrees with the cultural relativist in asserting that people's customs and beliefs differ. But this view further assumes that no one, not even society, can impose moral beliefs on another because there are no universal objective criteria for "right" and "wrong." The only way to judge the moral worth of an act is for a person to consult his or her own feelings about it. If, for example, a psychologist feels in a particular case that it is right to break a confidence, then it is right for that psychologist, but she can never say that it would be right for anyone else. A person may condemn another person for what he or she does but that condemnation is only an expression or statement of one's own unpleasant feelings[1] about that person's behavior and not a knowledge claim about moral truth. As does the cultural relativist, the personal relativist claims knowledge in ethics to be impossible since it entails the existence of ethical truths. A person can only know how he or she feels, which is psychological knowledge of one's own subjective feelings, not ethical knowledge. Since ethical questions are reduced to questions of feelings, the answers to such questions do not involve any objective truth. Thus if psychologists were personal relativists they would not have a set of ethical standards. But psychologists sometimes seem to endorse a personal relativist position when they insist that their personal view is irrelevant and force the client to decide for himself or herself what is right.

The theory suggests that factual considerations are not logically required in answering moral questions. Of course facts may influence a person's feelings but they are logically irrelevant to ethical decisions since facts point to something objective while moral questions are essentially subjective. It may be a fact that sexual intimacies with a client will have detrimental effects on the client and this fact may influence the therapist's feelings that he should not indulge in such intimacies. But according to this view there is no *logical* connection between that fact and the therapist's feelings. Consequently, an ethical decision cannot be evaluated as rational or irrational, correct or incorrect. It is simply a statement of or expression of one's feelings. Of course one may want to ask, "What *should* I feel about this action?" But to ask that question implies that there is some objective standard by which one can determine whether one's feelings about the behavior in question are morally appropriate or not. Any subjectivist would deny that there is such a standard.

What is objectionable about personal relativism is not so much its emphasis on a personal perspective in making moral decisions but its disregard of thinking as a necessary element in making such decisions. Thinking, as distinct from feeling, entails careful consideration of the facts, along with the ability to give a rational justification for one's decision. To be rational is in part to be consistent, which in turn can be expressed as a requirement to treat relevantly similar cases alike. We don't demand that feelings be consistent but we do require consistency in decision making. Hence consistency is required of a person's moral life—the way in which one harmonizes one's actions and tends to evaluate ethical situations, make moral judgments, and act on those decisions. The reason it makes sense to evaluate some behavior as moral or immoral is that most human beings can think about what they do. Hence they are expected to be rational and to be able to give good reasons for their decisions. In ordinary situations they can be held responsible for their behavior. But because personal relativism has no logical space for such considerations, "moral agent" can be translated into "emoting agent." Thus this model ignores the distinguishing feature of persons. Just as cultural relativism does not leave room for ethical inquiry, neither does this theory. A personal relativist has nothing to inquire about except one's feelings or the feelings of others. A psychological explanation for why a person has certain feelings might be relevant but an explanation or examination of the objective moral worth of an act is viewed as impossible. This theory ignores the fact that human beings in general are rational beings and that rationality is required in ethical decision making. And this theory is reflected in a "do-your-own-thing" attitude which does not encourage one to examine critically the worth of one's "thing."

The personal relativism model is often confused with two other views, *situation ethics* and *egoism*. According to situation ethics, even though the situation determines whether a person's behavior is morally correct, there is some absolute moral principle by which to make moral decisions and evaluate behavior (Fletcher, 1966). And this requires that one be able to identify the morally relevant features of the situation and take them into account before making a decision. From this view the moral value of an act is relative to a person's situation, but all relevantly similar situations dictate the same moral judgment, something not required by personal relativism. For example, if the staff of a mental hospital has wrongly judged a patient as not ready for home visits and the patient manipulates the staff to get the pass, then situation ethics could justify manipulation in this situation on the basis that the patient's autonomy was being violated. While manipulation of one person by another is not in general justifiable, a particular situation may justify it when a more fundamental principle is being violated. According to situation ethics, right behavior is determined by the situation based on a fundamental moral principle and right behavior would be right for anyone in relevantly similar circumstances.

According to egoism, what is right is what is in one's best interest. This may very well conflict with personal relativism because personal feelings can lead to behaviors which are not in one's best interest. An alcoholic, after detoxification, may feel that taking a drink would be all right when in reality it is not in his best interest.

The views of situation ethics and egoism are based on moral reasoning that takes into account relevant facts, something personal relativism does not.

Before discussing the next two ethical theories, we should point out that though many people consider themselves to be relativists of some sort, neither version discussed so far is really an ethical theory. An ethical theory is a theory about how we *ought* to behave. But ultimately neither personal nor cultural relativism deals in "oughts." Cultural relativism reduces to a study of what most people in a particular culture approve of, and personal relativism reduces to a study of what individuals feel.

UTILITARIANISM

Social living, if it is to be harmonious, requires that one at times put the community's interest ahead of his or her own. While everyone's interests cannot be accommodated at all times, we should at least try to see that the majority's interests are accommodated. This is the principle of utility which Mill (1861, 1957) discussed and attempted to defend in his book *Utilitarianism:* that act is right which promotes the greatest happiness for the greatest number. This ethical theory must not be confused with cultural relativism, for on that view it is possible in principle that an act might be approved of by society even though it did not make most people happy. The utility principle is an absolute moral principle which is not relative to a culture, though what in fact makes most people happy may be culturally determined.

No one person's happiness is more important than another's[2]—each person counts for one and no one for more than one. And so the utility principle requires that we strive equally to promote the happiness of others as well as our own. Mill thought it not unreasonable to demand of human beings an active concern for the welfare of others. He believed that selfishness makes us unhappy, that we naturally tend to have feelings for others and empathize with them, and that basically we want to see them happy. In this respect utilitarianism acknowledges a duty of beneficence. Mill (1861, 1957) would argue that the foundation of this duty "is that of the social feelings of mankind—the desire to be in unity with our fellow creatures" (p. 40). Thus it would appear that we have a duty of beneficence toward others, or at least toward those who can be affected by our actions. But as we shall see, this ignores special duties we may have to particular people by virtue of a special relationship in which we stand to them. This will have important implications in practice. For example, if a researcher were to assume that the duty of beneficence dictated increasing knowledge of human behavior for the welfare of the population as a whole and for future generations, any duty of beneficence the researcher may have toward the subjects will probably be ignored.

According to the utility principle, engaging in morally correct behavior is a matter of weighing alternatives in terms of their consequences, calculating which one seems more likely to produce more happiness than pain. This calculation involves considering the number of people who are likely to be affected and estimating (somehow) the amount of pleasure and pain each person affected by the action is likely to receive. Suppose, for example, that a mother and a child have developed a symbiotic psychotic relationship (one where parent and child share the same delusional system) but that there are several other children in the home who have not developed such a relationship with the mother. It could be that institutionalizing the mother may be beneficial to the one child but detrimental to the other children because she is still able to care for their basic needs. According to utilitarianism, the mother ought not to be removed from the home because her remaining benefits the greatest number of people.

However, such a calculation procedure not only has theoretical difficulties—can pleasure and pain be assigned numerical values?—but also practical difficulties—we do not always have time to weigh possible alternatives and to calculate their possible consequences. Suppose that a client is diagnosed as needing hospitalization but the therapist, being a good utilitarian, believes that he should take time to evaluate possible alternatives and possible consequences of those alternatives. The indications, however, are that immediate institutionalization is required. While the alternatives are being weighed, the client might harm himself or others.

While Mill did not seem to recognize the difficulty in actually weighing pleasure and pain, his answer to the problem of not always having time to calculate is that we have rules of thumb to go by—for example, to be honest, keep promises, and not hurt others. The *Ethical Principles of Psychologists* might be considered to be rules of thumb that in general provide answers to moral questions that arise in the profession. The reason there are particular rules is that past experience shows us that following such rules tends to produce more happiness than pain. But there are exceptions to these guidelines and we are at liberty to disregard them if we have good reason for thinking that another action would produce more pleasure than pain. The *Ethical Principles* attempt to build into the rules certain exceptions, but if a particular exception arises which the *Principles* did not anticipate, one may disregard the rule if in doing so more happiness would be promoted.

This view has *prima facie* appeal, for it certainly seems unreasonable to behave according to a rule simply because it is a rule, regardless of any consequences of doing so. This is why, for example, the *Ethical Principles* allow certain exceptions to the general rule to obtain informed consent from subjects in research. In some cases the advancement of science requires that subjects be deceived. It would seem unreasonable never to allow any deception at the expense of gaining knowledge which would benefit human beings in general. But to accept utilitarianism implies (1) that the utility principle is the one and only basic moral principle and one to which no exceptions are allowed, and (2) that no one's happiness counts for more than anyone else's. We will see that (1) justifies too much and (2) too little.

We recognize that special relationships with other persons entail certain duties and responsibilities to them that we don't necessarily have toward others. Psychologists are more duty-bound to promote a client's well-being than that of someone they meet at a party. But utilitarianism does not recognize any such personal priority. Consequently there is no *a priori* reason for promoting a client's well-being rather than that of a casual acquaintance. The utilitarian justification for preferring one over the other must be in terms of the utility principle and not in terms of any special relationship which is alleged to carry moral weight. If it can be shown that helping a casual acquaintance rather than a client would promote the most happiness, then utilitarianism would dictate helping the acquaintance. However, in practice we do not ordinarily allow what we think is our duty to be overridden by purely utilitarian considerations.

As Ross (1930) has argued, one possible relationship to a given person is that of being a potential beneficiary of that person's actions, but one may also stand in the relation of friend to friend, wife to husband, or therapist to client. In some cases a person may have to favor producing more good and thus temporarily ignore a duty that is based on a special relationship (though Ross says it is not utilitarianism that justifies doing so but rather the duty of relieving stress, which under some circumstances is more of a duty). Nevertheless we do have what Ross calls *prima facie* or conditional duties which we must fulfill under normal circumstances, independent of any utilitarian considerations.

Another common objection to utilitarianism is that it justifies too much—that in principle it allows anything to be done to a person or group of persons if the consequences of that act are beneficial to a large number of people. For example, society could demand psychosurgery for all violent criminals, justifying these actions using the utility principle. It could be argued that society at large will most likely benefit from the change in behavior, even if the clients were totally incapacitated as a result of this procedure. The famous Milgram study (1974) is another example of how utilitarianism can justify too much. Subjects thought they were volunteering for an experiment on learning, which in fact was an experiment on obedience. They were told to shock the learner (a confederate) if he or she gave a wrong answer. The subjects falsely believed they were administering painful shocks. Milgram wanted to find out the extent to which subjects would obey the experimenter who would tell them to continue if they decided they wanted to quit. Since they thought at the time they were causing pain to another, some subjects may have been permanently harmed (some required therapy) as a result of these experiments. But had the research not been done, it would not have been discovered that such a high percentage of "normal" Americans would be blindly obedient to authority figures. Deceiving the subjects was crucial but easily justified by utilitarianism in terms of the increase in knowledge. As this experiment shows, the basic problem with the utilitarian model is that the individual's rights can be violated if enough benefits accrue to a larger group of individuals. Thus it can be seen that while utilitarianism provides for a theory of obligation—we are obliged to promote happiness—rights have no fundamental role. This is a major objection to utilitarianism since "rights" talk is crucial in dealing with those who may be affected by the activities of psychologists. Though an adequate ethical theory should consider the rights of persons as playing a fundamental role in the theory, rights play only a secondary role in utilitarianism since the ascribing of rights to persons would depend on whether doing so would be in accord with the utility principle. In general this may be the case, but as we have just indicated, in a particular case there may be no guarantee that an individual will retain a particular right if retaining that right would conflict with the utility principle.

In order to answer such objections, some utilitarians have wanted to make a distinction (in terms of how behavior is morally justified) between two types of utilitarianism, act and rule (Rawls, 1955). Act utilitarianism, which we have been implicitly assuming in our discussion so far, holds that all moral rules are mere guidelines which may be broken if the consequences of following a rule in a particular case are not in accord with the utility principle. Rule utilitarianism holds that it is rules and not particular acts that define what is moral, and once the rule is justified by the utility principle, it must be obeyed without further appeal to that principle. Any exceptions must be built into the rule and since the rule *defines* moral acts, one is not free to disregard it in particular circumstances once it has been accepted. An example of a rule with exceptions built into it is this one, taken from the *Ethical Principles of Psychologists*:

> After the data are collected, the investigator provides the participant with information about the nature of the study and attempts to remove any misconceptions that may have arisen. Where scientific or humane values justify delaying or withholding this information, the investigator incurs a special responsibility to monitor the research and to ensure that there are no damaging consequences for the participant. (Principle 9.h)

Rule utilitarians argue that if anyone were allowed to break a rule on an ad hoc basis, much discord would result because no one would be sure when the rule should be followed. According to rule utilitarianism, moral rules are not mere guidelines or rules of thumb but rather they are definitive rules of moral behavior. They should be public and all persons are bound to follow them without any further appeals to the utility principle.

This version of utilitarianism also takes into account our ordinary belief that in many instances we should adhere to a moral rule regardless of utilitarian consequences. For example, psychologists are bound to maintain confidentiality. In ordinary circumstances the fact that a psychologist is in a confidential relationship with a client is the primary consideration, which would not be easily overridden by utilitarian consideration.

Unfortunately for rule utilitarianism, it has been criticized effectively both by act utilitarians and by other moral philosophers. Act utilitarians accuse rule utilitarians of rule-worshipping (Smart, 1956). Suppose that in following a rule, which has been justified on the basis of the utility principle, one will cause much unhappiness in a particular case. For example, if the rule stresses honesty as a moral principle, then being honest even when it hurts others would be obligatory. Thus if a client requests a diagnosis from the therapist who believes that such knowledge may have harmful effects on the client, the therapist would nevertheless be required to be honest with the client. The rule utilitarian has no choice but to follow the rule at the expense of the utility principle. Thus act utilitarians claim that rule utilitarians are not being true to the utility principle because it appears that they place more value on following the rule itself than on the utility principle. A true utilitarian must always hold the utility principle as fundamental, which means that no rule must ever override it. Therefore rule utilitarianism must either reduce to some moral theory other than utilitarianism or must go back to act utilitarianism in order to be consistent with the utility principle.

Other moral theorists have argued against rule utilitarianism. They claim that the problem is not so much the inconsistency in this version of the theory but rather the whole basis on which this theory tries to justify moral rules (Melden, 1966). The rule utilitarian argues that moral rules are justifiable on the basis that having certain rules produces happier consequences than not having them. If behaving in a particular manner produces greater benefits for a greater number of people, then that behavior may be required of all people by making it a rule. Once a rule is adopted, people are obliged to behave in accordance with the content of the rule. Thus on this view it is not so much respect for the privacy of the client which dictates the rule to maintain confidentiality but rather the fact that having such a rule promotes more happiness than unhappiness. Rule utilitarianism does not admit any intrinsic merit to having particular moral principles, and this puts moral rules in the same logical category as traffic rules. The reason for having the rule that everyone must drive on the right side of the road is not because that in itself is a good thing to do but only because the consequences are better if everyone drives on the same side. Without such a rule there would be no obligation to do so. The same kind of analysis would apply to the rule which indicates that material presented in the course of therapy is confidential. The rule to maintain a confidence is justified by the utility principle, but if there were no such rule therapists would not be required to maintain confidentiality.

But surely this goes against our ordinary way of moral thinking, from which point of view we tend to say that it is a special relationship that a therapist has with his or her client that provides the basis for many of the psychologist's moral obligations. This relationship results in certain duties on the part of the therapist towards the client and perhaps on the part of the client also. The client's well-being is (or ought to be) of prime concern for the therapist and *that* is the reason why psychologists have moral rules to that effect; the question of utility is quite irrelevant. A rule such as the above does not derive its moral justification from its utility, even though it may in fact be utilitarian to have it. Hence it can be seen that to give a *utilitarian* justification is not necessarily to give a *moral* justification, for one can agree that a certain rule has utility—it tends to promote happiness—but still question whether it is moral since promoting happiness may not always be the morally correct action. Moral rules specifying obligations and duties arise out of the fact that relationships *create* duties and obligations. To argue that there is no moral obligation unless there is a prior (utilitarian-based) rule to define it and hence create the obligation is not to capture our ordinary moral attitudes. We believe that we have certain moral obligations and rights regardless of the existence of definitive rules. We fulfill an obligation not merely because we believe that there is a rule which *defines* such an act as being right but because of the kind of relationship we have to another person. We believe that persons have rights independent of rules which may define those rights. Though we will give a more detailed analysis of the concept of right in Chapter 5, at this point we wish to examine briefly the role of rights in light of rule utilitarianism.

A rule ascribing various rights to people would be justified on the basis that it is in accord with the utility principle, not on the basis that it is inherently valuable. At least according to this version of utilitarianism, a client's right to confidentiality, for example, could not be as easily violated as it might be by act utilitarianism. However, rule utilitarianism does not give an *a priori* guarantee of rights for *all* people, and hence certain rights of clients and subjects—such as the right to privacy or the right not to be deceived—may not exist because there may be no rule which would define such rights into existence. Though such rights may be in accord with the utility principle and exceptions may be built into such rules, the major problem as we have indicated is that the justification for having rules which define rights into existence is utility, which is not necessarily a moral reason. But we want to say that regardless of the utility of having such rules defining rights into existence, there should be a guarantee of the rights of persons independent of utility.

The question might be raised as to just why it is that rights and moral obligations arise out of relationships among persons. Kant tried to give the groundwork for an answer to this question and it is to a moral theory based on his claims that we now turn.

A KANTIAN MODEL

The introduction to the *Ethical Principles of Psychologists* says that "psychologists respect the dignity and worth of the individual and honor the preservation and protection of fundamental human rights." Kant would applaud this statement on two counts. First, in *Groundwork of the Metaphysic of Morals* (1785, 1964) he claims that everything in nature exists as a means to some end except for persons, i.e., rational beings, who have intrinsic worth. Every thing in nature, except for persons, is merely an object which can be used for some purpose. Only persons exist as ends in themselves. He argues for this in the following way: the reason things have value is because of our needs and wants. These things are objects of someone's will, i.e., subjective ends, which have value only in being valued or willed. There are also natural, nonrational things which only have value relative to achieving one's subjective ends. If we had no needs and wants then nothing would be of value. And it is because things only have relative or conditional worth—worth relative to our subjective needs and wants—that they are called *things*. But rational beings are called *persons* because their very nature points them out as beings who are valuable in themselves. For Kant, only a free will is intrinsically valuable and only a free action is a rational action. Persons are rational beings; they are capable of acting freely and because of this they are intrinsically valuable. They are not to be treated as though they have only conditional value, for that would be to treat them as things. In other words, in pursuing one's subjective ends, one should not treat persons as though they were objects whose worth is only relative to one's subjective ends.

Second, "the preservation and protection of fundamental human rights" is a notion which also is fundamental to a Kantian ethical theory. As we shall see, a guarantee of rights follows in part from Kant's claim about the autonomy of persons.

The notion of free will is crucial in Kant's theory because of his emphasis on the autonomy of the person. Acting freely and hence autonomously does not mean acting on the basis of desire because we have no choice about our desires. Any action motivated by wants or desires has no moral value. A person is only truly autonomous when he or she acts independently of wants and desires. As we shall discuss in Chapter 4, this emphasis on free action, not being controlled but acting autonomously, is the goal of any therapeutic technique.

We might point out that this emphasis in Kant's theory surfaces in psychoanalytic theory where the goal is for the client to become more rational and free by bringing unconscious material, which controls the person, into conscious awareness.

From the claim that persons are intrinsically valuable Kant derives what he calls the practical imperative, which provides a basis or guide for ethical decisions. The practical imperative states that one should "act in such a way that you always treat humanity, whether in your own person or in that of any other, never simply as a means, but always at the same time as an

Practical Imperative

end" (p. 96).[3] Kant does not say we are never allowed to use other persons but that we must never treat them as *mere* means. While it is necessary to use others—physicians, secretaries, counselors, flight attendants—we must at the same time realize that they have worth independent of our need for them and treat them accordingly. For example, a psychologist may need to use deception in an experiment, but subsequent debriefing of the subjects is an attempt to show respect for them.

categorical
imperative This practical imperative is derivable from what Kant calls the categorical imperative, which is sometimes called the universalizability principle: "Act only on that maxim through which you can at the same time will that it become universal law" (p. 88). In other words, an act is morally acceptable if and only if one is willing to have anyone else (in relevantly similar circumstances) behave in a similar manner. For example, one would be justified in using aversive shock on a subject only if it would be acceptable to use aversive shock on anyone else (including the psychologist) in a similar situation.

We can see that the formulation of the practical imperative follows from the categorical imperative: I, as a person with feelings of dignity and worth, will be treated with respect and not as an object to be manipulated by others for their purposes. If I treat others as objects, then in effect I am saying that others may treat me that way (since as a rational being I must be consistent). But because I cannot consistently will to be treated that way, I cannot universalize a principle that allows me to use others. Hence a moral principle which allows persons to be treated as a mere means to some end is inconsistent because it is not universalizable and therefore is an invalid moral principle.

Here we can see how a theory of rights is derivative from both the categorical and the practical imperatives. The categorical imperative requires that our actions be universalizable; hence since I want my rights to be respected, I must respect the rights of others. The practical imperative requires respect for persons because they are intrinsically valuable, and because they are rational, respect for their autonomy is required. From this it follows that we must acknowledge that persons have certain *prima facie* rights such as the right to self-determination and to privacy. Thus the requirement that persons must give consent to have something done to them is basically the acknowledgement that persons are autonomous beings who have the right to make choices about what is done to them and hence the right not to be used as a mere object.

So the Kantian principle which requires that persons must never be used as mere means is justified, first, by a view about what a person is and, second, by what one can consistently will regarding one's treatment by others. Using the second justification we can see that one could not *consistently* will that persons be treated as mere objects for that contradicts the nature of persons. And the first justification relies on accepting the idea that persons are intrinsically valuable, which makes that claim more basic. However, if one does not accept the premise that a person is intrinsically valuable and thus rejects the conclusion that follows from it, that a person must never be treated as a mere object, moral argument comes to an end.

If someone questions the claim that persons are not things to be used for his or her purposes and hence fails to accept the claim that persons cannot be in the category of things, either that individual doesn't understand what the concept "person" entails or completely lacks a moral sense. Such an individual would not recognize others as persons "but as complicated objects involved in a complicated activity" (Rawls, 1958, 1975, p. 283). To recognize that we ought to treat others fairly and with respect "is simply the possession of one of the forms of conduct in which the recognition of others as persons is manifested" (Rawls, 1958, 1975, p. 283).

An objection may be raised to Kant's formulation of the practical imperative because it is worded in such a manner as to apply only to rational beings. Since Kant uses "rational being" as the defining characteristic of a person, most animals and profoundly retarded individuals would be classified as nonpersons. This would seem to allow the use of animals and human beings who lack the potential for rationality for any purposes whatever since their value is derivative from our needs and wants. However, we do want to acknowledge that such human beings and animals have some rights—e.g., the right not to be tortured, the right to be cared for if they are in our custody. Even if we cannot attribute moral responsibility to them as we do to rational beings, they would seem to be entitled to some basic rights because they have interests. ("Any creature that has interests has at least a *prima facie* right not to have those interests needlessly harmed." Rachels, 1976, p. 212.) An addition is needed to Kant's theory in order to require that we respect the rights of sentient nonpersons, that we be considerate of the feelings and well-being of all sentient creatures. Psychologists in fact assume this in Principle 10 of the *Ethical Principles*, which states that "the investigator ensures the welfare of animals and treats them humanely."

Adding to Kant's practical imperative in the way suggested would take some of the moral weight off "rational" (which is a happy consequence since it is difficult to specify exactly how "rational" should be defined). It also would justify the common moral belief that we have some duties toward sentient beings who do not qualify as persons because they cannot be held morally accountable for their behavior. Though we may be justified in using nonrational beings, we still have the duty to them to respect their interests.

Kant's theory would seem more adequate for psychologists than their relativism or utilitarianism, since those theories fail to account for the special worth of persons, an assumption psychologists make. While relativism must be completely rejected for reasons discussed earlier, we may at times have to appeal to utility. Suppose a child has a serious medical disorder which will result in mental and physical disability but which the parents refuse to recognize. Leaving the child in the home respects the parents' right but costs the child, whereas taking the child out of the home for treatment helps the child but violates the rights of the parents. In this case there is no right decision and hence an appeal to utility is in order.[4] Benefits accorded the child by removing her from the home outweigh any benefits to the parents by allowing her to remain in the home. But to hold as basic a moral principle which demands respect for persons and their autonomy is to say that purely utilitarian considerations may never override that principle. The Kantian model would seem to serve psychologists as a fundamental principle which provides the basis for what they see as their primary obligations. The awareness of and adherence to the practical imperative would function to define the nature of the psychologist-client/subject relationship. It would focus the psychologist's work on those factors which would be most respectful of the individual's autonomy. This emphasis on the individual's value reduces the importance of cultural and utilitarian considerations in the psychologist's profession.

In anticipating some of the issues to be discussed in later chapters, we should point out that the chief duty of psychologists is to help people. The immediate question arises, "To help whom in particular?", and this is where there will be inevitable conflicts because the specific duties that follow from this general one are extremely varied. Though we have defended a Kantian-based ethical theory as the fundamental one for psychologists (and one which is reflected in the *Ethical Principles*), it appears that at times an appeal to utility will be necessary when a psychologist has to choose which course of action is the lesser evil.

Another point we should mention is that psychologists in different areas may have different primary duties that stem from the more general one of helping people and that follow from either a Kantian-type theory or a utilitarian-based one. For example, the people clinical psychologists help are their clients, which supports a Kantian-based theory for making moral decisions. In some cases researchers aim to help the general public by attempting to increase our knowledge of human behavior. This conforms more to the utilitarian-based model for ethical decision making. But even within an area of practice there will be conflicts. The researcher will have to weigh utilitarian considerations against the Kantian principle not to use persons as mere objects. The clinical psychologist may have to weigh the duty of beneficence against the duty to promote client autonomy, for in some cases helping the client may require temporarily diminishing that client's autonomy.

To summarize, the duties of psychologists follow primarily from the Kantian model but in some cases an appeal to utility may have to be made. Because psychologists have many duties even within a particular area, they are bound to come into conflict. Often it is not easy to resolve the conflicts, but by being aware of the ethical basis for making a moral judgment, psychologists will be better able to take a rational approach to the conflicts they face and will be in a better position to make consistent ethical decisions.

Chapter 2

Ethical Decision Making
in the Psychologist's Profession

In addition to special training, what distinguishes a professional from a nonprofessional are special duties one incurs by virtue of practicing in that profession. These special duties in part define the profession and thus codes of professional ethics reflect these duties. Some professional duties stem from more general human obligations so any decision of professional ethics will undoubtedly involve general ethical considerations. As a therapist, a psychologist has a duty to keep client information confidential. This stems from the general human obligation not to violate a person's trust. As a researcher, a psychologist has the duty to obtain consent from subjects. This duty follows from the more general duty we have as persons not to use someone as a mere object. A psychologist who constructs job performance tests for a company has the duty to construct tests that are nondiscriminatory on the basis of sex or race, which follows from the general obligation to treat people fairly. And a psychologist who does evaluations of clients has the obligation to omit from a report any accidentally acquired or irrelevant information that could harm the client who is tested. This stems from the general obligation not to cause harm. Though such special duties of psychologists are derivable from general obligations, we expect more of a professional than of other people. The special duties define the role of psychologists in these professional activities. (The next chapter, which deals with consent, confidentiality, and competence, will be concerned with basic professional obligations.)

As a moral agent, a professional has the same basic obligations as anyone. Even though professional duties are derived from more general human obligations, the special duties that one incurs because of being in the profession will sometimes conflict with human obligations. For example, as a therapist one has the duty to keep appointments with clients. But if a family member were in a serious crisis and an appointment had to be postponed, the human obligation may outweigh this particular professional duty because the consequences of not helping the family member may be far graver than postponing client appointments. Reason would suggest that blind, rigid fulfillment of professional obligations can have serious negative consequences.

When there is a conflict of duties, one must make a decision as to which duty takes precedence. We have discussed some possible bases for making moral decisions, but merely being aware of the ethical theory on which a decision is based does not guarantee that the decision is correct. Moral reasoning is a complex process which involves many factors. And it is more complex in the case of professionals because, as we pointed out, professionals have both human obligations and professional duties. Psychologists, as professionals, often will have more considerations to weigh than one does in making decisions in ordinary life because of the special duties dictated by that profession.

One important factor in moral decision making is the context. General moral claims most likely will have exceptions. "Never break a confidence," "Always be honest with research subjects," "Never give advice in therapy" are general claims to which exceptions can easily be imagined. The reason for this is the specific circumstances in various cases. Hence the correctness of a moral decision cannot be discussed without taking the context into account. And the context may even determine whether or not an issue is an ethical one. The use of four-letter words, for example, is not unethical *per se* and a psychologist who uses such language may not be subject to moral criticism. However, if a psychologist uses such language in therapy with the intention of offending a client, the issue is then an ethical one because the psychologist's behavior affects the welfare of the client. This case does not raise a moral *problem* because there is no conflict of obligations. The *only* obligation in this case is not to offend a client. If there is no *conflict* of obligations but merely a matter of fulfilling the obligation at hand, then of course what one should do is clear.

In order to solve a problem that is ethical in nature, one must be acquainted with the steps in the process of reaching a moral decision so that the decision is rational and consistent. These characteristics can be said to be criteria for proper moral decision making.

So far we have discussed the nature of moral problems and have argued for the superiority of a Kantian perspective when making ethical judgments. We will now focus on the steps in moral decision making. The steps in proper moral reasoning are ones that anyone should use but we will focus on the point of view of psychologists because their special duties complicate moral decision making.

As in any type of problem solving, one should strive to make a rational decision. That requires making a decision based not on some feeling but on some kind of logical order. We want to be able to defend a course of action and this requires showing how a decision was reached.

The first step in solving a moral problem is to identify what the problem is. It is not always easy to recognize that a problem is ethical in nature. But the increasing interest of psychologists in ethics implies that they are becoming more readily able to identify ethical problems.

An ethical problem is identified by specifying the obligations one has that are relevant to the problem. The obligations that conflict must be identified and weighed in order to determine what is the primary obligation in a particular case. An example of conflicting professional obligations would be a case where confidentiality and the welfare of the client come into conflict. Suppose a psychologist is engaged in therapy with a depressed adolescent who admits to contemplating suicide. The duty to protect the welfare of the client by informing the parents conflicts with the duty to maintain confidentiality. An example of a conflict between human and professional obligations would be a case where the human obligation to be honest conflicts with the professional obligation to do research. Because deception is sometimes required to get valid experimental results, the two duties come into conflict. In each case one must determine one's primary obligation. As we pointed out earlier, context is important. In the first case, the welfare of the client takes precedence but before confidentiality is broken the therapist must determine whether there is reason to believe that the client may in fact carry out the threat of suicide. In the second case, a problem that will be dealt with extensively in a later chapter, one would have to determine whether deception is necessary to the experiment.

As implied in the preceding examples, when weighing one's obligations the immediate and long-term consequences of fulfilling an obligation must be considered. This does not mean that the primary question is one of utility, for one must first consider fulfilling the primary obligation and the initial choice should be made in terms of it. Consequences are not irrelevant but they should not be the sole factor in reaching a moral decision. Only when the consequences may be severe should a utilitarian approach be considered. If the severity of the consequences warrant sacrificing one's primary obligation to a secondary one, consideration must be given to making reparation for doing so.

While it may not be possible to list every consequence of alternative actions, major consequences can be considered, given knowledge of the case and past experiences. Based on available knowledge the effects must be weighed in terms of the good or harm they produce to those involved. We should note that despite some ethical theories that claim that consequences have no bearing on the rightness or wrongness of an act, it is unrealistic in professional practice or from the point of view of morality in general to ignore consequences altogether.[1] Consequences must be considered when determining what one ought to do when obligations conflict. However, as we indicated, this is not to say that consequences should be the *sole* determining factor in resolving conflicts of duties. One must first determine what one's *prima facie* duty is. A therapist's *prima facie* duty is to the client and if that duty conflicts with a duty the therapist may have in a secondary role as a consultant for some agency, the therapist should not resolve the conflict in terms of consequences, in terms of what action would promote the most happiness for the most people. Nevertheless, moral decisions must be acted upon and one's action must be placed in the context of the actual world. Suppose a psychologist or psychiatrist receives a court order demanding the records of a client. To relinquish them is to break a confidence, but to refuse to do so would mean a jail sentence. To preserve confidentiality in this case could result in the therapist's other clients being without help. That consequence and the obligation one has to other clients must be weighed against the duty to maintain confidentiality.

While this could be interpreted as a utilitarian approach to resolving the conflict, as we indicated in Chapter 1, Ross (1930) would say that in a case such as this there is an overriding duty, the duty of beneficience to the other clients.

Fulfilling a certain duty may not always be practical but being moral does not always require ignoring practicality entirely. In the above case, ignoring the consequences, or ignoring the fact that one may have a duty which overrides the duty one has to a particular client, may be neither practical nor realistic for the therapist, and doing so may be detrimental to other clients. As Wright (1981b) points out, "We do our clients ill if we lead them to believe in our absolutism when ultimate circumstances forces the abandonment of an unrealistic position" (p. 1539).

Nevertheless, the fact that consequences don't always figure as the major factor in moral reasoning can be seen in the attention given recently by psychologists to the problem of deception in psychological research. Some psychologists oppose deceiving subjects despite the potential for gains in knowledge.[2] Some therapists claim that they would serve a jail sentence rather than relinquish client records by court order. This shows that it isn't *only* the consequences that are taken into account in making ethical decisions.[3] Nevertheless, in the process of arriving at a decision at least some thought should be given to the possible consequences of alternative decisions where there is a severe conflict of duties.

Once a choice has been made, it must be examined objectively. The psychologist might consult with others who have faced a similar problem in order to validate his or her decision if there is some uncertainty. If there is the possibility of legal action being taken against the psychologist, such consultation also could provide some legal protection if the psychologist were asked to justify the action. At least it would show that the psychologist had not acted impulsively.

While consultation may be an aid to reaching a correct decision, the choice made by the psychologist must also be evaluated in terms of moral consistency to ensure that it will not be a subjective choice. For if a decision is subjectively based, the concept of *defending* one's decision will have no meaning. That concept implies giving rational reasons, but an entirely subjectively-based decision is merely a matter of personal preference which does not logically require that it be based on such reasons. The fact is that we try to give reasons for our moral choices which would be reasons for anyone to make the same choice in a relevantly similar situation. One is then committed to moral consistency, for part of what is meant by "good reasons" is reasons that are objective and hence are reasons for anyone.

To test for moral consistency one should ask "Would it be acceptable for anyone in relevantly similar cases to do the same?" This question implies an impartial observer and concerns universality, the Kantian categorical imperative. But Kant did not bring in the crucial notion of relevantly similar cases and hence the categorical imperative is perhaps too simple. In Chapter 1 we added the idea of relevantly similar circumstances to the categorical imperative and now we can elaborate. To say that a situation is *relevantly similar* to another is to say that it has features which are similar in ways that have a bearing on the question. For example, in obtaining consent to do something to another, the competence of the individual is a relevant factor in determining similarity of situations because the ability to consent depends in part on the individual's competence. To take another example, whether advice ought to be given in therapy may depend on the client's capacity in general to make independent decisions. Capabilities or competencies of psychologists also may enter into determining similarity of cases. Suppose two psychologists have a contract with an agency and are asked to administer a certain test. One agrees to do so and the other refuses. This does not automatically mean that one is fulfilling the contract and the other is not, for a refusal would be justified if the psychologist were not competent to administer the test. Hence there is a relevant difference between the two which makes the two cases dissimilar. When trying to determine if one could universalize a particular decision, it is important to emphasize that the features of the case must be relevant ones. There are irrelevant differences—the race of a client, for example, is irrelevant to deciding in a particular case whether breaking a confidence is justified—and there are irrelevant similarities—for example, that two psychologists attend the same church is irrelevant in determining whether one should refer a client to the other (assuming church preference has nothing to do with the client's problem). If there is no logical relation of some feature of a case to determining whether one's action could be universalized, then that feature is not a relevant one.

To return to the test question for moral consistency in decision making, if the answer is yes, the action under consideration is morally permissible, though not morally obligatory. But if the answer is no, to perform the action would be morally inconsistent and a different decision must be examined. If that question is used as a criterion for consistency and hence a necessary condition of a valid ethical judgment, it follows that social norms or personal feelings are not appropriate considerations in moral decision making. For the use of social norms or personal feelings does not by any means guarantee universalizability. In universalizing a decision one will want to take into account how much good vs. harm the action produces. But as we pointed out, this is not to say that evaluation of consequences in terms of positive or negative effects is the *only* feature of moral decision making.

In the process of moral reasoning psychologists must be aware of and examine their personal values, for these values influence their choice of action. Personal hierarchies of values may not be uniform, but adherence to the basic value of promoting welfare of the consumer should be. To say that this is a basic value is to say that other professional values are secondary to that one. Hence if a psychologist's primary activity is teaching, the welfare of students should take precedence over other professional activities. And if one's primary activity is consulting, then that should take precedence. Likewise, if one does private therapy, then obligations to clients take precedence over other professional obligations. However, two psychologists may disagree on what action best demonstrates adherence to the fundamental value. For example, suppose a client has decided to leave her husband and comes to therapy asking advice on how to tell him. In the past the client has not usually asked advice on how to handle certain problems, but has managed to make decisions on her own. One psychologist may decide not to give advice on the grounds that the client responsibility takes precedence over immediate help to the client. Another psychologist may place more importance on the immediate welfare of the client rather than on long-term client responsibility in making decisions. Both psychologists may be able to universalize their decisions but because they differ as to what is the best means of adhering to their fundamental value, they arrive at different decisions. This shows that in some cases different psychologists may validly arrive at incompatible decisions because of their different fundamental values. Either decision would be morally permissible as long as the client's autonomy is not violated.

Where other professional values are concerned, the ranking of those values may be a matter of personal preference. For example, one psychologist may prefer to do research rather than teach. Another may place higher priority on doing therapy with individual clients rather than evaluating clients for an agency. But it is important that psychologists be aware of what their personal priorities are within the profession. The ranking of one's personal professional values may be evaluated by considering various cases in light of one's priorities and seeing what decisions that ranking would dictate. If any of those decisions dictate a course of action that would not be acceptable for others to do in a similar situation, then that ranking of values needs to be rethought. Suppose a clinical psychologist who teaches places a greater priority on therapy than on teaching. That ranking of values would have the consequence of her devoting more time to clients than to students. In that instance, the classes may be ill-prepared, the teacher rarely available to the students, and she would only fulfill the minimum commitment to the university as a whole. On the other hand, this psychologist may be quite successful with many clients. To evaluate the values in question, the psychologist must ask whether it would be acceptable for other psychology teachers to behave similarly. If it would not be found acceptable for other psychology teachers to give preference to therapy, the psychologist must either rearrange the present values so that teaching has priority or give up that profession entirely.[4]

Ideally, good ethical reasoning should result in a correct decision. However, not only is it the case that sound reasoning may justify more than one decision, but all too often no decision is correct in the sense that all actions will have negative effects. In such cases one must choose the action with the least undesirable consequences. Though we argued in the first chapter that utilitarianism was inadequate as a fundamental ethical theory, when every possible decision one may make in a case has some negative effects, it will be necessary to use utilitarian considerations so that a decision is made in terms of producing the least amount of harm. For example, in order to qualify a client for vocational rehabilitation assistance from the government, the psychologist must assign a label to the client. As we noted earlier, this could have negative effects on the client, especially if the problem is severe. On the other hand, not to assign a label to the client would result in the client's not being able to receive government assistance for vocational training. There are negative consequences to either course of action. The context and relevant facts of the cases must be considered in order to determine what are the probable consequences of each course of action. The conflict in this case is between helping the client by assigning a negative label and not qualifying the client for help by not assigning a label. Where there is a conflict of obligations and there will be harmful effects no matter which obligation is fulfilled, utilitarian considerations would seem to be in order.

We can now summarize the steps in moral reasoning. Though the process is in general the same whether reasoning from the point of view of a professional or a nonprofessional, the special duties that psychologists have will enter into making a moral decision.

First, the moral problem must be identified in terms of the conflict of obligations. As a professional, the ethical problem a psychologist faces may be a result of conflicting professional duties or professional versus human obligations. One must then examine possible courses of action and determine the extent of one's obligations and which one carries more weight. Then the major consequences of each course of action need to be examined in light of one's obligations. Utilitarian considerations may be involved in choosing an alternative only if the good produced by not fulfilling one's primary obligation far outweighs that produced by doing so. But if utilitarian considerations justify an action other than fulfilling one's primary obligation, one must then consider how to make reparation for failure to fulfill the primary obligation.

After choosing among the alternatives one should then clarify and evaluate one's own values. Psychologists are professionally bound to place the welfare of the consumer first but the activities one chooses to engage in professionally are a result of personal values. One should then evaluate one's ranking of those values in terms of what decision would be dictated by them. That decision must be tested for consistency and universality by asking whether it would be acceptable for anyone in relevantly similar cases to do the same. If the answer is no, a different decision should be considered and one's ranking of values reexamined. To act on that decision would be inconsistent and the element of universality, which is essential to a correct moral decision, would be missing.

However, if no alternative yields a positive answer to the test question, one should choose that action which has the fewest undesirable consequences. In such a case, one could then universalize the action in the following way: "In any situation which is relevantly similar to this one, a psychologist should do X because the consequences of that action are more helpful or at least less harmful than the consequences of the alternatives." That one has reached a universalizable decision can be reinforced by consulting with other professionals in the field.

Moral reasoning is a very complex process and in reality we do not always go through all the steps we have outlined. Often we don't have the time, for a decision must be made quickly. However, by being aware of the process of reaching a moral decision and using it in cases where there is time to reflect on possible courses of actions, it may be that in those instances where there is no time for detailed reasoning, one will be better equipped to rely on one's quick decison and better able to defend it. Or if one later sees the decision was wrong, one will be able to cite the reasons why it was wrong and such knowledge will aid in making future decisions.

In discussing the nature of a moral problem, three commonly used ethical models, and the process of moral decision making, we have touched on some of the issues and problems that arise in the psychologist's profession. These and others will be explored in depth in the remaining chapters.

Chapter 3

Consent, Confidentiality, and Competence

The basic ethical obligations of psychologists can be summarized with three concepts: consent, confidentiality, and competence. Many specific moral problems that arise in psychology will involve at least one of these concepts. Before discussing them separately, however, we should first note how they are related.

Kant's principle to respect the dignity, worth, and intrinsic value of persons is compatible with the ethical orientation of individual psychologists and the profession as a whole. From this basic requirement certain others are commonly derived: an individual should never use another person as an object, should respect the autonomy of persons and their freedom to make choices, treat others fairly and hence not take advantage of them, and be honest. Specific duties of psychologists, such as to represent research findings accurately or to obtain a person's consent before doing anything to him or her, can be defined in terms of these more general duties. As in other professions, the nature of psychologists' work creates special duties and responsibilities. The aim and purpose of psychologists is to improve the well-being of human beings, for example, by doing research which will contribute to a better understanding of human behavior or by doing therapy with individuals so that they will be better able to function in personal and social life. Because psychologists' work can put them in a position of power and possible control over others, they must be aware of the ways in which they might take advantage of individuals. The special responsibilities incurred in professional practice, the requirements of consent, confidentiality, and competence, are designed to guard against such abuse. Thus the moral weight attached to these requirements is explained by the fundamental moral principle and those principles which it entails.

Obtaining consent is required before engaging in therapeutic or research activities and in doing so, psychologists are acknowledging the person's freedom to choose and are thereby respecting one's right not to be used as a mere object. This is why *informed* consent is so crucial. For uninformed consent can be dishonest and puts a psychologist in a position of being able to take unfair advantage of the person's ignorance, which in turn treats the person as an object to be manipulated. Similarly, the duty to maintain a confidence stresses the special relationship of therapist to client and researcher to subject, a relationship of trust in the psychologist to protect the well-being of the individual. The confidentiality requirement limits the risk of exploitation and reduces the power of the psychologist over the person.

Both the obligation to obtain consent and the obligation to maintain a confidence are further grounded in a person's right to privacy; acting without the person's consent is violating the person's right to be left alone, the right not to have his or her domain invaded. Disclosing confidential information without the person's permission obviously makes public what the person has a right to demand be kept private—information which is part of his or her personal, private sphere.

In acknowledging their duty to maintain a high level of competence, psychologists recognize that they cannot fulfill specific obligations unless they are generally competent. It should be noted that being competent entails recognizing the limits of one's competence. For example, using therapeutic techniques with which one is unfamiliar or unqualified to implement can result in harm to clients. As the *Ethical Principles* state, "Psychologists recognize the boundaries of their competence and the limitation of their techniques. They only provide services and only use techniques for which they are qualified by training and experience" (Principle 2).

In a certain respect competence is a more fundamental duty than the other two, since being competent implies not only having professional expertise in psychological techniques and research but also knowing what one *cannot* do. In addition, competence ought to imply not merely technical skill but also an understanding and fulfillment of the ethical obligations one has as a professional—a knowledge of ethical practice. Thus competence is an umbrella-type duty from which all the duties of psychologists follow. A competent psychologist will respect the rights of clients and will promote client autonomy.

The absolute nature of competence makes it unique, for while consent and confidentiality are only *prima facie* duties, competence is not. The former are duties which psychologists generally have but other considerations can take precedence over them. For example, while a psychologist may have to break a confidence in order to protect someone from harm, in no case would reason suggest that incompetence is acceptable. Apparent exceptions are not really exceptions. Suppose there is only one employed psychologist at an institution but that he is not competent to treat a particular patient. He may refuse to treat the individual and attempt to get special services for the person. Or if that is unsuccessful, he may make clear the limits of his competencies and still treat the person in hope that some treatment for the client is better than none. All of this can be done with a conscious understanding of one's limits and the awareness and consent of the client. In either instance, the psychologist is acting in a competent manner even though all of his specific actions may not be competent by stringent professional standards.

These basic requirements of ethical practice will now be discussed along with practical problems confronted by professionals in the field.

CONSENT

Because the work of psychologists is primarily concerned with doing things with or to other people, the basic justification for such actions lies in obtaining consent from those people. Consent plays a more prominent role in psychology than in some other fields and so it is especially important for psychologists to have a clear idea of what is involved in obtaining consent. The requirement of consent is a more complex one than might be realized. To explain consent in terms of a mere agreement is inadequate. An adequate analysis of consent includes three characteristics which must be present in every case: the consent must be *informed, voluntary,* and *rational* (Freedman, 1975). Since one ethical function of consent is to prevent individuals from being manipulated or taken advantage of, individuals need to make decisions based on relevant information. Often omitted is the fact that the individual *does not have to consent* and has the right to *withdraw* consent at any time. Even though consent is similar to a contract, the client or subject retains the prerogative to change his or her mind at any time; this privilege makes the consent contract different from other types of contracts.

Beyond this basic information, all aspects of the treatment or research procedure which might be related to willingness to participate need to be disclosed. The therapist or researcher is expected to disclose the practical details of the procedure in question. Details should address the following: what will be done, who will do it, how long will it take, risks associated with the procedure, benefits to be anticipated, alternatives that warrant consideration, possible inconveniences, whether the procedure is routine or experimental, and potential long- or short-term side effects. Beyond this basic information the psychologist is also required to clarify or expand on anything about which the individual inquires.

Equally important as conveying relevant information is conveying it in an appropriate manner and setting. The nature of the procedure must be explained in terms the person can understand, for the individual will not be informed if he or she does not understand the technical language of psychology. For example, if a psychologist were trying to verify that giving certain students more attention would result in high motivation, then he should not describe the experiment as an effort to validate the Hawthorn Effect. Since few if any students would know what the Hawthorn Effect is, the details might as well be in Latin. Psychology is a field with a detailed, often obfuscatory, technical language so it is not hard to disguise information in jargon. While we generally endorse the idea that information must be detailed, excessive detail can be problematic in that it can hide salient information.

In addition, the person's environment must be such that he or she can calmly reflect on what is being explained so that a rational decision can be made as to whether to consent. If a student is very upset about a test score and goes to the professor, who at the time happens to need research subjects, it would hardly be appropriate to ask the student to participate and to try to inform the student about the research. These three aspects of informed consent—conveying all relevant information, conveying it in language the person can understand, and conveying it in an environment conducive to careful deliberation—eliminate the subject's or client's

> "informational vulnerability" . . . a vulnerability which can, in obvious ways, give the psychologist an unfair advantage to be exploited in the manipulation of the subject [or client] toward the [psychologist's] desired end. (Murphy, 1975, p. 35)

A psychologist may have good reason to believe that a certain therapeutic technique will be beneficial to a client who might, if informed, reject it. In research, a psychologist may think that utilitarian considerations outweigh the duty to obtain informed consent from one's subjects. But to withhold the information is to show disrespect for the client or subject as it denies the person's autonomy and the individual's right to decide what happens to him or her. The paternalistic orientation ("father knows best") inherent in ignoring the consent requirement is antithetical to an autonomy orientation.

In practice, deception is rarely justified or needed in therapy but research often involves withholding information from participants so that meaningful data can be obtained. This area will be specifically discussed in Chapter 6.

As mentioned earlier, the requirement of consent is based on respect for a person's autonomy. From this it follows that consent must be given voluntarily; the client or subject must not be coerced into agreeing to participate. This is why it is so important in obtaining consent that the information be presented in an environment which is as stress-free as possible. Otherwise, the psychologist may be taking advantage of the person's anxiety when informing the person, which would be a form of coercion.

In therapy where psychologists use only noninvasive techniques, it is doubtful that any positive results could be obtained if the client is forced into therapy. Most psychological techniques depend on cooperation and thus the issue of voluntary consent may not be critical. However, to the extent that the procedure used is intrusive, there is the potential for compromising voluntariness.

When is participation coerced? It is sometimes thought that in making one alternative more desirable than another, the person choosing the more desirable alternative is not making a free choice. Thus it might be claimed that to offer money to people in exchange for participating in research, or to give students extra points if they agree to be subjects in an experiment, is coercion. If this is so, we would have to say that much behavior we ordinarily think of as voluntary is really coerced. But tempting a person is not the same as coercing (Murphy, 1975). In some cases, however, if the temptation is strong enough, the effect may be the same, for the person may go against his or her better judgment. "A temptation is said to be irresistible only if a man *could not reasonably be expected to* resist it, even though others might actually have resisted it in the past" (Benn, 1975, p. 232). Hence a temptation may be a form of coercion. A choice is truly free if it would be reasonable to expect a person to be able to withstand the temptation in a particular set of circumstances.

To coerce a person is to put him or her in a position where there is no meaningful alternative, a position in which the person can do nothing about the options and is forced to make a strongly biased choice. For example, to say to students, "Either you agree to participate in my experiment or you must write a research paper" is not to give them a meaningful choice if they could not be expected to resist the temptation of not writing a paper. Thus it is to take unfair advantage of their vulnerability. Here is a case where temptation may be a form of coercion, at least in the case of some students. Nevertheless, a conceptual line can be drawn between coercion and mere temptation. Coercion differs from temptation in that the former involves taking unfair advantage of a person's situation whereas the latter involves using an influence which the person can resist. Because in the context of research the use of coercion involves taking unfair advantage of a person's situation, "a coercive offer must be an immoral offer" (Murphy, 1975, p. 38).

As is true of the requirement to inform, requiring voluntary consent is also, in effect, requiring respect for a person's autonomy. Coercion involves not allowing the person a real choice and thus diminishes the extent to which the individual has control over what happens to him or her. Hence to act on the basis of coerced or involuntary consent violates the fundamental moral principle, to treat a person with dignity, because the person is being manipulated.

If an individual's consent is to count, that individual must be able to understand and reflect on the information given and to make a rational decision in light of it. In other words, a rational or competent person knows what counts as relevant in making a decision and is influenced by such considerations. Because people ought to have control over what is done to them, paternalistic measures are justified only when the individual is judged to be clearly incompetent. Now the question is, what qualifies someone as being clearly incompetent and hence not able to make rational decisions? First of all, we must take care to note the distinction between incompetence and eccentricity. Not all behavior that is at odds with how most people behave can be used as evidence of incompetence. Care must be taken in judging an individual as incompetent, for such a judgment has moral implications:

> To be judged incompetent often results in one's status as a full-fledged *person* being taken away or at least greatly altered. Basic human rights (including the right to do stupid and dangerous things if one so desires) may be set aside, and the incompetent person may simply be treated as the object of someone's (usually the state's) benevolent concern and management—a clear demotion from the status normally thought proper for an adult person. (Murphy, 1974, p. 465)

Consideration of the individual's capacity for rational decision making may or may not be related to the legal classification of "mental incompetence" or "mental illness."

> In most states, the label "mental illness" means that the person so labeled is unable to take care of his *personal* affairs (his health, personal safety, etc.), and the label "mental incompetence" means he is unable to take care of his *business* or *legal* affairs (his bank account, taxes, or property, etc.). (Ennis & Siegel, 1973, p. 74)

Legally speaking,

> labeling a person "incompetent" has a profound effect on his private life. No longer can he enter into legal relationships with others. His signature becomes worthless. His most basic rights of citizenship are removed. The constitutional right to privacy, in addition to the right to due process of law, requires that an alleged incompetent receive a full court hearing, with legal counsel, before he is declared incompetent. (Ennis & Siegel, 1973, p. 77)

While the legal definition of incompetence can be clearly punitive, it is not necessarily related to rationality. Turnbull (1977) introduces the notion of "capacity" in determining rationality. The criteria suggested include "the ability to engage in a rational process of making decisions" and having "the mental process or faculty by which he acquires knowledge" (p. 7). He points out that individuals may be competent to make some decisions but not others. A handicapped individual may be competent "to enter into a contract for the purchase of a shirt but not for the sale of all his assets for a nominal sum" (p. 8). This analysis suggests that notions of "blanket" irrationality or incompetence require further evaluation because rationality and competence are relative concepts. Somone who is irrational about some matter or who is incompetent in one area may very well be competent to do other things.

CASE STUDY 3.1

A middle-aged homemaker and mother has been in therapy with a psychologist for three months, suffering from severe depression. Before she began psychotherapy, a physician had prescribed an antidepressant drug, which had no positive effect. Her children have left home and she does not feel as needed as she did, nevertheless she does not see that as the real cause of her depression. In fact, she cannot find any reason for being depressed—her husband is a well-paid professional and they have a very comfortable life.

At the end of three months, the psychologist sees no improvement in her condition. The client is becoming increasingly frustrated over the fact that she feels just as depressed as she did when she began therapy. She tells the psychologist that she would be interested in any kind of treatment which might alleviate her depression. The psychologist says that his treatment seems to be ineffective and recommends that she see a particular psychiatrist whom he knows to be a strong advocate of electroconvulsive therapy (ECT). The psychologist then refers her to the psychiatrist, who agrees to treat her. She signs a consent form for ECT and says to the psychiatrist, "I don't care what is done—I just want to feel better." Because the psychiatrist assumes she has prior understanding of the nature of the treatment, he then proceeds to administer a series of twelve treatments over a period of three months. At the end of the series, the client shows no improvement and claims to have suffered severe memory loss. She returns to the psychologist and says "Those damn shock treatments didn't help—in fact, I feel worse because I can't even remember where things are in the house." The psychologist reviews the fact that she requested some other form of treatment and that she did sign an apparently valid consent form. He sees nothing he can do except reestablish their therapeutic relationship or refer her to another therapist.

It may appear that one could give voluntary and rational yet uninformed consent. A person could choose not to have the relevant information because he or she feels that it won't make any difference or he or she simply does not feel like taking the trouble to listen and understand. But if a person chooses voluntarily not to be informed, there are no grounds for complaints later that a rational choice could not be made because the relevant information was not given. A person who is characteristically rational or competent can be allowed to act without relevant information but the rationality of the decision can be questioned. Such a person exposes himself or herself to risk in not getting the information.

Research with institutionalized individuals presents a somewhat different situation. If an individual has been declared incompetent, then consent from the appropriate guardian would be necessary. Obtaining consent from the appropriate source would not necessarily release the researcher from the responsibility of subsequently obtaining consent from the patient himself or herself. For example, a patient may be able to communicate either verbally or nonverbally that she does not want to participate. Psychologists ought to respect this type of refusal regardless of its basis (rational or otherwise) since even incompetent individuals have the right not to be used. Similarly, children should not be assumed to be necessarily incompetent. For if a child has reached the age of being able to understand what is said, capable of reflecting on the information and rational enough to make a decision in light of it, then his or her wishes bear consideration. We are not suggesting that children have the reasoning ability and sophistication in decision making that most adults have; we only wish to point out that at a certain level of development children are able to comprehend what is said and make decisions based on information. These developing capacities need to be considered when working with children even though legal precedents forbid children under the age of majority from independently entering into contracts.

We can assume that most people are competent to make their own decisions about what happens to them or what is done to them. Thus it should not be assumed that institutionalized people cannot give rational consent simply because they are institutionalized. Psychologists who work with individuals in an institutional setting should assume that the patient is competent unless there is obvious evidence to the contrary. Therefore the patient should have the right to participate in the treatment plan to the extent that he or she is able. And because psychologists are in a more powerful position in such a setting than in private practice, they must make special efforts to obtain vaild consent before engaging in any activity with these individuals.

To treat individuals as rational and competent is to see them as beings who have the right to choose what happens to them and thus to have respect for their decision and their autonomy.

CONFIDENTIALITY

The duty to maintain confidentiality has both a practical and a moral basis. From a practical point of view, the confidentiality requirement is necessary for the good of the profession. People must be able to trust psychologists if they are to seek psychological services and be willing to participate in psychological research. If a client or subject cannot expect the psychologist to keep confidential all information regarding his or her private domain, no one would interact with or trust psychologists.

The moral basis for the duty to maintain confidentiality is a person's right to privacy, which thereby imposes on others in general and psychologists in particular the duty to respect that right. Not only is this right a moral right, but a legal right as well. However, from both moral and legal perspectives, this right is not absolute, for there are circumstances that justify violating a person's privacy. Thus the duty to maintain confidentiality is only a *prima facie* duty. It is true of any such duty that one has an obligation to fulfill it in ordinary situations. And so the question is not when to fulfill that obligation but rather what circumstances qualify as extraordinary and justify making an exception.

It should be noted that a legal justification for making an exception is logically distinct from a moral justification. The two may or may not overlap. In some instances one may have a legal duty to break a confidence (by court order), but it may or may not be a moral duty to do so. For example, a psychologist who is ordered to testify in a divorce proceeding regarding a client's fitness for parenthood may decline to do so for moral reasons.

In discussing disclosure of confidential information, two types of situations present different concerns: (1) situations in which a psychologist must make a conscious moral decision regarding breaking a confidence, and (2) situations in which confidences are carelessly or unwittingly revealed.

Regarding confidentiality problems of the first kind, the most obvious question is, what types of circumstances justify breaking a confidence? One situation which would justify doing so concerns the safety of others. For example, a psychologist working in a hospital for the criminally insane may learn from a client that he is obsessed with killing his wife. If in evaluating circumstances and intentions, the psychologist recognizes this as a real possibility, breaking the confidence would be justified—appropriate authorities in and out of the institution and the wife should be notified. Even though there are no accurate predictors of dangerousness, the psychologist must make educated guesses based on past experience with other clients and knowledge of the behavior of the client in question. Those who lack experience need supervision in this kind of case. The psychologist must be able to tell the difference between the client's *wishes* or *possible* behavior and what the client may *actually* do. An example of when the psychologist has reason to believe that the client may actually carry out a threat is the following case: A psychologist had a client who thought he was a dog. He crawled around growling and snarling at his family. When law enforcement officials were called to the scene, the client bit one officer on the leg. Later, during the psychologist's evaluation, repeated violent themes toward family members were expressed. The psychologist's report arrived on the counselor's desk at the same time that a phone call revealed an attempt by the client to drown his wife in the bathtub.

There are other cases, however, where clients may express wishes upon which there is no reason to think they will act. Some clients may say they wish a certain person were dead but the psychologist, based on knowledge of the client's past behavior, has no reason to think the client will take any action.

Because predicting actual behavior is difficult, it should be assumed that cases in which the therapist believes that the client poses some real danger to others are unusual cases. But what types of threats made by a client justifies revealing the information to the person concerned? Though a threat of physical harm is the most obvious, would other types of threats also justify

---

CASE STUDY 3.2

A 41-year-old man has been in therapy for two months. The presenting problem was his obsessive thoughts about the impending death of his mother despite the fact that she is in good health. This obsession had interfered with his productivity in work and his relationships with his wife and children. Because of his obsession, he nearly had three automobile accidents, since his attention in driving was severely disturbed. It was the last of these near misses that motivated him to seek psychotherapy. During the two months of therapy the focus of the sessions had been on his obsessive thoughts about the impending death of his mother. In session eight, which was a very emotional one, he broke down and sobbed silently for five minutes, after which he admitted to raping a woman three years before. The woman committed suicide soon after. No one was arrested for the rape. He tells the therapist the name of the woman, where it took place, and gives the therapist graphic details of the circumstances surrounding the rape. The therapist had followed the newspaper account of this rape and realizes the client has revealed information never reported by the newspapers. She is convinced that this is not a compulsive confession. The client is well respected in the community and has an excellent reputation as a family man. Due to an extensive battery of psychological tests administered early in the course of therapy and information gained from therapy sessions, she has no reason to suspect that he will commit rape again.

---

breaking a confidence? For example, suppose a client is plotting to ruin someone financially. Would such a threat constitute justifiable grounds for revealing such information to the relevant person if the therapist has grounds for believing that the client will do so? It could be argued that threats of that nature do constitute physical harm and would justify breaking a confidence. But the point is that there is a lack of specificity regarding "threat" which would justify revealing confidential information. Nevertheless, without strong restrictions on breaking a confidence, confidentiality may become the exception rather than the rule. On this basis Justice Clark presented a dissenting opinion in *Tarasoff v. Regents of University of California* (1974). But the majority ruled that the therapists, the defendants in the case, had a duty to warn a woman that a former client intended to kill her. When the client carried out his threat, after terminating therapy, her parents sued. The *Tarasoff* court held that

> when . . . a psychotherapist, in the exercise of his professional skill and knowledge, determines, or should determine, that a warning is essential to avert danger arising from . . . the psychological condition of his patient, he incurs a legal obligation to give that warning. (555)

Justice Clark agreed with the majority that if therapy is terminated, there is an increased risk of violence and the therapist must warn the potential victim. But as he pointed out, without a guarantee of confidentiality,

> many people, potentially violent—yet susceptible to treatment—will be deterred from seeking it; those seeking aid will be inhibited from making the self-revelation necessary to effective treatment. (567)

If clients cannot assume confidentiality, and there is a duty to warn, according to Clark, this duty "will likely result in a *net increase* in violence . . . " (568). He said that "By imposing such a duty on psychiatrists, the majority contributes to society's danger" (568). And, said Clark, "given the decision not to warn must always be made at the psychiatrist's civil peril, one can expect all doubts will be resolved in favor of warning" (568).

But even where breaking a confidence would seem to be justified, it might be argued that the psychologist must not look beyond the therapeutic relationship and hence, no matter what threats the client makes, the duty to maintain confidentiality cannot be overridden. While this is an extreme view, which seems to be implied in Clark's dissenting opinion in the *Tarasoff* case, it does point to the important aspect of the therapeutic relationship that such a relationship is between therapist and client, not between therapist, client, and outside world. And because of the difficulty of trying to tell the difference between the client's *wishes* and what he or she may *actually* do, this may be a further argument that the confidentiality requirement ought to be exceptionless.

Even if one does not want to take this extreme view and were to argue that in some very unusual cases breaking a confidence would be justifiable, we should emphasize that the decision to break a confidence cannot be made in a vacuum. To know merely that a client admits homicidal thoughts is not sufficient to decide whether breaking the confidence is justified. Much more information is needed. Without all the relevant details of a case, an answer to such a question is impossible. Nevertheless, even given relevant information, a decision regarding what and whom to tell will not be easy. The therapist's decision will depend not only on background information but also on one's clinical ability.

The *Tarasoff* Court, however, seemed to think that the problem therapists face as to whether a confidence should be broken and a potential victim warned is not terribly difficult. The majority opinion stated that

> the judgement of the therapist . . . is no more delicate or demanding than the judgment which doctors and professionals must regularly render under accepted rules of responsibility. (560)

What the majority did not take into account is the fact that dangerous behavior is extremely difficult to predict. In his dissenting opinion Justice Clark pointed out that "This predictive uncertainty is fatal to the majority's underlying assumption that the number of disclosures will necessarily be small" (568). He went on to say that "unlike this court, the psychiatrist does not enjoy the benefit in seeing which few, if any, of his patients will ultimately become violent" (568). As Wright (1981b) correctly notes,

> Few experienced mental health practitioners would seriously argue that we can predict specific and individual human behaviors with a high degree of probability. Yet that is precisely what the courts and public expect of us. (p. 1539)

If the therapist decides that some relevant person ought to be informed of the client's intention or behavior, an attempt should first be made either to convince the client to reveal the information himself or herself, or to obtain the client's permission to do so. At least the client should be informed that disclosure is imminent. Suppose it is learned that a father has been having an incestuous relationship with his adult daughter. The psychologist should first try to convince the man to tell his wife or get his permission to inform the wife. If neither alternative is possible, the therapist may be warranted in breaking the confidence. But in doing so, the information disclosed should be as minimal as possible. In the example just cited, what should initially be disclosed is not the incestuous relationship but a suggestion that the mother be more observant about the daughter's behavior and ask her to keep written records of her observations.

Third-party payments may pose a problem for maintaining confidentiality. Is the psychologist's first duty to the person who is paying the bill and who may wish to obtain information on the client, or to maintain confidentiality of the person receiving psychological services? Regardless of who is paying the bill, most psychologists would probably agree that the latter duty usually overrides the former. But the person receiving the services certainly should be informed of the limits of confidentiality and of any commitment the psychologist may have to the paying party.

One such case of third-party payment is a psychologist's employment by a company. Suppose the psychologist finds out in therapy that an employee in a management position is an alcoholic. Should the therapist inform the relevant person in the company of this since it is the company which hired the psychologist? The answer to this question depends on the answers to some other questions: Is the safety or well-being of other employees dependent on the client? Can the problem be treated without disclosing that information? What would be the consequences of disclosing the information? Whether or not this particular case is one in which the psychologist's *prima facie* duty is overridden by loyalty to the employer depends on the nature of the psychologist's contract, which should anticipate such situations. We assume that a competent psychologist would not sign a contract requiring him or her to divulge to the employer just any or all information obtained in therapy. When a psychologist is employed in this type of setting, the person who seeks psychological services should be informed of the exact limits of confidentiality.

Another case of third-party payment is when parents pay for psychological services for a child. Suppose a teen-aged client informs the therapist that he has been experimenting with numerous types of drugs. Should the therapist tell the parents? Again, some other questions must be answered first, such as: How frequent is the experimentation? Is the client aware of the possible dangers? What would be the consequences of informing the parents? There may be a conflict between the psychologist's duty to fulfill the parents' wish for the adolescent to become better adjusted and the duty to respect the autonomy of the young client.

So far we have been pointing to cases where the concern is for some third party. Now another question arises: Is a concern for the (adult) client's own well-being (as judged by the psychologist) a type of case in which consent may not be necessary to break a confidence? If the client is rational, the psychologist must respect the autonomy and the right of the client to make decisions about his or her own life. To take a paternalistic attitude toward the client implies a denial by the therapist of the client's right to choose. Even if the client is contemplating suicide and the therapist has reason to believe that the client will carry out that wish, that still may not be sufficient reason for breaking a confidence. It should not be assumed that anyone who is seriously contemplating suicide is *ipso facto* not competent to make a rational decision about his or her life and that a breach of confidence is *automatically* justified. Though some reasons for suicide may be better than others, serious suicidal thoughts do not alone render a person incompetent to make such decisions. But a psychologist who is treating a suicidal client or a client who is behaving in a way which is detrimental to his or her well-being will probably find it difficult *not* to take action. For one thing, we feel morally uneasy about sitting back and watching another person ruin or end his or her life when breaking a confidence could prevent that. For another, we may wonder if that is what the person really wants to do. It is this latter consideration that causes the real problem.

> The dangers inherent in acting on behalf of others from inferences about non-conscious wishes are great. Yet, if these wishes are disregarded or rejected by preferring to act only on conscious messages, equally important non-conscious messages will be left unacknowledged. Thus a decision to listen to non-conscious voices can lead to an abuse of power, while a decision to heed only conscious voices can abandon persons to an unwished fate. It is a dilemma for which there is no simple solution. (Katz, 1969, pp. 761-62).

Perhaps all that can be said is that the competent psychologist must use his or her training and sense of judgment (which may be no more than an educated guess) to determine what the client really wants by paying attention to both direct and indirect communications. That may not be saying very much by way of a solution. The point is that breaking a confidence on the basis of what is considered to be in the best interests of the client is not *obviously* a morally sufficient justification unless the client is clearly irrational.

Despite the fact that there are only a few unusual situations which justify breaking a confidence, the *Ethical Principles* and the *Standards for Providers of Psychological Services* (1977) suggest that the psychologist inform the client that confidentiality is not something the client can expect absolutely. The *Ethical Principles* state that "where appropriate, psychologists inform their clients of the legal limits of confidentiality" (Principle 5). And the *Standards for Providers* require that

> users shall be informed in advance of any limits in the setting for maintenance of confidentiality of psychological information. For instance, psychologists in hospital settings shall inform their patients that psychological information in a patient's clinical record may be available without the patient's written consent to other members of the professional staff associated with the patient's treatment or rehabilitation. (Principle 2.3.5)

While it is only fair to inform clients of such limits, there is another side to this which may result in a conflict between fairness and therapeutic progress. For suppose the client is informed that if the therapist judges some information revealed in therapy to be necessary either for the client's well-being or for the safety of others, that information will be disclosed to relevant persons (e.g., family or some legal authority). It is possible that in trying to be fair to the client by informing him or her of the limits of confidentiality, the client's therapeutic progress will be stunted. For such an advance warning may result in the client's censoring his or her disclosures and avoiding information necessary for proper treatment, as the defendants pointed out in the *Tarasoff* case. This is a dilemma that is not easily resolved. If the limits of confidentiality are made known to the client, in order that such knowledge will not hinder the client's therapeutic progress, he or she must be made to feel that the limits will either be beneficial (as indicated in the *Standards for Providers*) or that the limits apply only to extreme situations. And what counts as an extreme situation must be explained to the client. Perhaps discussion of examples of extreme cases (suicide, contemplated murder) can help clients to be comfortable with the limits of confidentiality.

While the client's consent to disclose identifying information may not always be necessary, it may seem that such consent is sufficient to do so. However, that is not necessarily the case. In some instances the client's well-being may be jeopardized if certain information were made known to others, but the client may not realize this when he or she agrees to the disclosure. And, as noted in the "Position Statement on Guidelines for Psychiatrists: Problems in Confidentiality" (American Psychiatric Association, 1970), the therapist "must be aware that there may be unconscious determinants in the patient's agreeing to disclose all details" (p. 189). It is the responsibility of the therapist to counsel the client concerning possible consequences of such disclosure. The *Standards for Providers* are explicit on this point:

> When the user intends to waive confidentiality, the psychologist should discuss the implications of releasing psychological information and assist the user in limiting disclosure only to information required by the present circumstances. (Principle 2.3.5)

However, from a legal point of view such consent may be sufficient in cases of court action. In some states a client has what is called the right of privilege. This right is explained in the "Position Statement on Guidelines for Psychiatrists":

> *Privilege* is a legal concept; it is the right of a patient, established only by statute, to protect his physician from testifying about medical treatment and the content of communications disclosed in the treatment process. Privilege is a legal right belonging *only* to the patient, not to the physician. (p. 188)

But if the client waives this right, legally that is sufficient to disclose any information regardless of possible detrimental effects on the client. In this same position statement it is stated that in a jurisdiction where privilege exists, a patient may, in legal action, waive his privilege of privacy, but it is to be noted that when the privilege is waived in such actions, all relevant information available to the psychiatrist must be disclosed by him in court; that is neither the patient nor the psychiatrist may then willfully withhold particular items of information because of his opinion disclosure might be prejudicial to the welfare or advantage of the patient. (pp. 188-89)

For this reason the therapist has a responsibility to make certain the client understands the consequences of waiving this right. As the above guidelines suggest, therapists "should take particular care to appraise the patient of the connotations of his waiving the privilege of privacy" (p. 189). And so even though the client's consent to allow disclosure is sufficient from a legal point of view, from a moral viewpoint the therapist should not accept it as sufficient unless the client is aware of possible adverse consequences. Consent to disclose confidential information is legitimate, as is consent to treatment, only if it is informed, voluntary, and rational.

As we mentioned in the beginning of this section, not all situations where problems of confidentiality arise are ones in which the psychologist makes a conscious decision regarding it. There are instances in which a person's right to privacy may be violated unwittingly or carelessly. It is these kinds of cases that psychologists must be especially aware of, just because they are quite ordinary and do not usually generate the discussion that unusual cases do. Let us now look at some of these types of situations.

Clinical psychologists may also be university professors. In teaching it is often useful to cite cases to illustrate a point or a therapeutic technique, but unless care is taken in the presentation to disguise the client's identity, especially in a small community, the client's privacy may be violated. This may require a conscious effort and it is something that psychologists must make certain of doing. For if the information is not truly disguised, the psychologist is relying on the restraint of the student, which may be unrealistic, especially in provocative cases.

In centers that provide psychological services, there may be an open filing system. Clients' records would then be easily accessible and thus the psychologist may not be in a position to guarantee confidentiality. In such circumstances there are several alternatives. The obvious one is to change the filing system so as to limit record accessibility to the psychologist(s) directly involved with the case. If this is not feasible, the therapist should inform the client of the extent to which others have access to records, for this may have some bearing on the client's decision to accept treatment. Psychologists should also take care in writing reports on their clients. Perhaps they should try to make statements that are more benign than they might otherwise do while at the same time being as honest as possible.

It may be tempting for a psychologist who happens to have a personal interest in the client of an associate to review that client's records. However, unless the psychologist is directly involved in that person's treatment, that psychologist has no moral right of access to such records. To read reports out of curiosity or personal interest is to take advantage of one's position and in doing so is violating a person's right to privacy. Many psychologists work to avoid knowledge of friends' or at least colleagues' problems.

In many settings (both public and private), nonprofessional people such as clerical workers inevitably will have to deal with clients' records. Psychologists must make explicit to those persons that they have a duty to maintain confidentiality. It should not be assumed that everyone is morally sensitive to the issue of privacy. The *Standards for Providers of Psychological Services* state that

> all persons supervised by psychologists, including nonprofessional personnel and students, who have access to records of psychological services shall be required to maintain this confidentiality as a condition of employment. (Principle 2.3.5)

Two further points should be made regarding the care which psychologists ought to exercise in writing reports. One is that clients have the legal (and we might add, the moral) right to review their own records.

Though it may not always be advisable that a client do so—the client may misinterpret or become overly concerned—nevertheless it is a right which the client has. It might be thought that this right will interfere with the therapist's ability to be completely honest in the client's records. However, because no test or diagnosis points to absolute truth, the recognition of this right of the client may result in a more conscious awareness on the part of psychologists that they are only dealing in opinions which may or may not be true. Psychologists should keep that in mind when they record test results and diagnoses. Test results are not always accurate indicators and a diagnosis is tentative. If a client reviews his or her records and is left with the impression of being a hopeless case, that may have serious effects on any therapeutic progress. The other point is that in some instances the therapist may have to provide some information on the client to the insurance agency. Because this information will be read by people not involved in the client's treatment, the psychologist should give as little information on the client as necessary.

Often psychologists must share cases with other psychologists, either in staffing or for purposes of consultation in treatment. As far as possible, the psychologist should not reveal identifying data of the client and should take care to disclose only information that is relevant. Where the case necessitates revealing the client's identity, the psychologist has an even stronger responsibility to make certain that those to whom the information is presented understand its confidential nature and the fact that they have incurred a responsibility to maintain confidentiality regarding this case. Discussion of these points prior to case presentation is often helpful. The more individuals who know about a person's private sphere, the more vulnerable that person becomes.

When a client changes therapists, in order to insure continuity of treatment, the new therapist must have the client's case history. The information given should only be that which is relevant to the actual treatment plan. This means that perhaps not everything the client confided in therapy need be relayed to the other therapist. Again, this is a matter of limiting the client's vulnerability. For example, suppose the client's principal problem is a poor relationship with her employer. Would knowledge about the unusual sexual preferences of the client, as contained in the current therapist's files, be of any use to the next therapist? If the therapist has found no connection between that and the client's main problem, such information probably should not be relayed to the other therapist.

While the difficult cases involving confidentiality require careful deliberation on the part of psychologists, they should also be cognizant of the fact that in *ordinary* situations a person's privacy may be inadvertently violated. As Siegal (1979) points out.

> Breaches of privacy and confidentiality often occur in a seemingly innocuous manner . . . . Whether on the telephone or in person, a psychologist should simply not make patients or clients an item of casual gossip or chitchat. "I have a patient who . . . " is all too often the casual party-talk kind of potentially destructive conversation. (p. 256)

COMPETENCE

The last obligation to be discussed is competence, but its position in this chapter does not reflect its importance. As we have discussed, there are circumstances under which it would be necessary to compromise or violate the principles of consent or confidentiality; thus those principles state only *prima facie* duties that are not absolute. But no such circumstances would seem to exist for the principle of competence. This is to say that the duty to be competent and maintain competence is absolute. Because people consult psychologists for a wide variety of problems and have trust in their abilities, clients have a right to receive services of consistently high quality. In addition, the duty to be competent in the psychologist's profession, which consists of doing things to and for others, entails the duty to respect the rights of those individuals and in part to understand what constitute morally legitimate exceptions to the duties to obtain consent and maintain confidentiality. We might also point out that Kant's categorical imperative would prohibit a psychologist from knowingly or carelessly acting in an incompetent manner, for what the psychologist would be saying by such an action is that he or she could will that all psychologists do the same. And of course such a universal law would totally undermine the profession.

Adequately analyzing competence is not an easy task and there has been little agreement concerning what constitutes competent practice. Part of the difficulty arises from the nature of the profession. Psychology involves a rich diversity of orientations, approaches, and techniques. For example, various methods of therapy are effective depending on the kind of client or the nature of the client's problem, or even perhaps on the therapist who implements a technique. And outcome studies on therapeutic techniques are difficult to conduct and interpret compared to similar studies in medicine.

The APA Task Force (1978) on the role of psychology in the criminal justice system says that competence is not so much a characteristic of the psychologist, in the sense of having appropriate degrees or licenses, but rather an interaction between the abilities of the psychologist and the demands of a given setting. A psychologist may be competent in one setting and incompetent in another. (p. 1105)

Nevertheless, there have been attempts at general definitions of competence and due to the complex considerations, such definitions have equated educational experience and competence. However, factors other than education are relevant to the notion of competence. Practical knowledge, training experience, and self-reporting are factors to be considered. In addition, competent psychologists who do therapy must also have an ability to effect desired behavorial changes. Those who do evaluations must have proper training and experience, and research psychologists must know research design. But in all areas of practice, competent psychologists must be sensitive to the ethical issues which pertain to their areas of practice.

We will now examine some of the elements thought to be relevant to the concept of competence.

A commonly accepted requirement of competence emphasizes the training of an individual psychologist. This focuses on relevant formal schooling and supervised field experience. This is one of the primary criteria employed by state licensing boards. In order to determine whether an individual is competent to practice, a board compares the person's training to some standard set of training experience. However, this approach begs the question because it must first be specified what counts as relevant training.

Most licensing boards avoid dealing with the potentially problematic relationships between competence and training by specifying certain degree requirements, i.e., a master's degree or a doctorate in psychology or clinical psychology. But since the content of programs and the methods of measuring the amount of knowledge acquired by students in a program vary considerably, stricter and more specific approaches to identifying competence are often invoked. (Even if there were uniformity in these areas, relevant training alone does not suffice as a condition for competence.) The APA has vacillated about the basic entry requirement (the M.A. or Ph.D.) for professional practice. The current orientation is to establish the Ph.D. as the basic entry requirement. While some would argue that this is just an attempt to establish high standards and protect consumers, others would suggest that the real issue is insurance reimbursements. Once psychologists earned this privilege (previously available only to psychiatrists and other physicians), M.A. level psychologists were quickly disenfranchized. While standards for training and APA approval of programs are available at the Ph.D. level, they are not for M.A. programs. This is unfortunate since M.A. psychologists provide most of the services in rural areas, especially in public facilities.

When someone is awarded a graduate degree in psychology, it is assumed that the individual has a grasp of facts, theories, and methods of research. But as we pointed out, there is diversity in program content and methods of assessing psychology students' knowledge and ability. Hence there is no guarantee that the individual has acquired such knowledge simply because he or she has completed a graduate program. And so most state licensing boards use a conjunctive definition of "competence" which includes both training and objective knowledge as criteria for identifying competent psychologists. This approach has the advantage of being easily measurable, through the administration of objective tests, which accounts for its frequent use. The licensing exam employed by almost all the states is a general psychology exam. Experimental psychologists and clinical psychologists take the same examination. The emphasis is on objective knowledge, rather than on practice issues. Thus such a test does not necessarily identify *competent* psychologists if "competence" is understood more broadly than mere training and knowledge of the field. Gross (1978) says that licensing boards "restrict themselves to the administration of examinations" (pp. 1012-13) and even then they only measure minimal competence. He notes that "If there is a tie between competence and licensing, there ought to be some evidence of that tie in the work of licensing boards. Unfortunately, there is not" (p. 1012). However, the APA has made an attempt to address the issue of competence in the various specialty standards.

An additional criterion and method for determining competence is self-report and self-restraint. At first glance, self-report may not seem very crucial, but it is important for two reasons: (1) from a moral point of view, it reflects honesty on the part of the psychologist, and (2) from the consumer's point of view, frequently it is the only criterion available. This requirement focuses on some of the psychologist's verbal behavior when interacting with a client. Honest self-report entails accuracy in representing one's skills, training, and expertise. "Competence" therefore is partly understood in terms of a psychologist's ability to identify his or her strengths and weaknesses and, in the case of clinical psychologists, a willingness to refer or to refuse to treat a client whose problem is beyond the existing competence of the psychologist.

Self-reporting or monitoring is important because the principle of professional practice relies on the practitioners as the primary means of enforcement. Perhaps this is because most psychological services involve private interactions; at least this is the case with therapy. The incidence of malpractice claims is quite low. [From 1976-80 the ratio of claims to insured was approximately .002, which represents a decrease in claims from previous years. (Wright, 1981a)] And the other avenues of redress are also infrequently used. Individuals with complaints about ethical violations can either take their cases to state licensing boards or APA's Committee on Scientific and Professional Ethics and Conduct (CSPEC). At the state level the sanctions are more potent (revocation or suspension of an individual's license to practice) but these agencies often lack the financial resources to follow up on cases where the individual practitioner chooses to take the issue to court. At a national level the sanctions seem impotent. In reviewing cases adjudicated by the CSPEC, the most serious sanction is being removed from the membership rolls of the APA. Prior to revision in 1980, individuals could keep the case against them from even being heard by voluntarily dropping their membership, an approach which was frequently used by the accused (Hare-Mustin & Hall, 1981).

This particular requirement of self-reporting emphasizes the autonomy of individual psychologists and assumes that they are responsible in their practice. Because it is virtually impossible for a board to monitor individual psychologists in their private practice (nor should there be a need to do so), psychologists must take it upon themselves to ensure their own honesty and responsibility to consumers. This particular feature of competence might be summarized simply as knowing what one can do effectively, what one cannot do effectively, and acting on that knowledge.

However, while it is true from a moral point of view that psychologists should limit themselves to practices in which they are skilled, this is not always the case in practice. At present, once a psychologist is licensed, he or she can engage in any kind of therapeutic and evaluative activity for which a consumer can be found. A psychologist trained in child psychology may believe he is competent to do marriage counseling and proceeds to do so. Or perhaps the psychologist merely has an opportunity to do marriage counseling and does so without thought about his ability to handle such cases. The effects could be harmful or at least unproductive. In order to protect the consumer, it might be advisable on the part of licensing boards to look to the medical profession as a guide—to take a specialty licensing approach. (The American Board of Examiners in Practicing Psychologists does use a specialty approach but this level of certification is voluntary.) Just as a general practitioner of medicine can deal with physical problems which are not too severe, so a psychologist licensed in general psychology can deal with clients whose psychological problems are not too difficult to solve and that do not require very specific knowledge of complex techniques in order to be maximally effective. But just as the general practitioner will refer a patient who has a severe problem of a particular nature to a specialist in the field, so would the general psychologist refer a client to a psychologist with the relevant specialty license. Should a psychologist discover that a client has severe problems, she should refer the client to a trained psychotherapist with the appropriate specialty. That the psychologist does so would, of course, depend on self-report, which might be better guaranteed if psychologists had malpractice suits brought against them as frequently as physicians do.

In order for competence to be analyzed adequately as applied to clinical and counseling psychologists, two more but rather complicated criteria must be specified. They concern therapeutic ability and clinical judgment. However, it should be noted that "it is fruitless to attempt to assess the global competence of psychologists in treating psychological disorder. The question needs to be much more task-specific: '*How* competent are *which* psychologists at treating *which* people for *what* problems?' " (APA, 1978, p. 1106).

Therapeutic ability is being able to understand what counts as improvement and to change behavior in light of that. While the ability of a psychologist to help an individual with a particular problem is surely a necessary condition for competence, it is difficult to specify precisely what is involved in this and in identifying this ability. Mere knowledge of therapeutic techniques is not sufficient. What is important is that the psychologist is able to determine which technique is most appropriate for a client's particular problem. This requires a diagnosis that is based on interviews with the client and that is a result of trained intuition or insight

CASE STUDY 3.3

A clinical psychologist with training in individual therapy and who has a private practice has read a couple of books on growth groups. He is a personal friend of the chair of a university department. The chairperson has been interested in growth groups and would like to have the faculty of her department participate in a group encounter. She tells the psychologist about her interest and informs her that there is money available for such a workshop since she believes it would aid in faculty development. She asks him to conduct the growth group and he accepts. Arrangements are made without informing the faculty of the nature of the workshop. They are simply told that they will be expected to participate in a faculty development workshop. During the sessions the psychologist encourages the group members to express all positive and negative feelings toward one another. Some are reluctant to do so, yet the psychologist pressures them into revealing their feelings. In addition, a couple of male faculty members make sexual innuendos toward one of the female faculty members. After the growth group experience, some of the feelings expressed in the workshop affect the working relationship among several people in the department. Because of their concern, they relate this to the psychologist and tell him they would like a follow-up workshop to alleviate the tensions in the department. The psychologist replies, "I really don't think I'm interested in doing any more group work. But I will be glad to see you individually in my private practice."

---

into the nature of the client's difficulty. The competent psychologist is able to go beyond the client's statements if necessary in order to get as clear a picture as possible of the case. Admittedly this is a vague characterization of therapeutic ability, and there are disagreements among psychologists concerning which insight is correct. There is no quick or easy way to resolve these differences. Thus it is understandable why licensing agents so seldom use this criterion. Besides, how can such an ability be identified even if there were agreement regarding correctness of insight? The preferred method would be to observe a psychologist working with a client. This approach (along with others) is used by the American Board of Examiners of Practicing Psychologists. But it is time-consuming and expensive. It also relies on the judgment of the examiners, who may be biased in favor of their own school of thought.

Another possible way to test this ability would be to examine transcripts or tapes of therapy sessions. This procedure is more frequently used but it too is problematic. This method suffers from a selection bias since a therapist will, of course, select a good case to present. To remedy this, it would be necessary to choose at random several of the psychologist's cases.

A third possible test would be to interview clients or former clients (or perhaps a questionnaire would suffice) regarding improvement in behavior, mental health, or goal achievement. However, the many problems associated with the evaluation of therapeutic success in general present difficulties for using therapeutic ability as a practical requirement for competence. Consumer feedback is not always a reliable indicator. There may be cognitive dissonance on the part of the client or former client concerning the effectiveness of therapy. A person who has invested much time and money in therapy might view herself as improved in order to justify the investment, even though there is no behavioral evidence of improvement. This problem could perhaps be solved by a representative sampling of the psychologist's clients, which should produce an overall picture of his or her therapeutic ability. This approach does raise questions concerning confidentiality in that clients may not want to be contacted.

The other ability which is necessary for competence is clinical judgment. By this we mean an ability to make reasonable judgments in resolving the dilemmas which arise in therapy. For example, a competent psychologist must know what kinds of circumstances justify violating a principle such as consent or confidentiality. This ability also requires insight since decision-making problems arise in cases where the correct decision is not obvious. Evaluating this ability of a psychologist would be done either through interviewing or through testing in which the psychologist is given the opportunity to demonstrate his or her method of moral reasoning.

We should point out that therapeutic ability and clinical judgment do not entail each other. A psychologist may be quite successful in improving clients' behavior yet may do so in ways that are too intrusive. Or perhaps the psychologist is careless with confidential information. This would indicate a lack of moral sensitivity that can be expressed as an inability to make correct clinical judgments. On the other hand, a psychologist may reason correctly in cases of conflict of principles but be unsuccessful in promoting positive behavioral changes and thus lack therapeutic ability.

Until now most of the discussion on competence has centered around psychotherapy. Competence is also required in teaching, testing, consulting, and research.

The teaching of psychology shares much with teaching in any other area insofar as the minimum requirement of competence is having adequate education and training in one's specialty. Competent teaching requires keeping abreast of new developments and knowledge in the subject to be taught. In psychology, doing field work can help to upgrade academic knowledge. New evaluative devices or better testing procedures are being developed rapidly. The psychology teacher who does nothing but teach can (and often does) ignore these improvements. In addition, a competent psychology teacher should be aware of the ethical considerations of the content of a course. For example, it would be considered incompetent as well as unethical to present case history material which readily identifies subjects.

In testing, the minimum competency requirement would be properly supervised training on those tests that are complex, e.g., the Rorschach, the Thematic Apperception Test (TAT), or any of the Wechsler tests. This requirement is over and above a basic understanding of statistics and a solid background in tests and measurements. And new tests are developed on a regular basis. If there is any doubt whatsoever about the use or interpretation of a new test, a competent psychologist would consult with someone who has already developed proficiency with the new procedure. Competency in testing also includes knowledge of what to include and what not to include in a report. Certain labels or the inclusion of irrelevant details can harm the consumer. A sensitivity to others should be a part of the concept of competency.

Consulting activities in psychology are many and varied. Psychologists are asked to consult with schools, industries, and institutions. The skills required for one agency may be very different from those required for another. A minimal requirement for competency in this area is for the psychologist to recognize his or her limits as well as strengths. For example, a clinical psychologist may or may not have the necessary skills for industrial/organizational (I/O) psychology. And an I/O psychologist would not be considered competent unless he or she were firmly grounded in antidiscrimination legislation. In Chapter 8 we will show that even knowledge of legality is not enough; moral competence is also required.

Research ranges from simple to extremely complex designs. Once more, a competent psychologist will not undertake, or will consult with others before attempting, an experiment beyond his or her level of adequacy. And knowledge of impact on subjects must be considered. This requires a full knowledge of the procedure for obtaining valid consent from research subjects and what circumstances justify deceiving subjects.

In summary, "competence" must be analyzed in terms of a broad variety of features. While some of them may be difficult to identify accurately, they do reflect the expectation that psychologists must not only be skilled professionals in the strict sense but must also possess an ability to evaluate honestly and objectively their own skills and to make reasonable, responsible decisions of both a professional and a moral nature. Competent psychologists recognize and appreciate the position they are in regarding the well-being of those whom their actions may affect.

Chapter 4

Therapeutic Techniques

Psychologists who practice psychotherapy are engaged in a process that aims at changing a person's attitudes and/or behavior. Psychotherapy can be defined as

> the treatment, by psychological means, of problems of an emotional nature in which a trained person deliberately establishes a professional relationship with the patient with the object of (1) removing, modifying, or retarding existing symptoms, (2) mediating disturbed patterns of behavior, and (3) promoting positive personality growth and development. (Wolberg, 1977, p. 3)

For our purposes we will focus on the formal therapeutic activities of trained therapists. Not everyone seeks the aid of a therapist to deal with his or her problems; many individuals seek and utilize informal therapy or counseling instead. Informal counseling is done by friends, ministers, family members, bartenders, and taxicab drivers. People who do informal counseling have no special responsibility because their relationship to those whom they counsel is not a therapeutic relationship. Psychologists are often forced into informal counseling, for example with students or people asking advice. But a competent psychologist would recognize the problems inherent in such informal arrangements. If the problem is severe, psychologists often suggest that the person work with someone in formal therapy.

In formal therapy, certain values are presupposed. It would be unrealistic and naive to assume that psychotherapists can and ought to be completely value neutral. For at a minimum what is presupposed as a basic value is client autonomy and the promotion of it is a part of the goal of therapy. Even those who see a particular therapeutic technique as a mere application of a solution to a problem cannot deny that the reason they want to use the technique is that they value helping a person become a more autonomous and responsible individual with the ability to make free choices affecting his or her life.

While client autonomy may be the most basic and obvious value presupposed in therapy, there are other aspects of therapy which indicate that therapy and the use of a particular therapeutic technique is not value neutral and that psychologists who engage in the therapeutic process must deal with questions of values. In this chapter we will first explore some of these questions and then discuss several therapeutic techniques in order to examine which ethical problems they may have in common and which may be peculiar to certain types of techniques.

The fact that a person is in therapy suggests diminished autonomy at least to some extent. A person with claustrophobia is controlled by that fear. Someone who is sexually inhibited is restricted by that inhibition in a personal relationship. So one goal of therapy is to increase the client's autonomy so that actions are a result of free choice and not the result of some controlling influence. This is not to say that anyone who seeks therapy is completely lacking autonomy, for there are degrees of autonomy. The fact that a person voluntarily seeks therapy and implicitly, if not explicitly, contracts with the therapist indicates some autonomy. And the client's problem may determine the extent of that person's autonomy. A client who has a fear of snakes may not have his life greatly affected by that fear if he lives where there are no snakes. In all other ways this person may be a functioning, autonomous being. A client who suffers from depressive episodes that make it difficult to function in ordinary life has less autonomy. The fact that a person seeks therapy indicates that he or she is having trouble coping with some aspect of life because of a problem. The amount of influence the problem has on a person's life determines the extent to which the client is able to make free, rational, and responsible decisions.

CASE STUDY 4.1

A client has been in individual therapy for six months. After five months the therapist believes that a great deal of progress has been made in the resolution of sexual problems which have greatly affected her marriage. However, during the last month the client has become enamoured with a minister who appears on a local TV station on a regular basis. This minister repeatedly claims that if a person has problems, "the sole remedy is to turn to God." Each session becomes more and more devoted to conversation about God, the Lord, miracles, etc. The psychologist is not a religious person but he realizes that for many people religion can be a source of comfort and security. However, in this situation, it appears to the psychologist that the client's preoccupation with the relationship between sex and sin is becoming detrimental rather than beneficial. Her relationship with her husband is deteriorating and her responsibilities as a mother are being neglected. She reports that "God has told me that sex is sinful and I should never indulge in sex again." When asked if she heard God's voice she replies, "No, it is just an idea but it is almost as if God is telling me what to do." During the fourth session after becoming enamoured with the minister, the client says that she is terminating therapy and that she is "going to put my destiny in the hands of the Lord." The therapist tries to convince her that in his judgment her situation is growing worse and that to terminate therapy would be irrational. He further informs her that if she continues this pattern of thinking, his only choice will be to recommend to her husband that she be committed to a mental institution.

It is often assumed that because a therapist attempts to help others become more autonomous, the therapist is already an autonomous individual. In order for that to be so, therapists need to examine their own values and be aware of blind spots. A client may encourage and succeed in having a sexual relationship with the therapist because the therapist is not totally aware of how he can be manipulated. Or a therapist may have the need to be paternalistic or to have some other emotional needs satisfied and thus may be reluctant to terminate therapy when it is appropriate. It may be expected that therapists should be free of problems that prevent the therapist from being autonomous, suggesting that therapists themselves ought to undergo therapy.

Historically, individual or group therapy has been a required part of graduate training programs in the clinical areas, and this practice is becoming more frequent in contemporary programs. If one expects therapists to have more autonomy and better mental health than average individuals, then this trend deserves support.

Since the goal of therapy is to promote autonomy, one basic issue is whether the therapist should exert any influence on the client in goal selection, since that would seem to be a further diminishing of client autonomy, or at least a failure to encourage autonomy. Before discussing this question, it should be noted that to influence is not to coerce. As we discussed in the previous chapter, coercion is forcing a person to do something against his or her will, which implies exerting pressure on a person. Influence does not have that implication. Both coercion and influence may result in a person's changing his or her behavior but the means by which that is accomplished is quite different in each case. When one person influences another, consciously or unconsciously, something of that person rubs off onto the other. Whereas a therapist can avoid *coercing* a client, a therapist cannot usually help but *influence* a client. To say that the therapist should not exert any influence at all on the client is both unrealistic and irresponsible. It is unrealistic because, as Stolz (1978) points out, "Therapists inevitably influence clients' decisions even when ostensibly leaving them free to choose" (p. 38). In any intimate relationship, there will be influence of one person on the other, and the therapist-client relationship is no exception.

But should the therapist *consciously* try to influence the client? To say no is irresponsible. For if the therapist exerts no influence on the client then one wonders why anybody should seek therapy in the first place or why a therapist should get paid for his or her services when in actuality no services are being provided. To claim that the therapist should not try to influence a client suggests that therapy is a waste of time. Controlling behavior is part of the therapist's job and, according to London (1969), "All forms of psychotherapy aim to control behavior . . . " (p. 41). He describes the goal of therapy partly in terms of restoring control of behavior to the client, which is to help the client become more autonomous. He says, "The goal of therapy in every case is to restore control of the disordered behavior to the patient or to eliminate it from the repertory of his behaviors by exerting a complex series of controls over him so that, either way, he will not be troubled by it any more" (p. 43). Even if the second means is employed— "exerting a complex series of controls over him"—the end result is still the same—a more autonomous human being, since the person no longer will be controlled by the disordered behavior.

Given that the therapist ought to exert influence on the client as a means of effecting behavioral change, what should be the extent of that influence in goal selection? It goes without saying that the influence should result in a positive change in the client's behavior and attitudes. But what counts as positive change? Is "positive change" defined in terms of what the client wants or in terms of the therapist's perception of how the client ought to be? When the client and therapist both agree on the accepted goals of therapy and hence what counts as positive change, the therapist is in a morally acceptable situation and can exert a great deal of influence on the client to help him or her achieve those goals. But what if the therapist's concept of positive change in the client does not coincide with the client's, that is, there is a difference in values? Should the therapist make a conscious effort to refrain from influencing the client in order not to interfere with the client's choice of goals? Suppose a client has as her goal to become less assertive because her assertiveness is causing problems with a job which she otherwise enjoys. She sees becoming less assertive as a positive change but the therapist disagrees with her goal and believes that finding another job is a more viable option. To respect the client's choice and her idea of what counts as positive change, the therapist may make a conscious effort not to influence her choice of goals and may even try not to exert any conscious influence at all. But in that case the therapist may not work very efficiently with the client. Even if a therapist could work equally effectively with a client whether or not he or she agreed with the client's goals, it may seem that to accept any value or goal of the client commits the therapist to personal relativism and the subjectivity of values. If the therapist tries to convert the client to accept his or her value system, the therapist is committed to the objectivity of values and assumes that his or her value system is correct. While this may be true, it doesn't follow that a therapist who believes in the objectivity of values is morally required to convert the client. For the therapist need not be paternalistic but instead may let the client choose his or her values and goals. Assuming the client is competent, he or she can be held responsible for the consequences of having those values and goals. This is to acknowledge the client's autonomy. Thus a therapist who accepts the values of the client even when they conflict with his or her own need not be committed to the subjectivity of values but rather to the autonomy of the client which is the therapist's basic value.

Given the preceding, does it follow that the therapist should acquiesce to any goal the client has? According to one view,

> except in very rare cases, the client should be given what he wants; the therapist should not impose his own values on the client. The therapist . . . may be thought of as a social engineer; his or her job is to decide which therapy is best suited to the client's problem. This raises an empirical, not a moral question. (Erwin, 1978, p. 173)

Two points need to be made here: (1) some specification is needed as to what counts as a "very rare" case, and (2) to imply that therapy itself raises only empirical questions is certainly naive. While therapy is not just a matter of applied values and ethics, neither is it just pure science (Karasu, 1980). This is to say that therapists at times may have to make value or ethical judgments regarding the client's goals. But to say that a value judgment may have to be made is not necessarily to imply that the judgment is purely subjective, for most likely there are objective grounds on which the therapist can question a client's goal. For example, the goal may be unrealistic and hence unachievable. A client may have as a goal to enter medical school and is suffering from anxiety and depression because his goal has been repeatedly frustrated. The therapist discovers that the client lacks the necessary intelligence and so, instead of helping the client to reach that particular goal, may try to get the client to set a more realistic goal. Or the client's goal may not be in his or her best interest. A client may want to adjust to a marriage in which his wife has repeatedly abused him. This indicates that staying married under any circumstances is a more basic value than his own welfare and the therapist may want to explore that ranking of values. In another instance a client may have a goal which is immoral, such as changing a spouse's behavior so that she can be more easily manipulated. Or the client may have a goal which is criminal in addition to being immoral. A therapist would certainly not be obliged to help a client achieve the goal of seducing a neighbor's child. In these cases, where the goal is unrealistic, not in the client's best interest, obviously immoral, or criminal, the therapist may engage in extended discussion of the goal and its sources in order to lead the client to reevaluate the goal. It is the job of the therapist to try to influence the client in order to assist the client in becoming a fully functioning person. But if the therapist is unsuccessful in getting the client to change goals, the therapist has the right to refuse to treat the person. This situation is not unlike situations in the medical profession. A physician who does not believe that abortion should be a method of birth control may refuse to perform an abortion for a couple who has repeatedly chosen abortion as a means of birth control. Or a psychiatrist who is opposed to the use of electroconvulsive therapy because of possible damaging effects may refuse to use it on a client who requests it.

In cases where a client comes to therapy with no goal or a misrepresented goal, the therapist must work on defining a goal. This may be frustrating for the client who may not want a diagnosis of the problem. But in order for therapy to be effective, the therapist must work toward helping the client define the goal of therapy.

If the client's goal strikes the therapist as being eccentric, the therapist must recognize that labeling a goal as eccentric reflects a bias on the part of the therapist which may be a result of adhering to cultural norms.

Therapists should be aware of the fact that a client's culture may pose a threat to autonomous goal selection. For example, women may tend to select culturally determined goals and therapists may encourage them to do so. In fact, in one study Broverman, Broverman, and Clarkson (1970) found that both male and female clinicians tend to see traits that are typically ascribed to men as the ones which indicate mental health in an adult. Among traits seen as indicative of healthy women were: more submissive, less independent, more easily influenced, less aggressive, less competitive, more emotional, less objective, and disliking math and science. They conclude that clinicians tend to have "a powerful, negative assessment of women" (p. 4) and that "a double standard of health exists for men and women, that is, the general standard of health is actually applied only to men while healthy women are perceived as significantly less healthy by adult standards" (p. 5). They go on to suggest that "clinicians are significantly less likely to attribute traits which characterize healthy adults to a woman than they are likely to attribute these traits to a healthy man" (p. 5). Clinicians tend to accept an "adjustment" notion of health and hence a healthy person is one who adjusts to the different social norms for male and female behavior in this society. This attitude perpetuates sex-role stereotypes. Hence if a female client chooses a goal that reflects a sex-role stereotype, the therapist should perhaps first examine the reasons for her goal selection to determine if it is an autonomous choice or if it is unduly influenced by social norms.

A person who deviates from the social norm may feel pressured into "voluntarily" consenting. And Erwin (1978) suggests that even if the request is voluntary, if the therapist agrees to the client's request, the therapist may simply be perpetuating society's unfavorable attitude toward those who deviate from the norm but whose behavior is not harmful but simply disapproved of. The fact that techniques exist that can change behavior and that therapists use indicates "that the behavior is undesirable and needs to be eliminated" (Erwin, 1978, p. 214). Of course if the client realizes that his or her decision is being coerced to some extent yet rationally decides that he or she would be better off if changed, "to withhold therapy merely because the decision is not wholly voluntary seems to be unjustified paternalism" (Erwin, 1978, p. 215).

It might be said that if the client is rational, morally responsible, and has freely chosen the goal, the therapist has an obligation to accept the goal and to help the client achieve it. But if a person is morally responsible and rational, why would such a person seek or need therapy? It might be that the person's life style is at odds with socially accepted standards and the person is suffering anxiety because of social pressure. Thus the person's goal might be to reduce the anxiety he or she feels because of being at odds with social standards. A person who chooses to remain a homosexual may suffer from anxiety due to the social unacceptability of her sexual preference and has as a goal to learn how not to be intimidated by people who are unaccepting. Or a wife who is divorcing her husband may not want custody of the children because she feels unable to cope with them, yet has guilt feelings over it. She makes a free, rational choice to give up her children, yet because of society's views about motherhood she feels guilty about her decision. Thus her goal in therapy might be to reduce the feelings of guilt. The therapist may not approve of homosexuality or of a mother giving up her children but because in each case the client appears to have made a rational, responsible decision, it would seem that the therapist ought to help the client. But as we mentioned, if the therapist doesn't approve of the client's goal, he or she may be ineffective as a therapist, in which case the client should be referred to someone who can be more accepting of the goal and hence more effective.

We have said that the therapist cannot avoid influencing the client and that furthermore the therapist *ought* to influence the client. Therapists need to recognize their influence, be it subtle or overt, and in doing so they can monitor it so that it does not become intrusive and diminish autonomy. But should the therapist actively advise the client? Since the goal of therapy is to promote client autonomy, it may be thought that advising would interfere with that goal and hence the therapist should refuse to give advice. However, it cannot be stated categorically that a therapist should never give advice on the grounds that doing so always interferes with promoting the client's autonomy. For whether or not a therapist should in some instances be directive will depend on the client. Suppose a client has the self-perception of being unable to make any decisions on his own and is accustomed to having others make decisions for him. In this case the therapist would only be perpetuating the client's dependency by being directive. On the other hand, if the client has typically been able to make decisions but in a particular case simply needs the opinion of an expert, the therapist may provide it without necessarily diminishing the client's autonomy. A truly autonomous person can still make a rational decision without being overly influenced by this expert opinion. Suppose a client doesn't know how to handle his exaggerated feeling of anger toward his wife when she has to bring work home from the office. In this case the therapist may offer several alternatives as to how to deal with his anger. Clearly, the therapist's opinion or judgment about the most effective means of achieving a goal is implied in the therapeutic contract.

In some instances it may be irresponsible for the therapist not to advise the client of options. For example, suppose a client is feeling suicidal because of depression and the therapist has some reason to believe that the client may act on those feelings. Here it might be irresponsible for the therapist not to suggest hospitalization or at least see a physician who can prescribe medication.

However, whether or not being directive is in order, the therapist might first get the client to explore possible solutions to the problem and examine the acceptability of those solutions. Thus in the cases mentioned above, the therapist might ask the client first what he or she thinks could be done. The therapist could have the angry client explore more positive means of expressing feelings. The therapist with the suicidal client might have the client think of ways to combat the suicidal feelings before advising hospitalization. The reason for this is to give the client a chance to arrive at a solution on his or her own in order to foster independent decision making and hence foster client autonomy.

Just as influencing is not coercing, neither is advising. While advising may impinge a bit more on a client's autonomy than does mere influencing (since the therapist is looked upon as an expert by the client), the client is still free to accept or reject the advice. But to coerce a client is to leave him or her without a real choice and hence is to deny the client's autonomy. Thus one of the most problematic issues in therapy is how to best increase client autonomy. The therapeutic setting is, to some extent, an indication of the extent of the client's autonomy and may color the therapist's perception of the client and therefore influence his or her ideas on the justification of coercion. In private settings, community mental health centers, university counseling centers, and in cases of voluntary commitment, more than likely the therapist will perceive the client as a basically autonomous person but one who needs help with a specific problem. Because of the voluntariness associated with these settings, coercion is rarely if ever justified. Perhaps the only time coercion could be used in an out-patient setting would be in cases of justifiable involuntary commitment. Because psychologists in any therapeutic setting have some degree of power over the client, they should be aware that coercion is possible since the client is in a vulnerable position. Hence coercion should be used only when the problem is severe—to prevent harm to others, or in the case of incompetents, to prevent harm to themselves—and there is no alternative.

Because the therapist's ultimate and basic goal is to promote client autonomy, any therapeutic technique that is restrictive or intrusive will at least temporarily diminish client autonomy. By a restrictive technique we mean a technique that imposes limitations on an individual's freedom to move about. The use of time out or, in the case of hospitalized clients, the use of the "Quiet Room" are examples of restrictive techniques. Such techniques diminish a client's autonomy because coercion is involved. However, the client is still able to resist behavioral change. By an intrusive technique we mean, rather broadly and in general, a technique which controls or modifies a person's behavior by impinging on his or her selfhood, which may do so rapidly and which the person cannot resist. Drug therapy is one of the most obvious examples of an intrusive technique. Certain drugs such as major tranquilizers may also be restrictive in that they may limit a person's ability to move about freely, but that is a side effect and is typically not (or ought not to be) the primary reason why they are used. While both the use of intrusive and restrictive techniques may at least temporarily diminish client autonomy, the use of intrusive techniques may be more morally problematic. Thus psychiatrists, who are in a position to choose drug therapy over other types of techniques, should be aware of the moral nature of such therapy. This is not to say that intrusive techniques automatically have the effect of diminishing client autonomy. Drug therapy may actually help the client become more autonomous. Though the client is being controlled by drugs, it may be that that control is what frees the person from another type of control which has diminished his or her autonomy. Intrusive techniques that enhance autonomy are acceptable, suggesting one criterion for evaluation.

Psychologists, too, have access to intrusive techniques in the form of aversive therapies. Such techniques can be thought of as intrusive because they seek to change a part of a person's personality, whereas a restrictive technique usually aims at dealing with an isolated piece of behavior. The use of aversive therapy is not *a priori* morally wrong since it may be that some aspect of a person's personality needs to be changed, either because it is distressing to the person or he or she wants to engage in conduct which is harmful to others. A homosexual may want to change his sex preferences for whatever reason and is willing to undergo aversive conditioning to accomplish that.[1] Or a person may have a very aggressive personality and acts out that aggression in violent ways. Aversive conditioning might change the aggressive part of the person's personality. If aversive techniques were effective in treating certain types of problems, they should be used only as a last resort because they are intrusive and rely on administering pain to an individual. However, this may be a moot point. There is a question of effectiveness because behavioral change due to such techniques are rarely generalized. Thus aversive techniques are seldom used.

Aversive techniques are usually thought of in terms of administering some type of physically painful stimulus to an individual such as an electric shock, which we have suggested is intrusive. But Stolz (1978) suggests that criticism of the client or open confrontation is also aversive. Perhaps the reason is that such techniques also cause the client pain, albeit psychological pain. However, we would not classify such techniques as intrusive because for one, the client can resist or terminate therapy, and for another, they are typically aimed at some particular behavior pattern. Hence an aversive technique may or may not be intrusive, depending on the nature of the change.

We have made a distinction between restrictive and intrusive techniques and from that distinction a point about client consent follows. If in some cases it is necessary to use a restrictive technique, the only moral justification for doing so is to control the client temporarily so that he or she will be in a state more suitable for the use of effective, nonrestrictive techniques. Hence, except in the case of an alcoholic who voluntarily goes to a detoxification center, which to some degree is restrictive, the client's consent to the use of a restrictive technique will, in most cases, not be possible.[2] But because the use of an intrusive technique seeks to change a part of the person, client consent would seem to be of utmost importance.

Assuming the client consents to the use of an aversive technique that is intrusive, is that sufficient to justify its use? Erwin (1978) says that this issue "cannot be disposed of simply by saying that we should give the client what he voluntarily requests; the request may not be voluntary, and catering to it may be wrong even if it is" (p. 214).

A variant of this problem is whether the client should be given *whatever* he or she requests. A client may request psychoanalysis for a problem which the therapist believes can be dealt with more effectively using some other technique. Or a client may request hypnosis to alleviate test anxiety when the therapist does not believe this will rid the client of the anxiety. Or the therapist may view this technique as more intrusive than other techniques, for example desensitization. To accede to the client's wishes may not be honest and may be a waste of the client's time and money. The therapist should suggest other alternatives and if the client rejects them, the therapist may be justified in refusing to accede to the client's request.

One question that needs to be addressed is truth-telling in therapy. Suppose a therapist is pessimistic about a client's overcoming depression. If the client asks the therapist what hope there is, should the therapist convey what he thinks? Since the therapist's main consideration should be for the welfare of the client, the therapist must ask what would best serve the welfare of the client. Salzman (1976) believes "that in the psychotherapeutic process an untruth is never justified, . . . but withholding the truth is quite different from telling a person a lie" (p. 102). He goes on to point out that

> In the present state of development of psychological theory our interpretations and observations are a long way from being verifiable, and consequently we may not be withholding a *truth* if we refrain from making an interpretation. (p. 102)

Another general problem that needs to be raised about psychotherapy concerns cost/benefit to the client. The question that arises is: should a therapist engage in lengthy, costly therapy which preserves more of client autonomy than the use of an intrusive technique, or should the therapist use an intrusive technique (or refer the client to a therapist who is competent in the use of such techniques) at the expense of temporarily diminishing client autonomy in order to accomplish the goal more quickly at less expense to the client?

Sometimes difficult choices must be made between these two courses of action. Any guidelines for decision making on this issue should fall somewhere in between always preserving client autonomy and always using the quickest, most effective technique. In the case of a client whose problem is not debilitating, the therapist should probably use a technique that preserves the client's autonomy even though it may take longer for the goal to be achieved. For example, a therapist whose client is suffering from depression that is not debilitating should use an autonomy-preserving technique rather than a technique that may prove temporarily effective in alleviating symptoms but is intrusive. A psychiatrist may have the option of prescribing a drug which eliminates the depressed behavior or working with the client to find the cause of the depression so that it is the client, in conjunction with the psychiatrist, who overcomes the problem rather than a drug.

But a client may have a problem that is so severe as to cause the person to be unable to function in everyday life. In that case a quick and effective technique should probably be used at the (temporary) expense of client autonomy in order to help the client function at a minimal level. Then a less intrusive or restrictive technique may be used. A person with an alcohol problem may go to a detoxification center that is restrictive but temporarily works on the client's problem. But the therapist may refuse to release the client immediately after detoxification even though doing so would seem to further client autonomy. The justification for doing so is that temporarily diminished client autonomy will result in long-term beneficial change. To cite another example, a psychiatrist may be justified in using drug therapy on a person suffering from psychotic depression (even without client consent) on the grounds that such intrusive therapy will get the client to a level where autonomy-preserving techniques can be used.

We have already discussed the obligation of psychologists to be competent, and in the context of this discussion, competence implies that the therapist is aware of the types of problems he or she can deal with effectively using a certain technique. A person may come to a therapist whose technique may work on the problem but the therapist sees that it will take too long and that another technique would be more effective. Or a therapist's technique may be effective in a short period of time in that it temporarily removes symptoms but will not achieve the larger goal. In each case the therapist should refer the person to one who is more suited to deal with the problem. Suppose a person with aquaphobia goes to a therapist who happens to be a psychoanalyst. Such a specific phobia can be treated without probing into underlying personality factors. In this case the therapist should refer the person to a therapist trained in behavior therapy since that kind of therapy has been proven successful in dealing with specific phobias. The cost to the person of treating the phobia would be phenomenal if psychoanalysis were used, whereas the cost would be much less if treated by a behavior therapist. Not to refer such a person might be irresponsible and an indication of incompetence if time, money, and client anxiety had to be considered. On the other hand, if a client-centered therapist has a client whose problem is anorexia nervosa, the therapist should refer the person to a behavior therapist with a psychoanalytic orientation. Such a therapist would initially apply behavioristic techniques but later would employ psychodynamic techniques. For a nondirective therapist to try to deal with this type of problem could be dangerous because lack of immediate intervention could lead to death.

As in any relationship, power can be misused, and in the therapeutic relationship we usually think of the power distribution as being unequal (in favor of the therapist). While there are many subtle ways that power can be misused, sexual activities with clients is a provocative and much publicized example. It has been commonly assumed that erotic interactions occur in conjunction with therapy but people were shocked when incidence figures became available. Holroyd and Brodsky (1977) found that 10 percent of the male therapists and 2 percent of the female therapists reported sexual interaction with clients, and these figures probably underestimate the prevalence. This is one practice which is clearly forbidden by the *Ethical Principles*. Some therapists justify this practice by suggesting that it has a positive impact on the therapeutic process, in that it makes therapy go faster or allows intimacy to develop more quickly. From the therapist's perspective this may be true but clients do not report similar experiences. Butler and Zelen (1977) contend that sexual interactions occur in times of personal crises where the therapists are experiencing adjustment problems themselves. Psychologists, like other people, have needs but therapy is expected to be a place where the therapist's needs are recognized and controlled. The suggestion that the psychologist is really the victim of lonely individuals who are perhaps motivated by the possibility of an insurance settlement is a little far-fetched. Even if we can assume that this is true, the psychologist's job is to avoid being "victimized" in this and other ways. Seductive clients do exist and this style is usually related to social adjustment problems. Sex with the seductive client is like playing any other "client game"; it fails to show the client that there are other options to achieve his or her ends. Since therapy is private and intimate, the development of erotic feelings is to be expected. If it is based on adjustment problems of the therapist, then therapy for the therapist is probably necessary. If it is just two people falling in love, then certain practical steps are necessary. Termination of therapy, referral of the client to another therapist, and perhaps a cooling off period would be appropriate. (When we refer to sex in therapy we do not mean sex therapy. Individuals practicing therapy for sexual disorders tend to be sensitive to the ethical issues involved and have worked out procedures which protect the client and themselves.)

The problem of erotic interactions with clients is basically a matter of dual relationships. Dual relationships are generally recognized as complicating and usually disturbing the therapeutic process. Dual relationships exist when, in addition to the professional relationship, there is some other relationship with the individual—friend, family member, student, or business partner, for example. The professional and nonprofessional roles create expectations or duties that can conflict. All experienced therapists have at some time received a request for therapy from a friend. Friends may expect that if they work with a therapist who knows them, they will feel more comfortable and that the therapist will already have significant information about the problem and perhaps its solution. Therapy with friends usually does not work out; either the therapeutic relationship or the friendship suffers. Objectivity from therapists should be expected and it is usually compromised when a therapist is involved with a client. Confrontation is never easy, but when a friend needs it, consideration of its impact on the friendship usually leads to avoiding it or watering it down. Practical problems such as fees or the impact on the friendship are enough to make therapists want to avoid this dual relationship. But the central issue from an ethical perspective is that it compromises the therapeutic relationship. Clearly, friends deserve better treatment, so referral to a respected therapist is in order.

The fact that therapists incur special responsibilities is evident, but what responsibilities do clients incur when they enter therapy? If the client agrees to the therapeutic process, he or she has the responsibility to follow through on recommended procedures that may be a part of a particular therapeutic technique. This is not to say that if therapy is unsuccessful the fault lies with the client, but it is to suggest that successful therapy is a two-way street. A client who places all the responsibility for the outcome of therapy on the therapist is not an active participant in the process.

Different approaches may have specific responsibilities. Behavior therapy may involve behavioral assignments or homework between sessions whereas psychoanalysis may require the disclosure of all thoughts. Any therapist who has unique expectations for the client needs to clarify these expectations before beginning therapy. And it is the client's responsibility to carry out these expectations if he or she consents to therapy. As we have indicated, one underlying goal of therapy is client autonomy, and this goal cannot be reached unless the client sees himself or herself as, at least in part, actively responsible for the outcome of therapy.

When confidentiality was discussed we focused on the therapist's responsibility. Therapists are bound to keep the content of sessions to themselves, but do similar duties exist for clients? Since the issue is the client's privacy,

---

CASE STUDY 4.2

A clinical psychologist who had just completed his internship was asked by his sister-in-law to provide some advice concerning a problem she was having with their two-year-old son. About three weeks before the child began to cry fiercely when put down to go to sleep. At the time the parents' schedule was irregular and the child was being put to bed much later than usual. The schedule had now stabilized but the child continued to express distress. It was now taking about three hours before the child settled into a restful sleep.

The psychologist has worked with similar problems in the past so he agreed to help, assuming that this problem would quickly respond to treatment. This notion was reinforced when he first met with his sister-in-law. She reported that both she and her husband would go into the child's room and try various things to calm or distract the child. When either parent picked him up he would stop crying and regain his composure. After playing with the child for ten to fifteen minutes they would put the child back down, but the quiet periods were usually followed by another episode of crying. The mother was concerned that the child was feeling abandoned and feared that permanent psychological harm might occur if the child was left to cry it out. The psychologist recommended an extinction program in which the parents would check the child's safety and comfort once and then allow the child to cry until he went to sleep.

The psychologist was away for two weeks and checked with his sister-in-law when he returned. She indicated that for the first week the program had started to work but her husband couldn't tolerate the noise so over her protests he would go get the child. At this point the sister-in-law began to discuss problems in the marital relationship that she saw as contributing to the problem. Having had similar problems with his brother's behavior, the psychologist was naturally sympathetic. He suggested that they all meet together to try to develop some consensus about how to deal with the child's crying. When they met that evening the discussion initially focused on the child but quickly shifted to the problems with the relationship. The husband felt that he was being ganged up on and refused to say anything. After a long silence the psychologist suggested that they go to the local mental health clinic since his treatment was going to be ineffective.

---

it is assumed that clients are free to disclose whatever they choose. Therapists who disagree with this view need to settle the issue before therapy is started as part of the consent agreement. Client disclosures can be problematic if the therapist is not careful. The therapist can suggest that the client also keep the interchanges in therapeutic sessions confidential. One of the authors was approached by a friend of a client at a party who apparently had been privy to a session-by-session account of what had happened in therapy. The friend was very complimentary of the therapist's skill and the unique approach used with the case (assertive training for anger control, which is not unusual). Both the client and the friend were graduate students in one of the helping professions so there were subtle factors suggesting that discussion of the case would not be inappropriate. One could interpret the client's disclosure as some kind of implied consent to violate confidentiality but this is quite presumptive. The author managed to "keep his jaws at rest" but this might have been related to spending most evenings writing and thinking about ethical issues.

So far we have discussed general problems relating to values and ethical issues that may arise in the therapeutic process. However, before turning to specific therapeutic techniques and examining them in light of ethical issues that might be peculiar to certain techniques, we should give a brief discussion of the ethical issues involved in group and in family therapy. We will not devote separate sections to them because they are not therapeutic techniques *per se*. Several techniques or variations of them can be used in working with families or with groups. But since we have pointed to some general ethical considerations arising in the therapeutic process in the discussion so far, we now want to show how some of those considerations arise in group and in family therapy.

While the ethical problems arising in group and in family therapy fall under similar categories, the nature of the problems are not always the same for both. For example, confidentiality presents a major problem for each. But the nature of the problem differs in each because unrelated group members may feel no strong obligation of confidentiality—hence a legally binding contract may be required (Bindrim, 1980)—while the family therapist is the one who may face a problem of confidentiality regarding what information revealed by an individual family member can be conveyed to other family members.

CASE STUDY 4.3

A family therapist has contracted to do therapy with a family of four. The couple has two daughters aged sixteen and fourteen. The father has agreed to participate in therapy only under the condition that there be a contract stating that all information received by the therapist from any one person in the family be revealed to everyone else. The therapist agrees, and the other members of the family consent to the terms of the contract.

The main problem is focused on the sixteen-year-old. The father believes her mother has been overindulgent and has not disciplined her enough, whereas he believes she needs strict supervision. This has caused problems between the couple which are now affecting the fourteen-year-old. The mother feels that his rigid attitude is driving the sixteen-year-old away and will do the same to the fourteen-year-old.

During the course of therapy, the fourteen-year-old finds out that her sister is pregnant and has made arrangements to have an abortion. She thinks this information may be revealed inadvertently in therapy either by her or her sister and is afraid her father would disown her sister if he found out. She telephones the therapist to relay this information.

Coercion is also a general concern for both that emerges in different ways. Parents may coerce children into participating in therapy, but group members, though voluntarily participating, may, for example, overtly or covertly coerce a member into divulging information at an inappropriate time.

A family in therapy differs from other groups in therapy insofar as family members usually must deal with each other on a daily basis whereas the group members need not. But because behavior change is a goal in any therapeutic process, such a change in one family member is more likely to have adverse effects on the others than in the case of those in group therapy. Hence the family therapist is more likely to have to deal with questions of priority regarding the welfare of an individual family member or members or the family as a unit, whereas the primary responsibility of the group therapist is to help everyone improve individually but does not have to be concerned with the group as a unit.

One final point needs to be made regarding group therapy. People who are in actual need of *therapy* rather than *personal growth* should avoid joining a group which is described as encounter or growth. It is not atypical for leaders of such groups to refuse to accept any responsibility for what happens to members of the group (Schutz, 1973). While this clearly is contrary to the "Guidelines for Psychologists Conducting Growth Groups" (APA, 1973), people who would agree to a contract containing a clause which relieves the group leader of any responsibility are responsible for what happens to them in the group—*Caveat emptor*.

We will now turn to specific therapeutic techniques and examine them to see what ethical issues might be peculiar to a certain type of technique. Our discussion will be devoted to psychoanalysis, client-centered therapy, behavior therapy, and rational-emotive therapy. We should point out that in our discussion of therapeutic techniques and the ethical issues, we will only highlight some of the aspects of the techniques. We do not pretend that a particular therapy will be practiced by every psychotherapist in precisely the manner described here. A therapeutic technique may be as varied as the therapist who uses it. Thus an individual therapist may face fewer or more ethical issues than we raise with a given technique, depending on how he or she uses it.

PSYCHOANALYSIS

Psychoanalysis is a form of psychotherapy which began around 1885 when Sigmund Freud began working with hysterical patients in Vienna, Austria. Through the years, some modifications in the theoretical constructs have been made, but most of Freud's basic theories are still maintained.

Many psychotherapists consider Freud's concept of the *dynamic unconscious* to be the most important principle in the entire psychoanalytic movement. Interactions between the conscious and unconscious must be seen as complex and ever-changing. When unconscious material is brought into awareness, the client[3] can make more rational decisions, suggesting that one goal of this technique is to encourage rational thinking. According to psychoanalysis, a principle difference between neurosis and normality is that the former causes a person to be "driven" by unconscious impulses (psychic determinism). This distinction is one of degree since even normal people have and repress unconscious conflicts. The more the unconscious is made conscious, the more normal, rational, and free the person becomes. As the unconscious becomes more and more conscious, there is an increasing emphasis on responsibility, which reflects the client's increasing autonomy. When the unconscious is made conscious, the client can move more toward self-actualization (which includes self-esteem, love, creativity, and productivity).

While other types of therapists also assume the importance and necessity of confidentiality, psychoanalysts seem to make more of a point to discuss it. Szasz (1965), in discussing some roles for psychoanalysts, goes so far as to say, "Do not communicate about (the client) with third parties, *whether or nor you have his consent to do so*" (p. 220, emphasis added). However, such a strong stand on confidentiality may cause problems because in some cases it may be beneficial to communicate about the client with a third party. And to refuse to do so even with the client's consent is to take a paternalistic attitude toward the client.

Psychoanalysis differs from directive therapeutic techniques in that "directive procedures such as advice, reassurance, or direct intervention in the patient's life are avoided except in certain extreme cases" (Fine, 1973, p. 20).*

However, as with most therapeutic techniques, acceptance of the client is essential. And

> with the acceptance by the therapist, and the growth of insights, the patient comes face to face with the conflicts between his feelings of love and feelings of hatred. In general, feelings of love when expressed meet with subtle or overt signs of approval from the analyst, while feelings of hatred, when expressed, meet with subtle or overt signs of disproval. As a result, the patient gradually begins to shift his whole emotional balance from hatred to love. This shift is accomplished in varying degrees in varying patients. (Fine, 1973, p. 21)

The psychoanalytic process involves many subtle interactions. According to Fine (1973), "the analyst is primarily conscious of the goals which the therapeutic process envisages, rather than precise routines" (p. 20). This means there is no exact, step-by-step formula by which therapy proceeds. Psychoanalytic therapy is a gradual unfolding process of bringing unconscious material into consciousness. Even though behavioral changes do occur in psychoanalysis, the major concern is much broader. The development of the total individual in terms of how she or he helps to create society is the ultimate goal. Psychoanalysis is now considered to be not just a therapeutic technique but a system for re-educating individuals to help restructure a better society and world. It is seen by some analysts as both a system of philosophy and a system of psychology:

> As a philosophy, it differs from others in that it is based on a sound scientific psychology. As a psychology it differs from others in that it offers a philosophical resolution to man's problems.

*The following excerpts are reproduced by permission of the publisher, F.E. Peacock Publishers, Inc., Itasca, Illinois. From "Psychoanalysis" by Reuben Fine in *Current Psychotherapies* by Raymond J. Corsini, 1973, pp. 20, 21, 22 and 30. *Current Psychotherapies* is now available in the Second Edition, copyright 1979 by F.E. Peacock Publishers, Inc.

As a philosophy psychoanalysis offers a view of happiness, expanding from the central concepts of love and work. Such a philosophy is of inestimable significance in the confusion of our times. (Fine, 1973, p. 30)

However, the ethical acceptability of making such grandiose claims based on limited empirical data is questionable. We are certain that both psychologists and philosophers would object to this contention. Furthermore, the use of psychoanalysis is not successful in treating all types of mental disorders. It seems to be most successful in treating neurotic and personality disorders and psychophysiological problems. It has not been too successful in the treatment of psychoses or habit disorders (though it does work with compulsives). Fine (1973) says that

> with the psychoses, those severe disturbances of personality which require hospitalization or some other protective steps to remove the individual from his immediate environment, psychoanalysis has been less successful . . . . the effort is so enormously time-consuming and so extraordinarily difficult for the therapist that relatively few have ventured into this field. In a recent publication, Marion Milner (1969) reports on the successful treatment of a schizophrenic which required daily sessions over a period of 20 years. (p. 22)

One tenet of psychoanalysis is that if the therapist cannot work with a given client, he or she is encouraged to refer the client to another therapist or to receive additional personal analysis for himself or herself. However, to receive additional analysis is an ideal and from a practical point of view it is unlikely that an analyst would be willing to undergo further analysis to deal with a given client. In spite of the fact that psychoanalysis is not successful with all types of problems, Fine (1973) says that

> historically, psychoanalysis was the first psychotherapeutic system that had any value. Currently it is the most complete, the most highly developed, the one with the greatest theoretical sophistication and by far the most effective. (p. 30)

However, some psychotherapists (e.g., Ellis, 1973; Wolpe, 1981) say that effectiveness may be a function of the number of sessions and the financial cost to the client.

In psychoanalysis, the individual is given primary consideration, but the overall value system is in a social framework. This is evidenced by the fact that Freud defined normality as the ability to love and to do productive work. Thus the work-love ethic is central to psychoanalysis. He also touched upon making the normal individual better than normal. Fine (1972) elaborates the work-love ethic to include creativity, open communication, the relationship of the individual to the larger society, and the pursuit of happiness. The work-love ethic implies certain values, namely consciousness, rationality, productivity, self-esteem, and heterosexual (marital) relationships.

As is the ultimate goal of any therapeutic technique, autonomy of the client is what the analyst strives for, an emergence from dependency. The analyst achieves this by making the client look at himself or herself, which may temporarily result in the client's feeling worse. But because consciousness is one of the stressed values of psychoanalysis, adhering to that value may have as a consequence an uncomfortable experience for the client. This in itself may not be morally objectionable since from a utilitarian view pain is justified as a means to happiness that outweighs the pain suffered. But unlike in the medical profession where the patient can be informed of how painful a procedure might be and what the risks are and can give informed consent, in psychoanalysis the client can give only limited informed consent. Due to the fact that some material is unconscious, the client cannot consent to making specific material conscious since he or she does not know what the material is precisely because it *is* unconscious. Also unlike medical treatment, for which the patient can be given some idea of the length of time for recovery and the cost involved, the length of time necessary for successful psychoanalysis cannot be predicted. Psychoanalysts are usually specific about most details and clients must be willing to tolerate some ambiguity regarding the process, its duration, cost, and potential effectiveness.

Because a heterosexual (marital) relationship is a value of psychoanalysis, it may seem that psychoanalysis would merely support society's norms. Our society does not approve of promiscuity and psychoanalysts see promiscuity "not as a sign of maturity, but of the use of genital sexuality as a drainage system for other emotions, e.g., the fear of being unlovable, which is assuaged for the moment by each affair" (Levine, 1972, p. 283). Thus to stress heterosexual (marital) relationships implies that a client who does not value such a relationship needs to be changed. And if a homosexual were to seek therapy from a traditional psychoanalyst, not because of a desire to change sexual preferences but to overcome feelings of anxiety due to social pressure, it may be thought that the therapist might refuse to treat the person or would try to change the person's value system.

However, it is not that the therapist would refuse to treat the person but rather would refuse to ignore that aspect of the person's life. And the therapist may well appear to try to change the client's value system by providing information or interpretation. However, the client is still free to choose what value system to accept. For example, if in analysis a homosexual client comes to realize that his sexual preference is really an attempt to rebel against his father's macho image, this knowledge, arrived at with the help of the analyst, may cause the client to change his sexual orientation.

Because traditional psychoanalysis seems to support what society approves of, it is particularly important for psychoanalysts to be aware of their own values and take care not to impose them unwittingly on the client. As Hartmann (1960) points out, "The analyst must be clearly aware of his own valuations and must know how to distinguish them from statements of fact" (p. 55). Though he goes on to say that the analyst should concentrate only on health values, it should be noted that what counts as health may be determined by the analyst's own ideas of how a person *ought* to function if he or she is to be healthy.

Therapists of all orientations have an obligation to clarify their value system to their clients. As Stolz (1978) says, "Ethical responsibility . . . requires that psychologists inform the clients of their own motives and biases . . . " (p. 38). Otherwise a therapist may, intentionally or not, try to manipulate the client into accepting the therapist's underlying values without the client being aware of it. Breggin (1971) notes that Freud warned "that the analyst should not try to make the patient over in his own image or ideals . . . " (p. 62). According to Szasz (1965),

> psychoanalytic insight or understanding may be put to various uses; the choice rests with the patient . . . . This is like giving a tourist a map of a strange city: the analytic traveler may, with a map, orient himself, but not find out where he should go. (p. 52)

But Breggin (1971) says that therapy "becomes moral reeducation" and that according to Freud, "the therapist is a 'spiritual guide' " (p. 60). So on the one hand it appears that choices are entirely up to the client but on the other hand the analyst is a "moral reeducator " and a "spiritual guide." This may seem to pose a problem, for the therapist guides and reeducates yet at the same time leaves decisions up to the client. However, moral reeducation takes the form of a discovery. For according to Hartmann (1960), part of a person's moral system is conscious and another part is unconscious. Moral awareness can be increased and, he says, "such broadening of moral awareness occurs, often dramatically, in the course of psychoanalysis, in the form of a discovery" (p. 39). Hence the analyst is not active in reeducating the client but rather helps the client discover his or her whole moral system and to be an autonomous moral agent. According to Hartmann (1960),

> the avoidance of what we consider moral value judgments, characteristic of the analyst's attitude toward the patient, is taken as a model by the patient who tries, then, to avoid moral value judgments in his own dealings with other people. All this we theoretically expect to come to an end with the termination of a successful analysis. (p. 75)

He suggests that many people who have not been in analysis adopt technical codes rather than accepting moral principles on their own. But, says Hartmann, what often happens "as a consequence of analysis is that the patient's own authentic moral values became dominant in his codes" (p. 92).

While the analyst must not give advice, "the analyst's conduct and values may serve as models which the patient may choose to imitate" (Szasz, 1965, p. 5). Advice giving is seen as diminishing autonomous decision making and responsibility from the client. And one goal of therapy is to increase the client's ability to make decisions, including ethical ones. According to Englehardt (1973), psychoanalysis "is setting the stage for the possibility of ethical decisions" because it "is directed toward liberating the patients from the control of unconscious drives and acknowledged forces" (p. 441). He sees psychoanalytic therapy as advancing "a precondition for any particular way of handling one's life, any particular ethic" (p. 444). Psychoanalysis then may be one aid to ethical decision making because by making the unconscious conscious, the client can make rational decisions and therefore will not need advice. However, as we indicated earlier, it might be that not to advise in some cases may be irresponsible. Szasz (1965) indirectly acknowledges this for forms of nonanalytic psychotherapy which he says teach by advice: "If the therapist deals with an acute situation and if the therapeutic contact is brief, this might be legitimate . . . " (p. 51). This implies that psychoanalytic therapy cannot deal with acute situations that require being directive; rather it is best suited for those who do not need advice. If an analyst sees that a client needs direction, either the client should be referred or the analyst should go against a tenet of psychoanalytic theory and at least advise about options. But according to Szasz (1965), "helping a patient learn by psychotherapeutic education (i.e., metaadvice) eliminates his need for repeated advice" (p. 5). This may be true, but what *practical* effect does encouraging clients "to take more responsibility for (themselves) and (their) life situation" (Szasz, 1965, p. 302) have on a client? The therapist assumes that when a client better understands his or her wants, the client will be in a better position to decide what he or she wants to do (Szasz, 1965). But even then, a client may know what he or she wants to do but does not know how to go about doing it. For example, suppose a woman has decided, because of constant marital difficulties, that she wants to leave her husband but does not know how to go about doing so. This might be a case where advice about options is in order because of the client's lack of knowledge, which prohibits her from acting on her decision.

If analysts are against giving advice, they certainly are not against influencing their clients to have certain feelings and not others. In a passage from Fine (1973) quoted earlier, he remarks that "feelings of love when expressed meet with subtle or overt signs of approval from the analyst, while feelings of hatred, when expressed, meet with subtle or overt signs of disapproval" (p. 21). While such positive feelings ought to be encouraged, it is also possible for the analyst, by using such signs, to encourage or discourage the client's specific values.

Clients are expected to hold to the fundamental rule, to say whatever comes to mind. When the client does not abide by that rule, the therapist may insist that he or she do so, and may insist in an aggressive manner (Breggin, 1971). If, as was mentioned earlier, this may be considered an aversive technique, then analysts may in fact use such techniques. And the use of such a technique would be justified on the basis that it may get the client to stop censoring his or her thoughts. Once the client sees the moral distinction between thought and action, free choice and rational decision making will be promoted since that will be a "further step in the *ethical liberation* of the patient from his past guilt and anger" (Breggin, 1971, p. 61). Though insisting that the client adhere to the fundamental rule may seem to intrude on the client's privacy, by agreeing to the fundamental rule the client is consenting to such intrusion and may terminate therapy whenever he or she wishes. Hence any intrusiveness on the part of the analyst is with prior client consent.

Psychoanalysts apparently feel that any advice giving will hinder the client in making his or her own responsible decisions. Advice is not even given when it comes to choosing a therapeutic technique. For according to Szasz (1965), "There is no way of judging whether a particular person with problems in living should be 'treated' by psychoanalysis, religious counseling, drugs, electric shock, or any of a host of other procedures" and hence "the analyst is committed to viewing the patient's decisions, including his choice of therapy, as acts of self-revelation . . . " (p. 87). But the client is not always aware of the limitations of a technique. Therefore it is the responsibility of the psychoanalyst (as it is of therapists using other techniques) to inform a person seeking therapy of the limits of that technique and in what length of time the person can expect positive change, if positive changes can be expected at all. Should a psychoanalyst take a schizophrenic as a client, who, if curable, might take 20 years to be cured (Milner, 1969)? Or should a psychoanalyst attempt to work with a person whose problem is a phobia that behavior therapy has proven successful in curing and who only wants symptom relief? Despite Fines's (1973) claim, quoted above, that psychoanalysis is "by far the most effective (therapeutic system)" (p. 30), to accept any client despite the nature of the problem would not be honest, nor would it be a recognition of the limits of one's competence. For people with nondebilitating problems, and for those who can afford it, psychoanalysis may in fact lead to self-actualization. But even for those who can practically and financially afford psychoanalysis, there is no specification in the verbal contract between the therapist and the client of what the client can expect in terms of length of therapy and specific behavioral change. About all that is agreed upon is adherence to the fundamental rule (Breggin, 1971) and the fees (Szasz, 1965). One way to avoid this ethical dilemma is for the analyst to state that he or she cannot make a prediction about the length of therapy but would expect certain changes to occur. These changes should be specified. Just as physicians should not assume that their patients are aware of alternative forms of treatment and length of time for recovery, neither should psychoanalysts assume that people who seek their help are aware of alternative psychotherapeutic techniques and what specific changes they can expect in what approximate length of time. But because of the nature of the psychoanalytic process, the therapist most likely does not have this latter type of information to give.

Psychoanalysis has typically escaped moral criticism, probably due to a failure to recognize the subtle ethical issues involved in the theory and practice of psychoanalysis.[4] Psychoanalysts should be aware that: the presupposed values of traditional psychoanalysis may tend to support society's norms; there may be a conflict between trying to reeducate the client and insisting on the free choice of the client; giving advice may occasionally be in the client's best interest; their technique, like others, is limited and it is dishonest to claim otherwise, and; the issue of informed consent is not one that can easily or satisfactorily be resolved.

CLIENT-CENTERED THERAPY

Originally called nondirective therapy (Rogers, 1942), the philosophy and techniques of the system devised and largely predominated by Carl Rogers have been renamed client-centered therapy (Rogers, 1951). The change in name was a change in emphasis from technique to the client-therapist relationship. The technique is still largely a nondirective approach of dealing with human problems, but from 1951 onward emphasis has been placed on the qualities of the therapist as well as on the client. During the 1970s, Rogers (1980) began to talk about the "person-centered approach" because he wanted to include more than psychotherapy in the system. This has no bearing on this section. "Client-centered" will be used because our concern is psychotherapy.

The approach is an outgrowth of humanistic-phenomenlogical viewpoint. Rogers' ideas are humanistic in that the client is seen as innately good and possessing "actualizing" tendencies. Unless hampered by faulty learning, the individual is seen as capable of making rational evaluative judgments which lead to balanced, realistic, self-enhancing, other-enhancing behavior (Rogers, 1951, 1965). Faulty learning ("incongruence") leads to self-centered, ineffective, or hateful behavior.

The goal of client-centered therapy is to release the client's self-actualizing potential. This can be done when the therapist is (1) genuine and honest (congruent), (2) understanding (empathic), and (3) caring ("unconditional positive regard"). The therapist must genuinely care for and trust the client and must communicate this to the client. The client will not make progress unless these qualities are perceived in the therapist (Rogers, 1951, 1965).

Since helping the client to clarify his or her own feelings is the major goal of therapy, activities such as advice giving, diagnosis, prognosis, etc., are avoided. Meador and Rogers (1979) emphasize this point:*

> Any attitude or manipulation, such as the use of esoteric language, professionalism, or diagnostic testing is avoided. These measures are seen as removing the process of therapy from the control of the client to the therapist, transferring the locus of evaluation from the client's hands to that of therapist, and undermining the confidence of the client in his own ability to discover his pattern of growth. (p. 134)

Anyone possessing genuineness, warmth, and positive regard can use the technique. According to Meador and Rogers (1979), "the theory does not stress the technical skills or knowledge of the therapist" (p. 151). They go on to say that

> the elements of genuineness, empathic understanding, and positive regard promote and enhance a healthy relationship regardless of the circumstances in which they are present. Because they are simple, understandable attitudes, available at least to some degree to any human being, they can be practiced by *anyone*, and *are not the exclusive acquisition of professionals* through long years of training. The fact that they are simple and understandable does not mean that they are easy to achieve, and *their acquisition is not guaranteed by professional*

*The following excerpts are reproduced by permission of the publisher, F.E. Peacock Publishers, Inc., Itasca. Illinois. From "Person-Centered Therapy" by Betty D. Meador and Carl R. Rogers in *Current Psychotherapies*, Second Edition by Raymond J. Corsini, 1979, pp. 134, 135, 151, 171 and 177.

training, and in fact may take much longer than professional training. (p. 171, emphasis added)

While most systems of psychotherapy stress warmth, genuineness, and positive regard, client-centered therapy is unique in that these attitudes are *all* that is seen as necessary.

In spite of the claim that professional training is neither necessary—one doesn't need training if one has the characteristics—nor sufficient—training doesn't guarantee that one will acquire the characteristics—some client-centered therapists claim that the method is universally applicable.

While we can understand a practitioner being an advocate for the type of therapy he or she uses, to suggest that any therapeutic technique is universally applicable is not supported by empirical evidence. Some of the components of client-centered therapy (listening skills and reflective statements) may be used with a wide variety of clients but client-centered therapy is probably most effective with basically healthy individuals and not with severely disturbed individuals.

Most psychotherapists are aware that certain therapeutic techniques, for example probing into deep layers of the unconscious too soon or releasing guilt or shame too suddenly, can be dangerous. The idea that in therapy there exists the possibility of precipitating a psychosis has been accepted for years. Many therapists have chosen to use the client-centered approach because it is considered "safe." The assumption is that the client will move at his or her own pace. This illustrates the emphasis that client-centered therapists place on client responsibility rather than therapist responsibility.

The emphasis on being nonintrusive and requiring client autonomy is the ethical ideal for any therapeutic position but in practice it is difficult if not impossible to achieve.

While client-centered therapists deny the use of any manipulation or directive techniques (Meador & Rogers, 1979), in practice this is simply not so. They exercise influence more than they think. For ". . . the therapist reinforces certain verbalizations by cues of approval which may be as subtle as a fleeting change of expression. . . " (Frank, 1967, p. 186) or they may use silence as a sign of punishment. Thus a nod or an "Mm hmm" could serve to reinforce what a client says, and a failure to respond to a client's statement may be interpreted by the client as disapproval and hence would function as a subtle evaluation. Nor does it seem quite honest to say that "The therapist in person-centered therapy tends to avoid any expression which could have evaluative connotations" (Meador & Rogers, 1979, p. 135). A client-centered therapist may *try* to avoid expressing evaluations but this is something the therapist may do unconsciously. And while client-centered therapists may stand "firmly against the therapist being directive with his client" (Meador & Rogers, 1979, p. 134), such a therapist may in practice be quite directive. Hence the ethical issue that arises here is that client-centered therapists are not objective about their subjectivity. In theory they say that they are nonevaluative, nondirective—but in practice they cannot avoid being either. Unless they recognize this and share it with the client, they may be more manipulative than other therapists who describe to clients the exact nature of therapeutic influence.

This emphasis is also seen in the fact that rarely, if ever, is advice given. The problems we discussed in refusing to give advice apply here. But another point needs to be made on this issue and that is that a refusal to give advice may be a form of paternalism. In an interview cited by Meador and Rogers (1979), the client specifically asked for advice. Rogers refused to give advice and noted that his reply would sound evasive to the client. A refusal to give advice when the client asks for it implies that the therapist knows what is in the client's best interest but the client does not. Of course at times that must be assumed for if the client always knows what is in his or her best interest and acts on that knowledge, therapy would probably not be necessary. But on the other hand, clients are encouraged to make decisions on their own, while on the other hand if they decide they want advice, that is denied to them.

If we examine the role of the therapist in client-centered therapy, it appears to be dubious. There is supposedly no diagnosis and no prognosis. Nor does the client-centered therapist "interpret meanings for clients,...question in a probing manner,...reassure, criticize, praise or describe his client" (Meador and Rogers, 1979, p. 135). At this point one begins to wonder just what the therapist actually does and whether the refusal to do any of these is fair to the client.

What goes on in this type of therapy is an attempt to get the client to clarify his or her feelings. But what effect does this have on curing the client's symptoms? London (1969) remarks that if the treatment doesn't cure the symptoms, the therapist has to sell "understanding instead of relief" (p. 53). This seems to be the case in part of an interview Meador and Rogers (1979) quote when the client says, "Now I feel like 'now that's solved'—and I didn't even solve a thing; but I feel relieved" (p. 177). As London says, a client may say that though the symptom hasn't been treated, it is no longer bothersome: "Here, therapy has changed the patient's needs to suit the symptom instead of curing the symptom to suit the patient's needs" (p. 54). He criticizes therapists who do not focus on symptom relief and says that therapists

> must take some responsibility for relieving symptoms as long as they hang out shingles telling symptom-ridden people to come to them for help. And it is this responsibility which their gentle techniques will not support, and with respect to which they are ill-defended, regardless of how much therapists or patients think of them. Without a good technology for symptom relief or a disclaimer of the ability to provide it, the unrealistic refusal to manipulate becomes the ultimate manipulation because it is patently irrelevant grounds for keeping somebody in therapy. (p. 56)

Hence if the person wants some specific behavioral change, or if the problem is debilitating, some other technique would seem to be in order and the client should be referred. As we pointed out, client-centered therapy is seen as safe—no diagnosing, no evaluations, no prognosis, no criticizing, no interpreting, and no probing questioning takes place. This suggests that client-centered therapists are reluctant to take responsibility in therapy; thus their method is safe for the therapist as well. This appears to be the implication of Meador and Rogers when they state that using, for example, diagnostic testing is seen as "transferring the focus of evaluation from the client's hands to that of the therapist. . . " (p. 134). But evaluation is often necessary before developing appropriate treatment. Perhaps some individuals can cure themselves but not all. Recall, however, the claim that the client-centered therapist is not an expert.

In summary, client-centered therapy may be more manipulative, paternalistic, and evaluative than it appears on the surface. And client-centered therapists who claim to be nonexperts and who do not use typical psychotherapeutic methods need a moral justification for charging professional fees. Most people who enter psychotherapy have already had a warm and sympathetic listener. If this attitude is *all* that is needed in psychotherapy, then the method should have already worked and hence there would be no need for psychotherapy.

BEHAVIOR THERAPY

Behavior therapy is a system of psychotherapy which utilizes therapeutic techniques based on research findings from experimental psychology and learning theory. Wolpe (1958) is usually credited with beginning the modern behavior therapy movement but the basic principles used come directly from the early learning theorists including Watson (1920), Thorndike (1911), Pavlov (1927), and Skinner (1938). As with any therapy the purpose is to ameliorate human suffering and to promote autonomy, but behavior therapy is unique in that it has a well-developed empirical basis. The techniques used are diverse and include desensitization, self-management, token economies, cognitive restructuring, relaxation training, reinforcement programs, assertive training, and sometimes aversive conditioning. The techniques are based on either the classical (Pavlovian) conditioning or the operant (Skinnerian) conditioning model of learning even though theorists recognize that this distinction is somewhat arbitrary. However, Goldstein (1973) distinguishes the techniques as follows:

> Behavioral influence in therapy has evolved in two directions, one based on Pavlovian concepts of learning which has as its major focus emotional learning, and Skinnerian methodology with its emphasis on observable behavior and change through contingent reinforcement. The former has developed in the outpatient setting, is usually a one-on-one therapy regimen, and is applicable to neurotic problems, while the latter has developed in inpatient settings, such as state hospitals and institutions for the mentally retarded. . . . (p. 207)*

*Excerpts from Goldstein on this page and following pages are reproduced by permission of the publisher, F.E. Peacock Publishers, Inc., Itasca, Illinois. From Alan Goldstein, "Behavior Therapy" in Raymond J. Corsini (ed.), *Current Psychotherapies*, 1973, p. 207.

This chapter will be mostly concerned with the Pavlovian modeled behavior therapy. Behavior modification based upon the Skinnerian model will be discussed in the chapter on special populations.

There has been considerable criticism of the model on which behavior therapy is based. As Davidson and Stuart (1975) point out, "Because many behavior therapy principles are derived from laboratory research with animals, some observers mistakenly infer that behavior therapists regard people as *nothing but* animals" (p. 757). However,they say that

> this unfortunately misses the point of experimental work in a science. Laboratory experiments by definition attempt to isolate a phenomenon and study it under conditions that are more controlled than is the case in everyday life. To use a pigeon in an experiment rather than a human being and then to extrapolate the findings from the pigeon to human beings, is to engage in *analogue* work. Based on these experiments, inferences are drawn about human behavior. When these inferences are validated in clinical experiments with humans, they contribute to our increased clinical competence. When cross-species validation does not occur, the results of the animal research are ignored. Animal studies therefore have heuristic rather than literal implications for behavior therapists. (p. 757–58)

From an ethical perspective it would be undesirable to use humans for research on basic processes where lower animals could as easily be used. Wolpe's (1958) work on induced neurosis is a good example of how the work on animals has generalized to humans.

Behavior therapists clearly recognize the unique capabilities of humans which distinguish them from animals. While early behavior therapists focused on behavior and tended to ignore internal events, current practitioners clearly incorporate cognitions (thoughts, feelings, and images) into their work.

In addition to collecting information, initial interviews are used to establish a working relationship with the client and to find out what the client's feelings are. It is a "transparent absurdity" says Wolpe (1981, p. 162) that

> behavior therapists consider their patients' "subjective problems, feelings or thoughts" irrelevant to the psychotherapeutic process. . . . It is the subjective problem, the complaint, that drives the neurotic patient to seek treatment, no matter of what kind. The behavior therapist carefully probes all seemingly relevant experiences because consequent therapeutic actions depend completely on an assessment of what triggers what. The patient's "feelings and thoughts" are the main source of information, augmented by various questionnaires that the patient thoughtfully answers. No therapy is more "personalized" than behavior therapy; no other therapist knows as much detail about the patient as the behavior therapist does before commencing treatment; and nobody else tailors the therapy as explicitly to the individual's problems. (p. 162)

Behavior therapists have been characterized as "cold, impersonal, and mechanistic" but these contentions seem unfounded. Behavior therapists are as interested as any other therapist in establishing a warm, genuine, and honest relationship. Goldstein (1973) says,

> a working relationship is one in which the therapist and patient are working together toward a commonly agreed upon goal. If this is not accomplished, then in the vast majority of cases, therapy will be ineffective. With such a relationship established, the stage is set for therapy. (p. 220)

He is quick to point out, however, that "such a relationship in and of itself is not sufficient as a maximally effective therapy" (p. 220). Thus, unlike client-centered therapists, behavior therapists see the working relationship as usually a necessary but never a sufficient condition of therapy. To the extent that effective treatment procedures exist for specific problems, the nonspecific relationship variables become less important in effecting a cure. For example, studies which have shown that procedures can be effective in the absence of the therapeutic relationship (e.g., taped presentation of desensitization for test anxiety) lead to questioning the importance of the therapeutic relationship. In spite of these findings, behavior therapists recognize the establishment of a working relationship to be critical. Transcripts of behavior therapists in early sessions are hard to distinguish from other therapeutic orientations since they utilize similar techniques (listening, reflective statements, etc.). In later sessions the behavior therapist is likely to be more active and directive than other therapists.

The importance of a working relationship is illustrated by the use of contracts. Using contracts in therapy is not unique to behavior therapy but they are used more frequently in this type of therapy. The methods and goals are more explicit and therefore more amenable to specification in contract form. The purpose of contracts is to clarify expectations on both sides so that misunderstandings are minimized. Some behavior therapists have even utilized performance contracts where their pay is contingent on accomplishing the goal of therapy. From the consumer's point of view, the use of contracts is advantageous.

One criticism is that behavior therapists are theoretically committed to determinism. If that is so, it does not seem to make sense for them to talk about the voluntary consent or the free choice of the client. However, as Davison (1976) points out, "most of us fall into the habit of distinguishing between situations in which people are forced to change their behavior and situations in which people make free or voluntary decisions to change" (p. 157). Nevertheless, he says that "we must come to grips with the conditions surrounding even those decisions in therapy that have hitherto been termed voluntary or free" (p. 157). Thus behavior therapists may be more sensitive to the issue of free choice and may have more of a tendency to question the voluntariness of a client's choice, especially when there is reason to suspect that, though on the surface it appears voluntary, it may be the result of subtle coercion on the part of others.

When behavior therapists first started to practice with a variety of clients they claimed ethical neutrality because of their need for empirically derived methods with client-selected objectives. In practice, however, objectives or goals are not all equal or ethical and behavior therapists openly deal with goal selection issues. As with any therapeutic activity, values can be a central issue. Behavior therapists are unique in that they are more willing to share their personal values with clients when relevant. If there is a conflict in values between the client and the therapist, "treatment efforts are held in abeyance until consensus is achieved" (Davison & Stuart, 1975, p. 755). But this is not to say that both client and therapist must make the same value judgments on everything. For even if a behavior therapist does not personally approve of the means to helping a client achieve a goal, the therapist may suspend a value judgment (Yoell et al., 1971). For example, a therapist may not personally approve of extramarital affairs but may recommend this to a client if he or she thinks it would help the client's sexual problems. Wolpe (Yoell et al., 1971) says, "My own view is that people should be as happy as possible—that they should follow life plans that are most satisfying to them" (pp. 127–28) and that "anything which is not anti-social and can be considered likely to benefit the patient may be done" (p. 129). This illustrates clearly the duty of beneficence in therapy. In line with this is the focus on the happiness of the client rather than merely adjusting to whatever norm society has. The fact that behavior therapy is symptom-focused is quite different from the approach of the psychoanalytic schools. They argue that symptomatic relief fails to serve the client because it does not cure the underlying problem (which is, of course, unconscious). However, most clients come to therapy because of symptoms rather than unconscious conflicts, so to ignore the client's self-report is to be paternalistic. Psychoanalysts also contend that if the symptom is simply alleviated, the unconscious conflict will surface as another symptom. The notion of symptom substitution is very complex. In some cases removal of the symptom does lead to symptom substitution—for example, the elimination of smoking may lead to some weight gain. In other cases clients experience greater behavioral freedom and report better overall adjustment.

Psychoanalysts assume that bed-wetting is a passive way of expressing hostility toward the parents and that if this symptom is removed, the hostility will surface in some other form. When this behavior is eliminated, however, the parent-child relationship as well as the client's relationship with others usually improves. Current practice in behavior therapy recognizes the interactions between symptoms and tends to go beyond simply removing one symptom. Multimodal, broad-based behavior therapy (Lazarus, 1971) is more typical in contemporary practice. That is to say, it involves restructuring of affect *and* cognition.

The unique orientation of behavior therapists regarding assessment and diagnosis has induced criticism. Assessment is a major component in behavior therapy but the purpose is not to find the appropriate diagnostic label for the client's problem but to discover a plan for effective treatment. As Morganstern and Tevlin (1981) point out, the purpose of assessment is to discover "*everything* that is relevant to the development of effective, efficient and durable treatment interventions. And from an ethical (and economical) perspective, one could add, 'And no more' " (p. 72).

In the assessment process behavior therapists often seek out information beyond that reported by the client and this may compromise confidentiality. In other therapeutic models the veracity of the client's report is irrelevant; what is important is the client's recollection or impression of the situation, so other types of therapists are less likely to seek or receive independent information about a client's functioning. Concerns about the accuracy of self-report suggest that the observations of significant others in the client's environment may provide better data for evaluating progress. As long as client consent has been obtained, this practice is without problems but behavior therapists are more likely to be interested in independent reports that come to the therapist's attention. Respect for privacy would suggest that the information should not be received if prior consent has not been obtained.

In addition to the goal selection and assessment issues already discussed, moral objections have been raised concerning the treatment methods employed by behavior therapists. Specific concerns have usually focused on the intrusive techniques which might be used on individuals without their consent. The most intrusive technique that does raise ethical problems is the use of *aversive conditioning*. This method involves the presentation of a painful or noxious stimulus in conjunction with undesirable or maladaptive behavior. This technique has been employed in the treatment of such conditions as alcoholism and deviant sexual behavior and has been widely sensationalized by the media, which has led many to equate behavior therapy and aversive therapy. Linked with this technique and also sensationalized have been electroconvulsive therapy, brainwashing, and even behavioristic psychotherapy in general. These techniques, which are interpreted as punishment, are no more the province of behavior therapy than any other psychotherapy practiced in a medical setting. Most behavior therapists think that punishment ought to be used only as the means of last resort. Goldstein (1973) expresses the typical attitude of behaviorists:

> Punishment is used quite infrequently even though many patients seek help via punishment in curbing unwanted behavior. To begin with no behavior should be subjected to punishment when there is no alternative behavior available. . . . Such an approach is dictated not only by the moral imperative to employ the least unpleasant possible method when there is a choice, but also by the experimentally demonstrated futility of eliminating behavior through punishment when no alternative modes of satisfaction are available. . . . Alcoholics and other drug abusers, pedophiliacs, and other sexual deviants, compulsive eaters, and those who engage in other stereotype compulsive behaviors almost always concurrently present a picture marked by poor interpersonal relationships and a deficit of appropriate behavior yielding social rewards. To ignore this aspect in favor of punishment is to ensure the failure of treatment and perhaps to run the risk of actually making the patient worse by increasing conflict and subsequent depression and anxiety. (p. 231)

Punishment and aversive conditioning seemed like potent techniques for difficult behaviors when first developed but the current status of these practices suggests that the potency was overestimated. Most behavior therapists practice without utilizing these techniques, probably because of problems with generalization of effect rather than on ethical grounds. With noncoerced adults these intrusive techniques could be used with the valid consent of the client. If they were very effective the client would be making a cost/benefit comparison where he or she might choose the more painful but quicker means. These techniques are often not included among treatment options because of problems with effectiveness. Behavior therapists seek the least intrusive and most effective means. Previous reliance on these intrusive means often reflected a lack of creativity on the part of the therapist. Bed-wetting *could* be cured by shocking the client as she wet the bed but since this problem can just as easily be cured using positive reinforcement, it has become the treatment of choice. While aversive techniques are only a small part of behavior therapy, if often provokes criticism of the whole model. One of the authors delivered a speech on alcoholism to a local service organization. One brief mention of the use of electric shock in the treatment of alcoholics led to a newspaper headline CATTLE PROD USED IN TREATING ALCOHOLICS. The journalist devoted more than half of the article to a discussion of how aversive techniques have been employed in treatment of various maladaptive behaviors. In actuality, the reference to shock (with emphasis on the fact that this practice was tried and largely abandoned) occupied about one minute of a one-hour lecture.

What is the justification of the use of aversive painful simuli? We have said that it should be used only as a last resort and, in out-patient settings (and where possible, in institutional settings), only with the informed, voluntary, and rational consent of the client. When used as a last resort, utilitarian considerations may be appropriate since painful therapy may be the lesser of the evils. A certain piece of behavior may be undesirable but so is the infliction of pain. If the beneficial consequences outweigh the amount of pain, then painful therapy may be justified. But in obtaining the consent of the client to use it, the therapist is still treating the client with dignity and respect. We have already discussed the elements of consent in the previous chapter, but informed consent in this case means that the client understands the degree of pain, possible side effects, the specified goal, the likelihood of success or failure, and alternatives (Erwin, 1978).

If the client is informed, competent, and voluntarily consents, is that sufficient to justify the use of painful therapy? Suppose a client requests this type of technique in order to eliminate what she thinks is a drinking problem because her religion forbids the use of alcohol. The therapist discovers that though the client enjoys drinking, she does so only occasionally and rarely to excess and hence is not really a problem drinker. Should the therapist accede to her request? In this type of case the therapist might first try to get the client to see that her perception of the problem is exaggerated. And even if the client insists on the use of some aversive technique, the therapist does not have an obligation to grant the client's request. A therapist is not obliged to use whatever technique a client requests, especially if it involves the infliction of pain:

> . . . the most significant danger is the use of aversive conditioning in. . . that it will be used to cause (clients) unnecessary pain. In a therapeutic situation

it is easy to become convinced that the infliction of pain, if it is called therapy, is in the client's interest. . . . (Erwin, 1978, p. 188)

Thus behavior therapy, because it has painful therapy in its repertoire of techniques, is more susceptible to criticism.

This raises the point that competence is crucial in applying behavior therapy techniques. Unlike client-centered therapy, behavior therapy stresses the training of the therapist. But, says Wolpe (1981),

> it is unfortunate that a great many people who use behavior therapy techniques have not learned much about behavior analysis or have not understood the need for it. They fail to identify intricate stimulus-response relations, and they do not distinguish conditioned anxiety from cognitively based anxiety. They have trouble with complex cases. They give package treatments for diagnoses like aquaphobia. . . . Inevitably, these people have much less success with patients than they would with the help of behavior analysis; and then they write articles stating that the favorable reports of the efficacy of behavior therapy are exaggerated. (p. 162)

Indeed, one problem of behavior therapy does appear to be the apparent simplicity of the techniques. Many people think that the methods can be applied with little or no training.

> There has been a proliferation of training programs particularly in behavioral techniques, the appropriate use of which can optimize a retarded person's abilities. The inappropriate use of these techniques, however, can be cruel, punitive and harmful—as in inappropriate removal of food or attention from a child for long periods of time or in inappropriate administration of aversive stimuli. The issue is if a person attends a one- or two-day workshop on the use of behavioral techniques, is he/she then qualified to use those techniques with retarded? This person is not: however whose responsibility is it to ensure that he/she does not misuse these techniques? (Tymchuk, 1976, p. 46)

The person conducting the workshop should make sure that ethical issues of competence are part of the program.

· In considering intrusiveness we should point out that behavior therapists are likely to be more directive than other therapists once the goals of therapy are developed. Behavior therapists may focus on the individual's perspective when considering goals but they are more active than other therapists when means are being selected. While client input is considered, behavior therapists recognize their responsibility in making recommendations about treatment options. Because of this behavior therapists are seen as controlling rather than allowing the client to continue to struggle unsuccessfully with the problem.

> Objectives are often achieved more quickly and with greater frequency than other techniques. . . . Obviously, techniques which do not succeed in achieving predictable outcomes are not likely to be criticized as "controlling"; they do not, in fact, succeed in "controlling" anything tangible. (Roos, 1974, p. 5)

Behavior therapy is much more specific in defining objectives:

> Approaches which strive to accomplish such vague or ill-defined objectives as "fostering self-actualization," "fulfilling human potentials" or "serving society" are much less vulnerable to. . . criticism. These diffuse objectives do not threaten such constructs as "free will" and "autonomous man." (Roos, 1974, p. 5)

And because behavior therapists define their procedures in specific and objective terms, they "are vulnerable to criticisms of being 'mechanistic' and 'dehumanizing.' In contrast, approaches using esoteric and ambiguous procedures (often couched in humanistic and idiosyncratic verbiage) foster the impression of 'art rather than science' "(Roos, 1974, p.5). While there are some ethical issues that arise in the use of behavior therapy, as there are in the case of other techniques, most of the commonplace criticisms of this technique do not apply because they are based on misrepresentation.

Behavior therapists have been known to break some long-standing rules of therapy dealing with therapeutic disclosure and advice giving. Among all of the types of therapists, the behavior therapist is most likely to share his or her personal perspective or evaluate options actively in behavior therapy. In the usual case where a client needs advice from an expert and the therapist refuses to give it, there seems to be an unwillingness on the part of the therapist to take responsibility. But Wolpe (Yoell et. al., 1971) says,

> I think that frequently the therapist needs to make the decision for the patient. I have seen, in the course of the years, quite a number of catastrophes that could have been averted if the patient's therapist had been able to accept the responsibility for a decision and help the patient to carry it out. (p. 128)

He goes on to say that he accepts the responsibility to give advice and "to help in every practical way to bring (the decision) about" (pp. 128–29). We are not suggesting that if a person wants simple advice he or she should go to a behavior therapist. Advice giving has the potential for diminishing autonomy and behavior therapists use it selectively. If the decision mainly involves values, the therapists will insist that the client clarify and choose independently. If the situation is such that the client does not seem to be able to decide yet there is clear reason to believe that one action will be most beneficial, then behavior therapists are more likely to exert influence. If a client needs short-term hospitalization and is ruminating over the decision, if asked, the behavior therapist will probably answer quite frankly. This would not seem to make the decision any less autonomous. However, because behavior therapists are willing to advise, and do so openly, on the grounds that they believe that sometimes a client needs advice, there is left open the possibility of the therapist coercing the client into acting on the advice by saying, "I can't treat you any more if you don't do what I want". While Wolpe (Yoell et al., 1971) claims that it is not often done, "occasionally it is justified" (p. 131). In one sense this is not really coercion since the client is free to seek another therapist. But if a client genuinely wants to stay in that particular therapeutic relationship, an element of coercion is involved. What would justify coercion in one of these rare cases is either that a client is not fulfilling his or her part of the contract or when the therapist sees that by not following the advice the client will be frustrating the goal of therapy. The important point to note, however, is that the behavior therapist is willing to assume responsibility for therapy, which is not the case in client-centered therapy where the therapist fears shifting the responsibility from the client to the therapist. Nor is the psychoanalyst willing to assume responsibility if therapy is unsuccessful. Behavior therapists such as Wolpe (1981) have been critical of psychoanalysts on this account:

> Psychoanalytically oriented therapists rationalize lack of progress by saddling the patient with the responsibility for it. The patient is told that failure to improve is due to his or her "resistance" and not to anything wrong or inappropriate about the therapy. (p. 163)

But, he continues,

> To keep patients interminably in chancery is an immoral practice and a social blot on the psychological profession. . . . it is a moral requirement of any health professional to know the state of the art in his or her field and to be able to offer patients alternatives when the methods used have failed. (p. 163)

As we discussed earlier, any therapist who is competent will fulfill the moral requirement to refer a client when the therapist's technique proves ineffective or when another technique will be more effective and less costly. Wolpe (1981) contends that behavior therapy is more effective and less costly:

> It has been applied with success not only to phobias and sexual problems but to the whole range of neurotic problems, including the most complex social neuroses and so-called existential problems. Again and again, in a modest time span, it has secured recovery in neurotics for whom lengthy psychoanalysis has failed. (p. 162)

Client-oriented therapists must also deal with the cost effectiveness problem for as we mentioned in discussing client-centered therapy, it, like psychoanalysis, can be a lengthy process. Nevertheless, no psychotherapeutic theory ought to make sweeping claims about what can be done with that technique. Behavior therapists are becoming more selective about the types of clients they are willing to treat. The client must be willing to take risks and this would be part of the contract. A behavior therapist would probably refuse to work with a client who is unmotivated and, for example, is not willing to change an environment that is part of her problem. Or a client who has anxiety about dating and refuses to ask a woman for a date because he is afraid he will be turned down is not willing to take a risk and hence a behavior therapist would probably be unwilling to work with him. The cost/benefit issue is important to behavior therapists and if their treatment program does not appear that it will be successful with a given client, they probably will not agree to engage in therapy.

We pointed out how therapists employing psychoanalysis and client-centered therapy deny that they try to guide the client. But in fact they really do exert subtle forms of influence and manipulation. Because of the subtlety, clients in either type of therapy may not be aware of this, which is a form of deception on the part of the therapist. But Goldstein (Yoell et al., 1971) says, "I try very hard to influence people. After all, that's what therapy is all about. But even those who say they are not influencing their patients do it covertly. I think the best and most honest way to operate is openly" (p. 129). Thus behavior therapists tend to be more out in the open than is a therapist who does not take a direct, straightforward approach with the client. In behavior therapy the client knows exactly what he or she is getting into when consenting to therapy. And as Stolz (1978) points out, "The selection of the goals of the intervention should be made in the context of as full a specification as possible of the consequences of their decision for the client's lives and the lives of others" (p. 38). Behavior therapists are more apt to do this because of their commitment to being fully open and honest with their clients. Whether or not a contract is used in the clinical setting, "the goals of properly conducted behavior therapy are always explicit" (Davison & Stuart, 1975, p. 775).

In carefully examining behavior therapy, one can see that despite the fact that this technique has been subjected to more moral criticism than any other, much of that criticism is unfounded. The use of intrusive techniques does present an ethical problem but as we have indicated, the use of such techniques is not widespread and they are typically used only on adults and with their valid consent. Where a method of positive reinforcement is available, that is the option behavior therapists most often choose.

Behavior therapists tend to have warmth toward and positive regard for their clients just as other types of therapists do. But behavior therapists are more explicit and honest with their clients; hence their clients are more likely to know exactly what is going on in therapy. They are willing to take responsibility for therapy rather than shift it on to the client. There is also an emphasis on self-management in their attempt to get clients to manipulate their own environments. This of course increases client autonomy. Responsibility for the outcome of therapy, however, is not placed entirely on the client. This seems to be more ethically respectable than therapies that place total responsibility on the client because, after all, the therapist is supposed to be the expert who has the ability to help the client. And unlike psychoanalysis and client-centered therapy, which tend to have rigid guidelines regarding what can or cannot be done in therapy, behavior therapy has no *a priori* rules except to do whatever is likely to benefit the client as long as it is not antisocial and does not cause unnecessary pain. According to Wolpe (1981), "nobody else tailors the therapy as explicitly to the individual's problem" (p. 162) as does the behavior therapist.

RATIONAL-EMOTIVE THERAPY

Rational-emotive therapy (RET) is a philosophy, a theory of personality, and a technique of psychotherapy developed by Albert Ellis in the late

1950s and 1960s (Ellis, 1962, 1973, 1979; Ellis & Harper, 1961). The system has its origins in the Stoic philosophers of ancient Greece and Rome, especially in the works of Epictetus (c.60 A.D.). In *The Enchiridion*, Epictetus wrote: "Men are disturbed not by things, but by the view which they take of them." Self-sufficiency also was stressed by the Stoic philosophers. Self-sufficiency and minimizing unhappiness are two central themes in rational-emotive therapy.

Ellis (1979) summarizes the basis of rational-emotive therapy as follows:*

> According to the theory of RET, emotional disturbance occurs when an individual *commands*, *insists*, and *dictates* that he *must* have his wishes or desires satisfied. Thus, he *demands* that he succeed at important tasks and be approved by significant others; he *insists* that others treat him fairly and ethically; and he *commands* that the universe be more pleasant and less rough than it often is. (p. 202)

Essentially, RET is a cognitive restructuring process in which irrational beliefs leading to negative self-talk (e.g., "This is awful," "I can't stand it any more," etc.) are brought to the client's attention and, in turn, are changed to rational beliefs.

Ellis (1973) lists the A, B, C, and D of RET as follows:

A—Activating Event
B—Belief
C—Consequence
D—Disputed (belief)

When an Activating Event leads to a Consequence, many people feel that A causes C directly. In actuality, most events are filtered through a Belief system. Beliefs may be rational (rB) or they may be irrational (iB). Much emotional discomfort is the result of (iB). People tend to impose "musts," "shoulds," "must nots," and "should nots" on the situation. When these musts or must nots are introjected, a situation that may be merely uncomfortable takes on a stronger emotional meaning and becomes "terrible," "horrible," or "a catastrophe." This awfulizing or catastrophizing is an indication that irrational beliefs are in operation. For example, a man's girlfriend decides to break up with him (A). He believes (iB) that this is a sign that he is worthless, no good, and a failure in relating to women. He also may believe (iB) that there will never be another woman as good for him again or that all women will see him as worthless. This belief (iB) about the (A) Activating Event now leads to (C) deep depression. Or, he may believe (iB) that his girlfriend is out to get him or that she represents every woman in the world (Ellis, 1972). In this case, (C) would be hostility. Whatever the situation, the person would feel "awful" or "terrible" and would want to assign *blame*. In the first instance, he would blame himself. In the

*Excerpts from Ellis on this page and following pages reproduced by permission of the publisher, F.E. Peacock Publishers, Inc., Itasca, Illinois. From "Rational-Emotive Therapy" by Albert Ellis in *Current Psychotherapies, Second Edition* by Raymond J. Corsini, 1979, pp. 172, 174, 202, and 226.

second situation, he would blame her. And blame rarely, if ever, solves any emotional problem. At this point, a rational-emotive therapist could step in and begin to (D) dispute the unfounded evidence. There is no empirical evidence that one person's judgment is the final, or even accurate, judgment. The girlfriend could be very wrong or she may not even have intended to make the man feel worthless. She may simply have found a better relationship *for her*. Even if she did want to hurt the man, she is not representative of *all women*. And even is this were the case, a person's worth is not determined by a group of misguided people. It is not the end of the world. Many people have survived a broken relationship and some have even learned to live happily alone. The situation may be uncomfortable but it is not a catastrophe. The therapist, by (D) disputing the (iB) irrational belief, guides the client into (rB) more rational beliefs. Many things in life produce discomfort, but few are "the end of the world."

There are a number of irrational beliefs that are perpetuated by most cultures. In fact, these beliefs are so common that few people ever take time to examine their irrationality. Some examples of irrational beliefs are: "It is terrible when I am not liked or respected by everyone;" "I am not worthwhile unless I am perfectly adequate, competent, or achieving;" and "It is a catastrophe when things don't go the way I want them to." (See Ellis, 1962; Ellis and Harper, 1961.)

This is only a sample of "crazy" things people tell themselves. When the uncomfortable event (A) occurs and a person begins to feel the (C) consequence, he or she often forgets that it is (iB) the irrational belief(s) that is (are) causing much of the discomfort. The object of RET is to intervene at (D) and dispute the "insane" belief. Humans are capable of being rational, just as they are capable of being irrational, and RET therapists work toward making the client's belief system more rational (rB). The approach is hardheaded and no-nonsense. The therapist attacks irrational beliefs head-on and does not spend a lot of time establishing a deep relationship with the client as do client-centered therapists. Nevertheless, even though RET therapists may not spend a great deal of time establishing empathic relationships, they are deeply committed to full acceptance or tolerance of the client (Ellis, 1973) as is the client-centered therapist. However, unlike the client-centered therapists,

> the rational-emotive therapist does not believe that a deep or warm relationship between the counselee and the counselor is either a necessary or a sufficient condition for effective personality change. He believes, instead, that it is highly desirable for the client and therapist to have good rapport, and especially for the therapist unconditionally and fully to accept the client: to tolerate and to refuse to down *him* even though he may well criticize and point out deficiencies of his *behavior* . . . . To keep the client from becoming and remaining unduly dependent on him, the RET therapist often deliberately eschews "paid friendship" and uses, instead, firm, hardheaded methods of convincing the client that he'd damned well better resort to more self-discipline. (Ellis, 1973, p. 172)

Also, the rational-emotive therapist does not hesitate to give advice or direction, as Ellis (1973) indicates:

The rational therapist differs radically from the Rogerian therapist in that he actively *teaches* them (1) that blaming or damning is the very core of emotional disturbance; (2) that it inevitably leads to dreadful results; (3) that it is quite possible, though difficult, for a human to learn how to avoid rating his *self* or his *being* even while he continues to rate his *traits* or *performance*; and (4) that he can give up self-rating by a specific process of questioning and challenging his magic-based self-evaluating assumptions and by deliberately risking (through activity homework assignments) many kinds of failures and rejections. The rational-emotive practitioner, consequently, is more persuading, more didactic, and more information-giving than the client-centered practitioner; and in that respect they are probably almost at opposite ends of the therapeutic continuum. (p. 174)

Advice giving and directive therapy have been discussed at other points in this chapter. Total refusal to give advice can pose problems but so can too liberal advice giving. Some clients are looking for a club to hang over the therapist's head: "I followed your advice and look at how terrible things worked out." Balanced judgments are required to know when and where not to become directive. RET therapists have been criticized for being too ready to teach and direct. This can present a problem of paternalism and a denial of client autonomy.

Since RET does not employ the use of aversive techniques in the form of physically painful therapy, it does not have the ethical problem of deciding when such therapy is justified. However, aversive techniques in the form of open confrontation are a central part of RET. Though the client may get upset by the blunt manner of the therapist, that does not prevent the therapist from continuing in the same manner. In fact, the therapist may appear to be insensitive to the client's feelings, at least from the client's point of view. However, it would seem that the therapist has some responsibility to be sensitive to the client's feelings in order to establish a comfortable working relationship. Teaching the skills of RET before establishing rapport could be viewed by the client as painful. Rapport is what one client in an interview was expecting to establish first and apparently this is what she wanted initially, for she says, "I didn't expect to be put on so *fast*. I expected a moment to catch my breath and see who you *were*; and to establish some kind of rapport" (Ellis, 1973, p. 186). But the therapist sees that as a waste of time and implies that the client does not know what is in her best interest. This seems to be paternalistic. The therapist wants to help the client as quickly as possible. This justifies paternalism in terms of utilitarianism (efficiency) and what is beneficial to the client.

RET has much in common with behavior therapy and Ellis (1973) agrees that his system is similar to "broad spectrum" behavior therapy (e.g., Lazarus, 1971), but he rejects the idea that his approach can be classified in the conditioning-learning or behavior modification tradition. There is overlap, but the Ellis approach stresses cognitive restructuring more than do traditional behavior therapists.

Like behavior therapy, RET employs many therapeutic strategies, e.g., role-playing, suggestion, directing, modeling, assertion training, support, etc. RET assigns "homework" even more often than do behavior therapists. Unlike all other psychotherapies, the theory of RET stresses humor as an extremely useful adjunct to therapy. Among other forms of humor, strong language is sometimes used in therapy to help break through inhibitions. When a person is emotionally upset, there is a tendency to think certain "taboo" words. RET therapists believe that the use of these "street" words by the therapist makes it easier for the client to express himself or herself emotionally.

Humor, along with informal dress and simple office settings, are deliberate attempts to emphasize the humanness of *all* people, therapists included. The modeling of tolerance and respect for fellow humans is considered important. Clients are also taught to be tolerant and respectful of themselves. These points illustrate an implicit adherence to a Kantian ethical model. But emphasis is also placed on minimizing unhappiness in the individual:

> Rational-emotive therapy is a method of personality change that quickly and efficiently helps people resist their tendencies to be conforming, suggestible, and unenjoying. It actively and didactically, as well as emotively and behaviorally, shows how to abet and enhance one side of their humanness while simultaneously changing and living more happily with (and not represssing or squelching) another side of their humanity. It is thus realistic and practical, as well as idealistic and future-oriented. It helps individuals more fully to actualize, experience, and enjoy the here and now; but it also espouses long-range hedonism, which includes planning for their own (and others') future. It is what its name implies; rational *and* visionary, empirical *and* humanistic. As, in all their complexity, are humans. (Ellis, 1979, p. 226)

Rational-emotive therapy, though it values the happiness of the individual, does not promise to give happiness; it only hopes to provide some of the conditions necessary for happiness. Thus there is emphasis on the individual becoming more rational and taking responsibility in the conquest of happiness. It is up to the individual to exercise his or her rationality, with the help of a therapist, to achieve happiness, for rationality is a faculty unique to persons. As Bertrand Russell (1930) said, "The happiness that is genuinely satisfying is accompanied by the fullest exercise of our faculties, and the fullest realization of the world in which we live" (p. 110).

The primary emphasis in RET is on rationality as the means to achieve autonomy and happiness. RET is unique in this respect because it appeals to an essential characteristic of personhood to achieve behavioral change— one's ability to be rational and to be able to restructure one's belief system in a rational manner.

Ellis (1973) states that RET is most effective with mildly disturbed clients and thereby recognizes its limitations. He points out, as did we, that this is true of most systems of psychotherapy. No sweeping claims about effectiveness are made for all types of problems. Although RET therapists have worked with the full gamut of problems, there have been differing degrees of effectiveness. The method seems most appropriate with mild depression, problems involving situationally induced anxiety (e.g., marital or family problems), and mildly neurotic or deviant behavior. For these types of problems, RET seems to be cost-effective in that problems generally are

cleared up in few sessions. As with other psychotherapies, the more complicated the problem, the more sessions are required.

While there is some overlap between behavior therapy techniques and
rational-emotive therapy, the latter has not been subject to as much moral
criticism, partly because it does not get as much publicity and partly because
it is not in the conditioning-learning tradition. Being directive and confrontive can be aversive and therefore painful. Thus, as in behavior therapy, a
sensitivity to these issues is central to an ethical approach to psychotherapy.
Ellis (1973) does not believe that a warm relationship is a necessary or a
sufficient condition for effective therapy· He does, however, believe that
it is desirable (though not necessary) for the therapist and client to have
good rapport and that the therapist accept the client fully and uncondition-
ally. If that is so, open confrontation too early in the interview would seem
to be detrimental to establishing rapport with the client and hence not in
the client's best interest. It may be that what a client needs initially is the
type of relationship client-centered therapists advocate. But rational-emotive therapists seem to rule out this *a priori* as necessary to effective therapy.
It does not follow, as Ellis (1973) suggests, that if a therapist establishes the
type of relationship advocated by client-centered therapists, at least initially,
that the client will become dependent on the therapist· While openly con-
fronting the client with his or her irrational belief(s) at some point in therapy
may in the long-run be beneficial to the client, rational-emotive therapists
should be aware that doing so at the wrong time could have negative effects.

Despite the blunt approach taken by rational-emotive therapists, it should
be noted that they do show deep respect for their clients as persons (a
Kantian approach). They show the client that they tolerate and fully accept
him or her and that it is the behavior or irrational belief, not the client,
which is subject to criticism.

As do behavior therapists, rational-emotive therapists take an active part
in therapy, and thus must be willing to take responsibility for the outcome
of therapy rather than shift it to the clients. However, the burden of therapy
is not entirely on the therapist for the client must cooperate in carrying
out homework assignments. But even if the client is willing to do so, the
therapist must be careful not to move too soon in the type of assignment
given to the client. Suppose a sexually inhibited client is given the assignment
to seduce a man. If the client is not ready for such an encounter, the effects
could be quite harmful to the client and therefore morally wrong. Thus
RET has a problem similar to that of behavior therapy, and that is the
possibility of it being ineptly or inappropriately used. But as we said regarding behavior therapy, that is not so much an ethical issue which pertains
to the technique but rather to the individual therapist who has the moral
responsibility to be competent in the use of RET. Because it can be ineptly
used, therapists who use this technique need more thorough training than
those who take a passive approach and thus incur more responsibility in
training. Hence it would be irresponsible for someone who participates in
a one or two-day workshop conducted by a rational-emotive therapist to
believe that he or she is competent in the methods. The therapeutic moves
in RET are too subtle to be taught in such a short period of time. Further-

more, it would be irresponsible for an RET therapist to conduct one of these short workshops and leave the participants with the impression that they have become competent in the use of this technique.

Though we have emphasized the positive aspects of RET and indicated that almost any problem would lie with the individual therapist, there are some theoretical problems we should point out. One is the de-emphasis in the theory on the necessity of establishing rapport with clients. A second is an inherent possibility of being overly intrusive psychologically because it is a confrontive technique. These two problems are not unrelated, for if rapport is not established, it is much easier for the therapist to be confrontive at an inappropriate time. There is also the possibility of this type of therapy being coercive because there is a high expectation on the part of the therapist in terms of the client's willingness to take risks. Finally, there is nothing in the theory that deals with the irrationality of *positive* emotions. RET focuses on "awfulizing" and the irrationality behind such an attitude but it does not entertain the possibility of "wonderfulizing"—that a positive feeling may also be based on irrational beliefs. Someone who is "high on life" regardless of misfortunes that happen to him would hardly have a rational grasp on reality. The saying "Don't trust anyone who smiles all the time" could be true, for that indicates a loss of touch with reality. Though such people typically do not come for therapy, maybe they should.

We have indicated that openness and honesty about what is going on in therapy is important from a moral point of view so that the client knows how the therapist is attempting to change his or her behavior and consents to that technique. In psychoanalysis and client-centered therapy the client is being subtly influenced despite the theoretical claim that these therapies are nondirective. A moral point in favor of RET is that therapists using that technique readily acknowledge that they persuade and will not hesitate to give information and advice. By acknowledging that they persuade, they put what they are doing out in the open. And in giving information and advice they are acting in the role of expert, someone who has services to sell.

Chapter 5

The Right to Treatment
and Involuntary Commitment*

If a person is in need of medical attention but cannot afford the services of a physician, most people would probably agree that the state should assist in paying the cost. But what about cases in which the need is not for the services of a regular physician but rather for a psychiatrist or a psychologist? Do persons have the *right* to such treatment? Or is it merely a privilege?

Before discussing these questions, a few remarks about what constitutes a right are in order. Since much has been written on the concept of rights (see, for example, Feinberg, 1970), we shall only deal with it briefly.

A right is a legitimate claim to something. When a person has a right to something, there is a corresponding duty on the part of others not to interfere with the person's exercising that right. In some cases it may be a duty on the part of some to make it possible for the person to exercise a right. Legally speaking, this may involve granting or specifying a further right on the part of the state. For example, everyone has a moral right to a minimally decent existence. Part of what is needed for such a life is education. In this case it is insufficient merely to say that others have a duty not to interfere with another's pursuit of education, for not everyone has the monetary means to pay for one. It then becomes the duty of the state to provide people with the means necessary to exercise the right to a decent existence. And so the state legally guarantees one's right to education.[1] While a person may have a *moral* right to something, in some cases (though not all), unless it is protected *by*, or made possible to exercise by means of, a *legal* right, that right (moral) may be meaningless in practice.

We would not want the state to interfere in *all* areas of moral rights—that would entail too much interference in private lives and would be impractical besides. Where, however, the right in question is one concerning basic necessities or in some cases of promise keeping (e.g., contracts) this claim holds true.

Privileges differ from rights in that a privilege is an advantage or benefit not everyone enjoys. A privilege is not something to which a peson has a legitimate, that is, protected, claim and is therefore not something which

*This chapter, with some changes, originally appeared in *The Journal of Medicine and Philosophy*, 1980, Vol. 5, No. 4, and is reprinted by permission of the Journal and the University of Chicago Press.

is guaranteed. Even if everyone has the right to earn a living, having a prestigious and well-paying job is not necessary for minimally decent existence.

A person's moral right to life[2] is also a (*prima facie*) constitutional right. But unless that legal right entails the right to the means of life—basic necessities—it would be a fiction in practice. And so the right to life must entail the right to a minimal degree of health, a claim on others not to interfere with one's health and, when necessary, a claim on the state to provide the means to health, that is, the right to treatment. However, the right to health or to health care is not mentioned either in the Constitution or the Declaration of Independence despite the fact that "life, liberty, and the pursuit of happiness" can hardly be achieved without having a legal right to health.

While the right to treatment has been legally established, in fact, at least for those who have been involuntarily committed to a mental institution, not everyone agrees that this is a right which persons have and which ought to be acknowledged and protected by law.[3] It has been argued that even though a person may have a right to health, it does not follow that a person has a right to the means of health, the right to treatment. Such an argument has been based on the premise that "the right to health differs from the right to theft" (Szasz, 1976, p. 478). However, this claim mistakenly assumes that the right to health and the right to property are analogous when in fact they are not. Property is not something a person needs in order to have a decent existence. While we do have a right to own property, owning property in fact is a privilege. Others have a duty to respect the property owned by someone, but the state has no duty to provide it. But health,unlike property, is a basic need since some degree of health is necessary to a minimally decent existence. So unless there is a legal right to treatment, if the state does not have a duty to provide it, the right to health is a fiction. (It might be said that the right to property is a fiction in fact for those who do not have the means to acquire it. Even so, it does not follow, as it does in the case of the right to health, that the state has a duty to provide the means to property since property is not a basic necessity.) Treatment cannot be considered a mere privilege; it must be a right. To say that a person has a right to health but that the state is not under any obligation to provide the necessary means would be like saying that a person has the right to own property but no one has a duty to see that the person keeps any property which may be owned. The right to treatment is analogous not to the right to theft but to the right to keep what is legitimately owned.

In a society where people are equally well-off and able to provide for their basic needs independently, the state would not necessarily be under an obligation to provide health services. Such services might be viewed as any other market commodity. Under those circumstances, the claim that "medical care is neither a right nor a privilege; it is a service provided by doctors and others to people who wish to purchase it" (Sade, 1976, pp. 482-83) would make moral sense.[4] But since that statement presupposes that everyone is in fact able to purchase services necessary to a decent existence if they so desire, in our current society it is not at all true. For while services are indeed provided by professionals to those who wish to purchase them, some persons may be in need of and wish to purchase such services but are unable to do so. To apply the above claim across the board without taking into account the fact that there is poverty in our society reflects a morally insensitive attitude.

One reason for arguments against the right to treatment is that it is sometimes assumed that such a right denies the individual therapist the right to refuse to treat a particular person. And surely a therapist has that right.[5] But it is precisely because it is not the duty of any *particular* therapist to provide treatment that it must be the duty of the state to make treatment available by means of contracting therapists, given the present economic condition of many people. Thus the above reason for denying a right to treatment is based on the false assumption that that right entails a claim on particular therapists, not on the state. But since it is the state which guarantees the right to health by guaranteeing the right to life, the state is under obligation to provide the means to health, whether it be bodily or psychological health.

It is curious that while most people would agree that one has a right to medical care where the problem is obviously physical, psychological treatment sometimes seems to be thought of as a luxury or privilege. This may be due to the fact that mental illnesses usually are not detected in the way that other illnesses are detected. And this might account for the reason that right to treatment has been overlooked for so long, even for those involuntarily committed. The attitude seems to be that if one's illness is not detected by a regular physician, then the person has no illness. Perhaps it is mistakenly assumed that while the latter is not the person's fault, problems of a psychological nature are ones for which the person can be held responsible. If this assumption were true, there would be much less reason to expect the state to provide the means to treatment. However, such an assumption has no basis. Some forms of mental illness have been found to be associated with brain dysfunction and other forms may be the result of an unhealthy environment. If in some cases it can be shown that the person is responsible for his or her mental illness, a parallel can be found for regular illness. For example, a heavy smoker who contracts lung cancer can be said to be responsible for that. Responsibility (or lack of it) for illness cannot be determined solely on the basis of the type of illness.

While we want to argue that the right to treatment should be extended to everyone and not just to those involuntarily committed, the grounds for ascribing it to the latter should be rather obvious. Before examining those grounds, however, let us just point out one argument for a general right to treatment, one based on compelling state interest.

One justification for the claim that the right to treatment should be extended to everyone could be based on compelling state interest. This means that when it can be shown that the state has a compelling interest in some matter, then the state has a right to take necessary means to protect that interest. But in some cases it may be more than a state's right—it may be a duty since the state is obligated to protect itself and its citizens. This entails providing necessary services to those who cannot afford them. In fact, in *O'Connor vs. Donaldson* (1975) the Court stated, "That the State has a proper interest in providing care and assistance to the unfortunate goes without saying" (p. 4933).[6] It is to the state's own benefit to protect the health of its citizens. And it may even be more important to the state that it protect the mental health of its citizens, since any form of democracy can only be successful if its citizens can make rational and responsible decisions. (This should not be taken to imply that one who does not *always* make rational, responsible decisions should be committed.)

While it should be obvious that the involuntarily committed have a right to treatment, it was only in 1960 that that right was even suggested (Birnbaum, 1960).[7] The fact that it was suggested only in the context of those involuntarily committed is understandable, given not only the dreadful conditions of state mental institutions but also the fact that involuntary confinement is a denial of a person's autonomy. Thus treatment is a more pressing concern in such instances. Since supposedly people are committed because they are in need of treatment, to confine them involuntarily and then fail to provide adequate treatment destroys the moral justification for confinement. There is no justification for depriving mentally handicapped individuals of their freedom without providing necessary services unless one is a utilitarian. It is conceivable that a utilitarian might argue that providing treatment is too costly for society and thus mere confinement of individuals presumed to be in some way harmful to others is sufficient. While this is true of utilitarianism in principle, Mill in *On Liberty* (1859, 1947) was very concerned with protecting the liberty of individual persons on the basis that such protection in the long-run would result in a healthier, happier society. For this reason he would not in general defend involuntary commitment simply on the basis of what seems good for a particular person or on the basis of what one *might* do. However, if such confinement in a particular case could be shown to be dictated by the utility principle, in order to be consistent Mill would have to say that the person's liberty should be sacrificed. Utility and liberty are not always compatible values. (From a legal standpoint, confinement for custodial purposes was ruled unconstitutional by the *O'Connor* court.)

If a person has been involuntarily committed to a mental institution, then adequate treatment (and thus a decent environment) must be provided, for nothing else justifies involuntary commitment. It is primarily on this basis, and not on the basis of compelling state interest, nor even for the protection of others, that the courts have recognized the right to treatment. But before discussing that basis in detail we must ask what justifies involuntary commitment in the first place.

Such a commitment is not justified by a prediction about what a person might do since predictions in those matters are rarely accurate. (See, for example, von Hirsch, 1972; Ennis & Litwack, 1974; Steadman and Cocozza, 1974; Perlin, 1976a.) Steadman and Cocozza contended that psychiatrists are inclined to overprediction: "Judging a healthy person sick . . . is seen as preferable to judging a sick person well" (1974, p. 108).

Also, depriving a person of liberty requires a better justification than the mere fact that it would make others feel more comfortable. In *O'Connor v. Donaldson* the court made this clear:

May the State fence in the harmless mentally ill solely to save its citizens from exposure to those whose ways are different? One might as well ask if the State, to avoid public unease, could incarcerate all who are physically unattractive or socially eccentric. Mere public intolerance or animosity cannot constitutionally justify the deprivation of a person's physical liberty. (p. 4933)

While all dangerous behavior is aberrant, not all aberrant behavior is dangerous. Even though we may believe that a person would be happier if he or she were not a misfit who engaged in aberrant behavior that is merely eccentric, that is still insufficient reason for involuntary commitment because that belief is difficult to verify.

We believe that no one would want to be a misfit in society. From the very best of motives, we wish to fix him. It is difficult to deal with this feeling since it rests on the unverifiable assumption that the aberrant person if he saw himself as we see him, would choose to be different than he is. But since he cannot be as we, and we cannot be as he, there is simply no way to judge the predicate for the assertion. (Livermore, Malmquist & Meehl, 1976, p. 175)

Thus, what we believe to be the person's own good is an epistemologically doubtful basis for denying a person's autonomy and freedom to live as he or she chooses. But more importantly, it is also a morally doubtful basis.

The only freedom which deserves the name, is that of pursuing our own good in our own way, so long as we do not attempt to deprive others of theirs, or impede their efforts to obtain it . . . . Mankind are greater gainers by suffering each other to live as seems good to themselves, than by compelling each to live as seems good to the rest. (Mill, 1859, 1947, pp. 12-13)[8]

We are now faced with a dilemma that is not easy to resolve: accurate predictability of dangerous behavior is unachievable, but besides recent dangerous behavior, that seems to be about the only justifiction for involuntary commitment. The *Lessard* court recognized this also but said:

Although attempts to predict future conduct are always difficult, and confinement based upon such a prediction must always be viewed with suspicion, we believe civil confinement can be justified in some cases if the proper burden of proof is satisfied and dangerousness is based upon a finding of a recent overt act, attempt or threat to do substantial harm to oneself or another. (p. 1093)

Thus, although prediction of dangerous behavior is often inaccurate, recent past behavior may indicate that the individual is in need of psychological help at present, which makes prediction irrelevant.

In most jurisdictions, and as noted by the *Lessard* court in the quotation above, a person may be committed not only on the basis of posing a physical threat to others but also on the basis of posing a threat to oneself, either by attempting or threatening suicide.

(1) the person in question must be proven, on the basis of convincing scientific evidence given at a fair hearing with appropriate due process guarantees, to

CASE STUDY 5.1

A 45-year-old male had applied for vocational rehabilitation assistance. The psychologist was to evaluate the client to determine if he was eligible for this assistance. Previous psychological records were available on the client but the psychologist did not have the time to examine them before the interview. During the testing session the client drifted off from time to time. He seemed to be responding to hallucinogenic voices. During these silent periods the psychologist glanced through the client's records. He noted that there had been a major change in medication recently. At the end of the session, he said to the client, "I notice that your medication was changed recently. How is the new medicine working?" The client replied, "Oh, it's doing fine. I still hear the voices but I don't pay as much attention to them as I used to."

"What are the voices saying?"

"They are telling me to do awful things to little girls."

"Like what?"

"Oh, it's too awful to talk about. I don't want to talk or think about it."

This was the only observation of the client's mental state. After the client left, the psychologist read the previous records carefully. It was determined that the man had been in a mental hospital for several years because he had assaulted several young girls in response to having heard voices.

Two weeks later, the psychologist is contacted by a social worker at the mental hospital. The client had been committed for 72 hours because he was found wandering along a rural road completely nude. The hearing required a psychologist as an expert witness. The psychologist agrees to attend the hearing as one of the witnesses. The psychologist and other mental health professionals all agree that this individual has the potential for violent behavior and strongly recommend at least a 90-day commitment for the client.

lack capacities of rational choice and deliberation; and (2) these incapacities must be *shown* to be highly likely to lead to danger to the person's life and limb or to the life and limb of others (Richards, 1977, p. 219).

However, since the law is designed primarily to protect people from each other, it is not obvious that it is always justified in interfering with a person's decision to commit suicide. The state has the duty to make health services available, not to force people to be healthy. However, an argument based on compelling state interest, if carried too far, could justify the state's right to force people to be healthy. That is what we want to deny, for that violates a person's right of self-determination.

While it might be argued that the state has a compelling interest to protect the health and lives of its citizens and is therefore justified in interfering in cases where one's health is in danger, nevertheless it is not clear that it should be up to a court to decide what is best for a particular individual. And from a moral point of view, a protest against commitment by a suicidal person should be respected, which is to say that due regard ought to be given to the reasons for suicide. Persons ought not to be committed merely because they have suicidal wishes. This does not mean, however, that involuntary commitment is never a morally justified means to prevent a suicide, for in some cases a decision to end one's life is made in a temporary state of psychological stress.

In general, there are two conditions under which paternalistic interference is justified, each being a necessary condition and jointly constituting a sufficient condition: (1) a person's mental state is not conducive to rational decision making and therefore the individual cannot function as an autonomous being whose actions are the products of his or her rational choices[9]; (2) the consequences of an act are in some way irreversibly harmful to oneself.[10] The first may be only a temporary condition, and if so, involuntary commitment would be justified for a *limited* amount of time but only as a last resort. The purpose of committing an individual would be to provide him or her with a stress-free environment, which would function as a ' 'cooling off' period, in much the same way that we now require couples who file for divorce to go through a waiting period" (Dworkin, 1975, p. 183).[11] Though a decision to get a divorce is not so grave as a decision to commit suicide, just as couples who do so decide are not necessarily acting from a temporary emotional state, neither does it follow that a person who decides to commit suicide is acting from a temporary state. And so it would be unjustified to commit a person involuntarily for an indefinite period of time only on the basis that the person is suicidal.

Assuming that sometimes there are sufficient moral and legal grounds for involuntarily committing an individual to a mental institution, the right to treatment follows as a consequence. We shall now concentrate on the legal foundations that have been cited for that right. As we mentioned earlier, some moral rights, especially those concerning a minimally decent existence, without legal guarantee are worthless in practice.

The right to treatment has been defined as "the legal right of a mentally ill inmate of a public mental institution to adequate medical treatment for his mental illness" (Birnbaum, 1960, p. 499). A more pointed definition of that right is "the right of involuntarily hospitalized mental patients to receive adequate therapy as an exchange for their being deprived of their liberty" (Robitscher, 1972, p. 298). Involuntarily committed individuals who are mentally handicapped are not serving time, that is, are not being punished, but rather are individuals whose fundamental right to liberty has been suspended on the basis that they are unable to make free and rational decisions regarding themselves and/or others. Punishment presupposes some wrong act for which the doer can be held responsible. Not every committed person has done a wrong act, and those who have are not held accountable, which is indicated by their commitment to a mental institution rather than to a prison. Thus strictly speaking it may seem odd that the cruel and unusual punishment clause has been cited as one of the constitutional bases for the right to treatment. In *Rozecki v. Gaughan* (1972) the defendants claimed that inadequate heating of the correctional institution "could not constitute 'cruel and unusual punishment' since as the plaintiffs were patients rather than inmates (albeit involuntarily confined), the question of punishment was not involved" (p. 7). While this claim was rejected by the *Rozecki* court, the court was not specific as to why the Eighth Amendment could be used as a basis for the right to treatment or even as a basis for requiring decent living conditions. But in *Martarella v. Kelley* (1974) and in *Welsch v. Likins* (1975) the courts were very specific. The *Martarella* court stated that

> Eighth Amendment's prohibition of cruel and unusual punishment is not
> restricted to instances of particular punishment inflicted on given individual
> but also applies to mere confinement to institution which is characterized by
> conditions and practices so bad as to be shocking to conscience of reasonably
> civilized people. (p. 576)

The *Welsch* court made the same statement (p. 489).

Thus the Eighth Amendment is interpreted broadly as a right to freedom
from harm. But that in itself seems insufficient to show that there is a
constitutional right to *treatment*, only that there is a right to decent living
conditions while involuntarily confined. The due process clause must be
invoked to guarantee positive action. That clause has been used to argue
that involuntary confinement requires that such confinement be for some
purpose that is not served unless the facility provides adequate treatment.
In *Wyatt v. Stickney* (1971) the court held that

> there can be no legal (or moral) justification for the State of Alabama's failing
> to afford treatment—and adequate treatment from a medical standpoint—
> to the several thousand patients who have been civilly committed to Bryce's
> for treatment purposes. To deprive any citizen of his or her liberty upon the
> altruistic theory that the confinement is for humane therapeutic reasons and
> then fail to provide adequate treatment, violates the very fundamentals of
> due process. (p. 785)

The concept of adequate treatment partly consists of individualized treatment plans. This was recognized by the *Rouse* court (1966), which stated
that the hospital must show "that the program provided is suited to (the
individual's) particular needs. Treatment that has therapeutic value for
some may not have such value for others" (p. 456).

While the due process clause of the Fourteenth Amendment has been
the main basis for the legal right to treatment, it seems that the equal
protection clause also could be viewed as a foundation for that right. A
person who has been involuntarily committed is deprived of certain fundamental rights and should be protected just as other citizens are. (Because
of the nature of the confinement, perhaps there is an even stronger duty
to protect involuntarily committed individuals.) Thus to justify suspending
these rights the state must show good cause, which can only be that it is
providing adequate treatment.

The Fourteenth Amendment also would seem to require a provision
(which some states have) for periodic review to make certain that the purpose for confinement is being served and "to insure that the hospital does
not forget its patients and allow them to remain there year after year when
they might be suitable for discharge" (Ennis & Siegel, 1973, p. 47).

From a moral point of view it should be emphasized that the right to
treatment is not and cannot be fundamentally based on utilitarian considerations. This was implicitly recognized in *Roberts v. State* (1974) when the
Indiana court stated that there is a duty owed toward mental patients "to
preserve . . . their life, health and safety: beyond any duty owed to the
general public" (p. 505). While the right to treatment may in fact have

utilitarian consequences, to use that as a basic justification would not only fail to *guarantee* that right in all instances but could conceivably justify involuntary confinement *without* treatment. The primary purpose of involuntary commitment and the primary goal of treatment is (ought to be) to help the individual become able to function as an autonomous, rational being, which cannot claim to be self-justifying.

To say that the primary goal of treatment is to promote autonomy of the individual is to say that it is the therapist's duty to help the person become able to make free decisions that are a product of his or her own will, decisions that are not due to some debilitating mental condition, or to the decisions and choices of others. It is important that the goal of treatment be described in this way rather than in terms of normal functioning. For what is normal, understood in a nonevaluative sense, is what is taken to be typical behavior of people at large in a society. Such a goal may not be agreed on by the individual (a female patient may not want her goal to be the acceptance of the role of the "happy homemaker"), even though the goal is described as normal (according to cultural standards).

A person who is committed voluntarily surely has the right to specify goals. The real moral problem arises in cases of involuntary commitment. To the extent that the person is able, he or she should be consulted regarding the specific goal of therapy and perhaps some agreement can be reached. This should be possible in many cases[12] since, as has already been pointed out, it does not follow merely from involuntary commitment that the person cannot understand anything which is suggested or that the person cannot specify a reasonable goal. However, if the individual is so mentally handicapped that discussion of goals is not possible, the therapist in charge of the treatment program should keep in mind the general goal of therapy as leading to as much autonomy as possible. This is to suggest that in some cases it cannot be assumed that the autonomy of a particular client is a given but rather something that needs to be developed to the degree possible for that client, for example, to help the client become more self-reliant even if he or she is mentally handicapped to the degree that discussion of goals is not possible.

The treatment of involuntarily committed individuals raises two questions[13]: (1) what kinds of methods are legitimate to achieve the goal, and (2) to what extent does an involuntarily committed person have the (moral and legal) right to refuse treatment?

In answer to the first question we can say that the least intrusive or restrictive means ought to be used. This is in fact a legal right of the patient. The *Lessard* court quoted from *Shelton v. Tucker* (1972) that "even though the governmental purpose be legitimate and substantial, that cannot be pursued by means that broadly stifle personal liberties when the end can be more narrowly achieved" (p. 1095). While *Lessard v. Schmidt* was a commitment and not a treatment case, this passage is also applicable to treatment plans. The more intrusive or restrictive a technique the more the person's autonomy is diminished. If we assume that the client in some or many cases is already autonomous to some degree, then certainly no technique should be used which will not enhance what autonomy the client already possesses.

Perhaps an intrusive technique will, in the long run, prove to increase client autonomy, but the therapist must not ignore the dignity of the individual as a person.

While certain techniques may in the long-run enable the person to leave the institution and may thus be said to promote the individual's dignity, depending on the degree of intrusiveness, "it still may be the case that the methods used are not expressive of dignity of the agent. They may treat him as an object rather than a subject. Though leading to increased self-respect they are not expressive of it" (Dworkin, 1976, p. 27).

The second question is a bit more complicated. If a person has been involuntarily committed for the primary purpose of receiving treatment, it might seem to follow that the person has a duty to accept treatment. But whether that does in fact follow depends on whose right is at issue. To say that the patient has a duty to accept treatment is to imply not that the patient's right to treatment is at issue but is rather to imply that it is society's right to correct an individual's behavior no matter what. It would then follow that it is a duty on the part of the patient to accept treatment. But because it is the patient's right that is central, the duty arises on the part of society (the state) to make mental health services available. It is not the patient's duty to accept treatment, and thus the state in most instances cannot justifiably force treatment on someone. One can legitimately be coerced to fulfill a duty but rights can be waived; it would be an odd sort of right if one were compelled to exercise it. Thus the right to treatment entails the right of the person to waive that right, that is, the right to refuse treatment.

But the issue is not nearly so simple as that. On the one hand, coercing an individual to accept treatment is a further denial of the autonomy of the involuntarily committed person.

> To assume that institutionalized populations are incompetent to make any decisions affecting their lives would have serious consequences; it would erode the notion of personal autonomy and might well lead to a situation in which the State would invoke alleged incapacity as justification for its own judgment on a whole range of issues personally involving a patient. Such a situation would . . . involve bad therapy or rehabilitation hastening dependency and loss of control . . . . " (Friedman, 1975, p. 83)

On the other hand, it seems that we do have a duty to the individual who is genuinely in need of treatment even if it is refused; at times we do have a moral duty to be paternalistic. And so in some cases it would be insensitive to say that

> persons should be left to pursue their own fate if they so "state." Such a position can be as destructive of human life as its over-readiness to hospitalize . . . . [W]ithout coercion, society will abandon many people to their self-destructive and uncared-for fate. Such an approach is as insensitive as the abuse of power that leads to indefinite incarceration without treatment with treatments that are of not value or ineffective or even harmful. (Katz, 1969, pp. 770-71)

Thus, while in some cases a patient's refusal of treatment should be accepted, there are cases where the patient is not able to make a rational choice about treatment regardless of what he or she claims to want. In such cases it would be insensitive to accept that patient's refusal despite the fact that the courts have "agreed that a patient who is adjudicated as personally incompetent to exercise the right to refuse, nevertheless retains the right to refuse" (White & White, 1981, p. 958).

If a patient does refuse treatment, the first question that must be asked is why. The reasons a patient gives for refusal will shed light on whether the decision to refuse is a competent one. If the reasons given indicate that the person has sufficient understanding of the relevant information, then coerced treatment is unjustified. No doubt the objection will be raised here that determining whether the patient has sufficient understanding of the relevant information is a subjective matter, that to talk of what constitutes a rational decision "may express a value preference for a particular kind of thinking . . . " (Friedman, 1975, p. 78). Such an objection is based on two assumptions: (1) that there is no way to determine objectively whether another person has sufficient understanding; and (2) that because what is thought to be rational may involve value judgments it cannot be used as an objective criterion for judging competence.

To accept the first assumption entails that in no case can we ever tell whether a person sufficiently understands what is said. But unless we are willing to succumb to the traditional philosophical problem of the knowledge of other minds—that no one can ever know for certain anything about the mental state of another—that assumption must be rejected. Just because there are borderline cases, it would be absurd to assume that we can *never* make a judgment about whether or not a person understands what is said.

If the person's reasons as to why he or she rejects treatment are based on irrational reasons or indicate fundamental misperceptions of reality, surely it is reasonable to conclude that the person does not sufficiently understand or is not influenced by relevant considerations. What is meant by a rational or competent decision is simply that one understands and is influenced by the relevant information provided. Thus the second assumption is not entirely true. While one's goals may involve value preferences that may ultimately be subjective preferences, what counts as a rational pursuit of those goals is not. (This is not to say that a goal is never subject to considerations of reasonableness or rationality. There is an obvious difference between having as one's goal to become a college professor or a good truck driver and the goal to become a good murderer.) Determining what counts as a rational pursuit of one's goals involves determining whether or not the person acts on correct perceptions of reality and relevant considerations in light of the chosen goals. And it is the goal itself which generates criteria for relevance (Murphy, 1974). If the reason for refusing treatment is not based on irrational reasons or fundamental misperceptions of reality (as determined by the chosen goal), then coercing a person into accepting treatment would be difficult to justify, not only morally but legally as well. In *Scott v. Plante* (1976) the court ruled that, in the absence of an emergency, involuntary administration of drugs would amount to a violation of the right to bodily privacy and interference with the First, Eighth, and Fourteenth Amendments. The same could be said for other types of treatment that do not require client cooperation and hence could be coercively administered.

In the areas of commitment and treatment (as elsewhere), there will of course be borderline cases where determining competency is concerned. But the burden of proof will not be on the person who refused commitment or treatment but on those who believe that coercion is justified.

Chapter 6

Research and Experimentation

All types of psychological activities have been evaluated from an ethical perspective, but the area of research has received the most scrutiny. It is likely that ethical conflicts occur as often in therapy as they do in research but because research is more public it has been subject to closer inspection. Veatch and Sollitto (1973) cite some provocative examples of abuses. One study involved using electroconvulsive shock as a punisher for hospitalized mental patients and another investigated the use of succenylcholine (an injected drug which produces a short cessation of respiration) as a possible aversive stimulus for conditioning negative reactions in prisoners. In both cases the problems are quite clear—the subjects came from special populations, consent was intentionally not obtained, and the procedures involved risks. It is not surprising that these techniques were tried on an experimental basis but it is amazing that these studies were submitted and accepted for publication. Surely gross violations also occur in therapy but they are seldom publicized. The guidelines from both the American Psychological Association (APA) and federal agencies for research activities are more detailed and specific than those available for psychologists' other primary activities (teaching and therapy). The APA places the responsibility for ethical conduct with the researcher rather than relying on external enforcement, while the government's approach has been to use Institutional Review Boards (IRB) for approval and monitoring. Formal review and external monitoring are most frequent with large, funded research projects and less frequent with informal/non-funded research. External review not only increases the quality of the research but also ensures that the ethical issues are dealt with in a more open fashion. With informal research the ethical safeguards are often equally informal or non-existent.

There are three general problem areas of research—the subject-researcher contract, the use of animals in research, and professional practice. Each of these areas will be discussed separately.

SUBJECT-RESEARCHER CONTRACT

There are several areas where ethical concerns arise when doing research with human subjects. For example, when discussing a conflict between method and ethics or the issue of consent, deception will obviously be an issue. To raise a question about cost vs. benefit usually involves questions about risk. So though we have divided this section into various aspects of research that deserve consideration where human subjects are involved, overlap of issues will be unavoidable.

Method/Ethics Conflict

The conflict between desirable or recommended methodological practice and ethical considerations is the core of many of the critical issues. The reason psychologists may at times deceive subjects or expose them to risks is not that researchers lack sensitivity to and respect for basic rights of human dignity. Compromising ethical principles is often related to the desire to use the best methods available, thereby enhancing the value and interpretability of the obtained data. Historically, methodological innovations have been used without question; today it is clearly seen that the "ideal experiment" may have to be compromised to protect fully the rights of subjects. Inferential statistics allow us to generalize from sample to population only if random sampling is used, but subjects who exercise their right not to participate introduce a sampling bias which limits the ability to generalize. The finding in question may only be applicable for the subset of the population who volunteer willingly. This is one source or experimental bias or confounding that researchers will have to learn to live with. Deception is used when subjects are likely to bias their responses based on what they think the experiment is about. Reducing or manipulating the cues which produce response bias on the part of subjects in experiments improves methodology but the rights of subjects are violated by some of these procedures. Research involving "placebo groups" also illustrate this conflict. In order to evaluate accurately the effectiveness of a drug or a treatment it is necessary to leave the control group untreated and to keep subjects "blind" to which treatment they are receiving.

Ellsworth (1977) notes another area where methods and ethics conflict:

> Hypotheses that involve socially undesirable behavior may often be better tested outside of the laboratory, ideally in a situation where subjects do not know that they are being observed by a social scientist . . . . Where I say "ideally" I am speaking solely in methodological terms. Unfortunately, the "best" methods are not always the most ethical ones. (p. 607)

Several consequences of this conflict are apparent. West and Gunn (1978) suggest that researchers will shift their energies to the more acceptable topics. Should this become the trend, in the future we may have a psychology of "pleasant events," where knowledge of the negative aspects of human behavior does not advance. These authors point out that theories are likely to be restricted:

> The trend toward nonmotivational theories in social psychology is likely to be accelerated. If researchers are prevented from using manipulations that are capable of arousing motives, then it is unlikely that they will obtain results that support a motivational interpretation. (p. 38)

CASE STUDY 6.1

A counseling center had developed a treatment program for eating disorders that seemed very effective. The program lasted six months and was a comprehensive system of therapy with appropriate medical supervision. The program seemed to work well for bulimia. The center served primarily students, but clinicians from the city began to refer their clients based on reports of the clinic's success. The people involved decided to begin a research project to determine the program's real effectiveness. The design involved having half of the next twenty referrals serve as a waiting list control group while the other half were exposed to the treatment. Various physical and personality mesures were to be used as outcome measures. The experimental group met weekly and the control group came in twice a month to fill out quetionnaires and behavioral records of their eating behaviors. Subjects signed a consent form prior to participation and understood that assignment to the experimental or waiting list control group was random. Students who came to the counseling center with bulimia as the primary problem were encouraged to participate in the research project but were offered treatment by another staff counselor if they preferred not to participate.

After some time several members of the control group began to complain that their symptoms were getting worse and that they wanted to begin treatment sooner than promised. Since the experiment was the only way that true effectiveness of the treatment could be established, the researchers counseled patience. While this placated most of the group members, three individuals stopped coming for their appointments and would not respond to the clinic's requests that they become reinvolved. One of the dropouts then had a binge-purge episode which resulted in serious fluid loss and subsequent hospitalization. She was in critical condition but eventually began to recover. When her parents found out that she had been denied treatment, they retained a lawyer with the intention of suing the school. Their argument was that their daughter was a student at the university and should not have been deprived of services, especially since some nonstudents were receiving the benefit of university services.

Hopefully the response of the research community will be to search for creative solutions that are acceptable in both methodological and ethical terms.

Consent

Informed consent has been isolated as the basic requirement for ethical practice in research. As such, it emphasizes the contract between researcher and subject. Professional principles indicate that "the investigator establishes a clear and fair agreement with research paritcipants, prior to their participation, that clarifies the obligations and responsibilities of each" (Principle 9.d). The establishment of this "clear and fair agreement" is accomplished through obtaining valid consent from each participant. However, the idea of obtaining informed consent is easier to endorse as a principle than it is to accomplish in practice.

The concept of informed consent comes from the medical/legal standard which is used when treatment involves intrusive methods. The medical practice of requiring informed consent is derived from legal principles which deal with battery or inappropriate touching of others (Faden & Beauchamp, 1981). It functions to release the physician from some types of liability when risks are associated with treatment. As we discussed earlier, if consent is valid it must be informed, competent, and voluntary. In obtaining valid consent, respect is shown for the rights of the individual participants but there are situations where deception is a methodological necessity. Studies where observations are made without the individual's knowledge represent instances where some component of valid consent is missing. Ethical principles suggest that some compromise is acceptable.

> To the extent that weighing the scientific and human values suggests a compromise of any principle the investigator incurs a correspondingly serious obligation to seek ethical advice and to observe stringent safeguards to protect the rights of human participants. (Principle 9.a)

This introduces the idea of cost/benefit or risk/benefit comparisons into the deliberation of the researcher. The thrust of this kind of analysis is summarized by Blackstone (1975): "Tally the costs of an experiment, including that to the research participants. Tally the probable benefits. If the probable benefits outweigh the probable costs, then the experiment is ethically justifiable" (p. 409). However, consent and cost/benefit are in conflict since the former is based on a Kantian model while the latter is based on a utilitarian model. The conflict between the rights of the individual and society is a central issue, and one that is not easy to resolve. "Costs" in this analysis usually involve the subject, i.e., basic rights are compromised or the procedures involve risk. Advancement of knowledge, discovery of new potent methods or progress of science are the type of factors cited as benefits. Since this suggests future (potential) benefits, Blackstone (1975) warns against "visions of monumental gain" based on a single study. Future benefits are hard to predict and researchers (or their colleagues) may not be completely objective in making such predictions. This model seems more appropriate for clinical or medical research where both costs and benefits are more specific and can refer to the individual. Subjects and researchers view the cost/benefit comparison from different perspectives. Michaels and Oetting (1979) found that subjects' judgments about the ethicality of hypothetical expeiments and their willingness to participate varied as a function of costs (risks) but was unrelated to benefits whereas researchers focus on benefits, real or imagined. What is necessary is to define clearly and honestly what constitutes costs and benefits in this kind of analysis. Researchers, for example, may construe the ease of acquiring subjects as a relevant dimension in evaluating costs but convenience is probably not an adequate justification.

The cost/benefit comparison is more complicated when the research is of a clinical or applied nature. In pure research, costs refer to the subjects, and the benefits are generally an advancement of knowledge. This advancement of knowledge is utilitarian in that it is of benefit to society but not usually to the subjects who participated in the study. With clinical research the benefits apply to the subject as well as to society. If a study is investigating methods useful for reducing depression, depressed individuals probably anticipate some relief in their symptoms. While some unusual subjects may be willing to participate to advance knowledge, most expect some individual benefit. The desire for symptom relief among clinical subjects introduces an element of coercion into the consent contract. This aspect of clinical research needs to be carefully considered and the potential personal benefits need to be represented accurately.

The conflict surrounding the cost/benefit model is far from being resolved despite continuing debate. Kelman (1965) and Soble (1978a) both endorse a strong interpretation of the consent requirement. They argue from an individual rights perspective and conclude that without valid consent research should not be conducted. More moderate positions would suggest that it can be ethically acceptable to compromise consent under certain circumstances or even that consent is unnecessary if no risks are involved.

According to Principle 9.d, consent is informed when "the investigator informs the participants of all aspects of the research that might reasonably be expected to influence willingness to participate and explains all other aspects of the research about which the participants inquire." In practice this component of consent is difficult for researchers to comply with since it is often methodologically necessary to exclude some information. Two practices make adherence to this principle problematic. The first involves passive violation where some information (e.g., the experimental hypotheses) is withheld; the second involves more active manipulation where subjects are misinformed or deceived about some parts of the experiment.

Most research in psychology can be conducted without active deception but it is unusual to inform subjects fully. What information needs to be provided to potential volunteers? The practical details of the experiment need to be disclosed. What subjects will do, how long it will take, and where it will take place are examples of such details. If experiments involve any risks or costs, subjects would, of course, require this information. However, subjects also need to be "read their rights." Researchers have quickly developed sophistication regarding research ethics while most subjects lack basic information about the ethical issues involved. Some review of the subjects' rights with special focus on the voluntary nature of their participation and their right to withdraw is essential. The necessity of fully informing subjects about the research has been considered for both medical and psychological research. Technical details (such as the diameter of a small needle used for an injection or the type of respirator) are not considered essential to medical research. Full disclosure would require very sophisticated subjects to actually understand the information provided and, if carried to an extreme, might function to obfuscate essential information. In psychology one of the critical problems is how much information about the purpose, hypothesis, or expectations is required. While full disclosure of the purpose of a given study is ideal, there is little support for this idea from psychologists. If subjects develop expectations as a function of being told the purpose of a study, they may monitor and modify their behavior in a systematic fashion. Resnick and Schwartz (1973) manipulated the amount of information provided to subjects in a verbal conditioning study. They found conditioning only when subjects were uninformed about the purpose of the study. Fully informed subjects did not condition or negative conditioning was evident. In the interest of good methodology, information concerning the hypothesis is routinely withheld. Freedman (1975) concludes that "the informing of the patient/subject is not a fundamental requirement of valid consent. It is, rather, derivative from the requirement that the consent be the expression of responsible choice" (p. 35). This suggests that a responsible person will seek information on which to base decisions but that he or she can also decide without information (uninformed consent).

While information concerning the hypothesis is usually omitted, there are times when this information may be relevant. For example, if a study involves rape victims and the researchers expect or predict that there are common behavioral or personality characteristics among rape victims, the question arises whether the potential subjects should be told what the hypothesis is. Many volunteers in the case may choose not to participate since the hypothesis suggests that something about them may be partly responsible for the rape incident. The rape victims may find this suggestion of their being responsible for the rape quite offensive. This would seem to be a case where knowledge of the hypothesis is relevant.

The next sections of this chapter which deal with the researcher-subject relationship concern deception, risk, coercion, and privacy. While each of these issues raises unique questions, they also involve challenges to the idea of valid consent. Components of consent procedures and suggestions will be discussed under each topic.

Deception

No single practice has generated as much publicity, debate, and criticism as the use of deception. The debate focuses on the logical incompatibility of the concepts of consent and deception. How can subjects give valid consent if they have been deceived or misinformed about critical aspects of the study? Milgram's (1963) study on compliance with authority has been frequently used as an example of this practice. This study raises issues beyond that of simple deception. Milgram reports that subjects in this study experienced high levels of stress and a part of his method involved convincing (or, in some cases, even perhaps coercing) subjects who wanted to terminate their participation to continue. Deception is frequently used in social research to study problems such as conformity, obedience, cheating, and aggression in the laboratory. The purpose of deception methodology is to increase internal and external validity. Internal validity refers to the internal logic of the experiment itself. Deception has been used to simulate powerful social situations to arouse motivational states that are critical in controlling behavior. In addition to creating powerful variables, reducing demand characteristics is another reason for use. Experimenter instructions often mislead subjects about what aspect of their behavior is under study.

The fear is that if the subject knows what is being studied (e.g., honesty), he or she will then behave in socially acceptable ways.

The second justification for deception deals with external validity or how well researchers' findings generalize to behavior in other settings. As Miller (1972) points out, "Despite the fact that the behavior occurs in a setting formally defined as a psychological experiment, via deception the actual process investigated can be related or generalized outside the laboratory—what some might term the 'real world'" (p. 626). This advantage must assume that subjects are naive or at least that they are easily duped. Because of the publicity about deception in psychology experiments, subjects may be suspicious or expect to be deceived, in which case these procedures are probably ineffective and do not readily improve external validity.

We assume that deception will continue to be used, and if that is the case, what can be done to minimize the ethical problems involved with this practice? The strength of psychologists' interest in deception is clearly represented in recent APA principles which suggest that after a cost/benefit analysis, deception can be used. Soble (1978a) considers various arguments concerning the use of deception and concludes that accurate knowledge of purpose is critical. His position is radical in that his solution is that these studies should not be conducted; which is a strong expression of the Kantian perspective. Kelman (1967), in an early paper on deception, was critical about overuse. When deception was considered the methodology of choice, 40 percent of the studies in the *Journal of Personality and Social Psychology* and the *Journal of Abnormal Psychology* involved the use of deception. Kelman (1967) said,

> I sometimes feel that we are training a generation of students who do not know that there is any other way of doing experiments in our field—who feel that deception is as much de riguer as significance at the .05 level. Too often deception is used not as a last resort, but as a matter of course. (p. 5)

The reliance on deception is often a matter of convenience rather than a methodological decision. The Ethical Principles allow for the use of deception when it is a "methodological requirement" (Principle 9.e). If this criterion is strictly interpreted, deception is acceptable only in unusual and infrequent cases. This would eliminate deception being justified on such bases as convenience or the ease of acquiring subjects. As Soble (1978a) points out, this type of consideration reflects a paternalistic or utilitarian justification that might allow any kind of violation in order to save money or time.

If deception is used, investigators incur increased responsibility and accept certain limits in the range of variables that can be studied. Examples have been cited where subjects are deceived about the existence or magnitude of risks involved with the study. Knowledge of risks is a necessary condition for consent so the practice of disguising the risks is clearly inappropriate from an ethical as well as a legal perspective. The decision to use deception places a heavy burden on the researcher to show that the importance and quality of the study justifies its use. The study would have to make a significant contribution, considering the existing knowledge in the field. Considerations which are primarily personal (advancement in employment or in the profession) would, of course, be eliminated. The quality of the study would have to be excellent and other options for investigating the problem would probably have to be eliminated on the basis of methodological problems.

Researchers also accept some limitations in the range of the variables they study. For example, researchers who work with induced anger will probably have to accept the idea of working with low magnitude anger rather than the potent levels to which they have become accustomed. These constraints would suggest that replications, demonstrations, and poorly conceived research should not be attempted if deception is involved. While it would be interesting simply to replicate Hartshorne and May's (1928) studies on honesty, the methods used would not be acceptable by today's standards because of the level of deceit.

Both ethical and methodological issues need to be evaluated when deception is considered. The ethical issues focus on the rights of the subject; a clear and fair agreement is compromised when deception is used. Philosophers and psychologists have suggested options that will improve either the ethical or methodological problems which exist. These suggestions are practical and while there is no single solution that solves all problems, the use of several safeguards does improve the situation. Campbell (1969) suggests that the "subject pool" be informed that some of the experiments in which they will be asked to participate will involve deception. In this case subjects are forewarned, yet they do not possess specific information about individual experiments. This is similar to the idea of "informed deceit" suggested by Horn (1978). There would seem to be no compelling reason why individuals could not consent to being deceived. There are two possible variants of this procedure that apply either to a single experiment (specific) or to a set of experiments (general). When the general form of "informed deceit" is used, it reduces both ethical and methodological problems, while the specific form reduces only ethical problems. In both cases it allows individuals who object to deception to choose not to participate. This assumes that we are dealing with noncoerced subjects and that the deception does not involve misrepresentation of risks. Mixon (1972, 1977) supports this general idea but argues that subjects need to know if deception will be used in the specific experiment for which they are volunteering. While this furthers the ethical aspects, it destroys the methodological advantage. Arguments are offered as if this is the only source of protection available to subjects. If subjects understand their rights to decline or terminate participation, then they have options if the experiment disturbs them in any way.

Another option which Soble (1978a) labels "presumptive consent" is to anticipate informed consent by surveying a sample of subjects from the population to be studied (Berscheid et al., 1973). If sample subjects would agree to participate, then it is acceptable to use the procedure in question. However, asking subjects to predict their reactions is an imperfect approach since subjects know that they are not actually participating. The emotional response of real subjects may differ from the cognitive response of "mock subjects." Mock subjects may emphasize advancement of knowledge while real subjects may emphasize their rights. Veatch (1975) discusses this option and suggests that "if there is substantial agreement (say 95%) then it seems reasonable to conclude that most real subjects would have agreed to participate even if they had the information . . . " (p. 23). Deciding on the appropriate cutoff is a critical problem for this solution.

Ex post facto consent was used by Milgram (1974) as a part of the justification for his studies: "The central moral justification for allowing a procedure of the sort used in my study is that it is judged acceptable by those who have taken part in it" (p. 199). Often, as a trivial indication of sensitivity to ethical issues, the researchers offer to exclude or destroy data if there are serious objections. This is trivial since subjects care about what happens to them rather than the disposition of data. The problem here is similar to the question of how much risk a subject can agree to. Subjects usually are agreeable, especially after participation, so decisions concerning risks and deception should probably be made independently of what subjects are willing to endure. The problem with the *ex post facto* consent is that subjects' judgments after participation are probably positively biased. After participation, even if the subject behaved badly, he or she would seek to justify his or her involvement. The experimenter could focus on the value and importance of the study and de-emphasize the procedure and negative actions of the subject. Dissonance theory (Festinger, 1957) suggests that subjects will actively seek to justify, explain, and accept their participation or their actions. This does not suggest that subject perceptions and judgments are not important, rather that they are not sufficient.

Soble (1978b) suggests a combination of general consent in addition to using proxy consent. This procedure involves general consent on the part of the subject with a friend or relative who knows all of the details of the study giving proxy consent. This approach assumes that the friend or relative possesses more accurate information about the subject than a sample of peers. Both ethical and methodological advantages are offered by this procedure but costs will probably preclude wide usage.

Also, some suggestions which are mainly methodological in nature have been offered. Role-playing has been suggested as an option for eliminating the use of deception. Instead of deceiving subjects, the experimenter actively enlists the aid and cooperation of subjects in imagining the situation and acting out their responses. A researcher interested in impression management (the ability to appear sick versus healthy) with hospitalized mental patients could either deceive subjects by telling them that an interview would be related to discharge or have them imagine that this was the case and then role-play their reactions. The ethical advantages of the latter are obvious, and if the results of these studies were consistent with the findings from deception studies, then role-playing would find frequent applications. While some evidence indicates that role-playing can replicate general relationships, the expectation that the results would be comparable has not been supported. Role-playing may be appropriate for cognitive estimates of future behavior but this technique has been found to lack the power to induce involvement when motivational or emotional variables are studied

(West & Gunn, 1978). Field experiments and sophisticated correlational approaches (path analyses, regression, and time-series analysis) are also discussed by West and Gunn (1978) as possible options. The predictions of an "ecologically valid" psychology which was supposed to develop as psychologists move out of the laboratory have been greatly exaggerated. Laboratory experiments still represent routine practice, and field studies are exceptions. While field studies avoid the problems of deception, the ethical issue of privacy is raised. If issues of invasion of privacy can be avoided, then finding "real world" representation of researchers' variables offers advantages, especially in terms of external validity.

If deception is used (and it probably will be), the researcher is required to debrief the participants (Principle 9.e and 9.h). Tesch (1977) indicates that debriefing has educational, methodological, and ethical functions. The ethical functions are, according to Holmes (1976a, 1976b), dehoaxing and desensitizing. Dehoaxing refers to removing any misconceptions or illusions created during the experiment. In doing so, any negative emotional states experienced by the subjects also should diminish. But evidence for the effectiveness of dehoaxing is weak; self-evaluations, self-report measures, and behavior on subsequent tasks have revealed residual effects of the experimental manipulations. These studies have focused on short-term effects (immediate to two months after participation) where differences are most likely. The experience of being deceived probably accounts for difficulties with dehoaxing. Subjects enter the experiment expecting to be deceived, they are in fact deceived, and then researchers expect subjects to "shift gears" and accept as true whatever explanation the experimenter provides. If everything else is misrepresented, why should the subject now believe the deceiver?

Desensitizing refers to changing or ameliorating any negative feelings that subjects may have concerning their behavior during the experiment. This would be most important when subjects have engaged in "reprehensible acts" (Diener & Crandall, 1978). Milgram's study on obedience is an example of the kind of behavior which would require desensitizing. Holmes (1976b) suggests that experimenters attempt to justify the participants' behavior through claiming that situational determinants are powerful in the experimental setting or that this behavior is not related to behavior in the real world. While the intentions are noble (subjects should not leave feeling badly about themselves), the practice often involves another deception or distortion. If everyone is told that he or she behaved like most people, then the researcher would surely be lying to some.

The methodological and ethical functions of debriefing also are important. The debriefing interview is a rich source of information about preexperimental expectations, strategies in the experiment, and the effectiveness of the deception. This is critical information for developing effective methods. The educational functions often are completely ignored and represent an area of frequent malpractice. Subjects are told, "We can't tell you the purpose of the study, but when we are through collecting data we will get back to you and explain everything in full detail." While subjects accept this contract, researchers seldom fulfill their part of the agreement. Semesters end and intact classes disperse or the data reveal nothing important or interpretable, so the subjects do not get feedback. This is one area where self-regulation by the researchers has failed miserably, so some type of institutional regulation is probably necessary.

The problems with deception in research are not going to disappear nor are researchers going to stop using this approach to understand behavior. If deception is to be used, the quality of the research and the ethical safeguards need careful evaluation.

Risk

There is considerable agreement concerning the disclosure of risk but some uncertainty about what constitutes risk. To the extent that risks are involved, subjects need to be informed prior to obtaining consent. Principle 9.g states that "the investigator protects the participant from physical and mental discomfort, harm, and danger that may arise from research procedures." The specification of what constitutes physical and mental discomfort is not easily accomplished when we talk about psychological research. In medicine the risks are more easily understood since information is available on average mortality, probability of cure, and probability of side effects. If medical patients are making cost/benefit decisions, at least they can be provided with objective information on which to base their decision. In psychology the risks are not usually life-threatening but they are more difficult to measure and document. Physical injury and physical risks are infrequent in psychological research. Physically intrusive methods are unusual unless the psychologist works in a medical setting or works in human physiology. As Wolfensberger (1967) indicates, the relevant risks of interest are intrinsic (part of the experiment proper) rather than extrinsic (normal risks associated with life). While psychologists sometimes conduct studies where physically intrusive methods are used, it is assumed that qualified medical personnel supervise or carry out these parts of the research. For example, a researcher may need blood samples in a study of changes associated with exercise but the blood samples would be the responsibility of the medical collaborators. Physical discomfort poses more of a problem, since psychologists do study and research topics such as pain tolerance or reduction. The *Ethical Principles* do not forbid research of this kind but the importance of consent is paramount. Studies will continue in this area, and if procedures are clearly described, if subjects maintain control over their participation, and if the magnitude of the discomfort is within reason, problems should not occur.

The real issue deals with mental or psychological discomfort, harm, or risks. Experiments that deal with negative or unpleasant emotions (anxiety, fear, or depression) or allow subjects to behave in antisocial or pathological ways possess the potential for producing harm. As with deception, researchers incur increased responsibility when these types of manipulation are used. Replication would seem inadequate justification for inducing high levels of these states and generally we would assume some unique contribution to knowledge if this type of study is contemplated. Subjects' evaluation of frequently used procedures was studied by Farr and Seaver (1975). They found that procedures that involve pain, shock, inflicting pain on others, physical endurance, and bogus feedback about latent homosexuality were viewed as most discomforting. Sullivan and Deiker (1973) found that subjects and researchers do not necessarily agree about the risks of experimental procedures. While researchers generally rated various procedures as more aversive than subjects did, subjects were more concerned about procedures involving shock (even at low levels).

As indicated earlier, Michaels and Oetting (1979) report that subjects considered risks in deciding whether or not to participate, but were not concerned with potential benefit. It can be assumed that researchers are more responsive to the benefit side of this comparison. Faden and Beauchamp (1981) have looked at a similar issue in medicine. They distinguish between personal and professional standards for consent. The idea of a professional standard suggests that there is agreement among professionals about what information clients should have when consenting to medical treatment. The personal standard suggests that there may be unique, even irrational, concerns on the part of the patient that need to be disclosed prior to treatment. Clients with cancer phobia, for example, might require information on increases in risk of cancer, even if these chances are very small or remote. Faden and Beauchamp found evidence for a professional standard using beginning therapy with anticonvulsants as a concrete example. Physicians generally agreed about what information clients needed before beginning anticonvulsant therapy. Unfortunately, they also found that patients wanted information that differed from that viewed as important by the physicians. This suggests that the researcher is probably not the best judge of risks and that procedures approved by the average subject may be evaluated differently by individual subjects.

How serious are the risks in psychological research? While examples can be found where real risks do occur, most psychological research involves variables that are not very powerful. As Ellsworth (1977) indicates, there is a distinction between independent variables of the "chronic" and "acute" types. Most laboratory experiments involve acute manipulations of variables (e.g., anxiety) that are restricted in range and low in magnitude compared to the chronic version. It would be difficult to induce in the laboratory anxiety as powerful and pervasive as that experienced by the typical doctoral student waiting to begin his or her oral exams. Since many acute manipulations fail to affect logical dependent variables, most should have no long-term effects.

If risks are involved, the professional standards suggest that they must be minimized. Valid consent allows for some exposure to risk. Consent agreements have been referred to as release forms but they do not release experimenters from legal and ethical obligations. If subjects are harmed, the researcher is responsible for "detecting and removing" the negative consequences. Occasionally the idea of "shared risks" is offered to describe the consent contract. In reality most researchers recognize that subjects have the "lion's share" of the risks.

What steps can be taken to reduce, eliminate, or control risks? The use of peer review provides some safeguards but since subjects and researchers do not use the same standards in evaluating risks, this procedure alone is inadequate. Some representation of subjects in the review process is necessary. Information about subject evaluation of risks or discomfort is easily obtained and should be used. Screening subjects for personality characteristics or pathology that might interact with specific procedures also should be helpful. Anxiety induction is probably risky for individuals who are already chronically anxious, whereas the nonanxious subject may not be affected. Screening participants can be very helpful but it does not come with a guarantee of effectiveness and the subject shares some responsibility. An example from medical research documents this problem. A paid subject provided false information about her medical history in a study of an experimental drug's effect on sleep. In this case the subject died (from a coronary) as a function of complications induced by the experimental drug.

Coercion

Valid consent assumes that the individual giving consent is doing so on a voluntary basis. Coercion is viewed as a major problem when special populations are involved in clincial and nontherapeutic research projects. The idea of voluntary participation is based on characteristics of the subjects and environmental demands operating at the time. Competence or rationality refers to the process individuals generally use to make decisions rather than an inspection of the specific decision in question. Responsibility, according to Freedman (1975), is a dispositional characteristic rather than a situational response. Relevant criteria would be the ability to develop a life plan and to live with the consequences of one's decision. While these criteria lack specificity, we can generally assume responsibility or rationality unless there is compelling evidence to the contrary. Being institutionalized or being declared mentally incompetent would be examples of this type of evidence.

If competence is assumed, the environmental demands would seem to be most salient. The most frequent subject in psychological research is the college student enrolled in introductory psychology classes. In the 1960s schools required student participation in faculty and graduate student research. Even though it is often assumed that the required (or forced) participation is a thing of the past, there are no recent surveys to confirm this assumption. Psychology has been criticized as lacking ecological validity since much is known about the behavior of the college student and the white rat in a laboratory but such knowledge may not generalize to other settings or subjects. The choice of the college student is a matter of convenience rather than a methodologically based decision. Most researchers teach and students are used because they are available and cooperative.

Recent literature still contains statements such as "introductory psychology students, who were required to participate in research, volunteered for this study." Though it is recognized that required participation is inappropriate, there are still vestiges of this approach in practice. Many departments have settled on a compromise requiring participation but allowing individuals who object to being subjects to satisfy this requirement in some other way, e.g., writing papers, reading research, or attending movies. This still appears to be coercive. Freedman (1975) indicates that consent is not voluntary if grades are made contingent on participation. To the extent that the options are more aversive than research participation, this solution still involves coercion. If research participation is one of several reasonable and equally attractive options available to students, however, it would be hard to view participation as being coerced. Of course the most reasonable approach would be to use only volunteers and avoid making participation an academic requirement.

Another way to facilitate student participation is by offering extra credit. However, this practice is questionable. Teachers themselves disagree strongly on the value of extra credit activity. Unless one challenges the rationality of the student then there should be no conflicts. If extra credit is associated with participation, then other comparable options for earning credit need to be available. Surprisingly, students frequently pick research participation over other options.

There is nothing unique about research participation if it is structured as an educational experience. One primary requirement for educational participation would be structured feedback about the experiment. Since feedback is frequently omitted, this is a concrete instance where researchers can improve their performance.

It is unlikely that there will be a dramatic change in the type of participants in psychological experiments, so specific safeguards need to be developed and used. Obtaining subjects on a completely voluntary basis is not impossible. While the rate of volunteering would be lower, many people are still willing to participate. The practice of soliciting volunteers from classes taught by the researcher can present unique problems. Since the researcher and the subject are in a dual relationship, the researcher is in a position of power regarding the participants. Again, this practice has developed on the basis of convenience and requires caution on the part of the researcher. The best safeguard involves subjects who know their rights and insist on them.

Privacy and Confidentiality

Privacy and confidentiality are the last issues which deal primarily with the subject-experimenter contract. Both of these concepts (or rights) come from social, legal, and moral conventions dealing with individual rights regarding personal property. Ruebhausen and Brim (1966) indicate that

> the essence of privacy is no more, and certainly no less, than the freedom of the individual to pick and choose for himself the time and circumstances under which, and most importantly, the extent to which his attitudes, beliefs, behavior and opinions are to be shared with or withheld from others. (p. 426)

According to these authors, privacy involves the "right to be left alone" (p. 425), while confidentiality focuses more on the control of sensitive information. The distinction between these two concepts is somewhat arbitrary; concealed devices, for example, intrude on privacy and diminish an individual's ability to decide what information is to be made public.

One of the solutions offered to the social psychologist trying to avoid the ethical and methodological problems involved with deception research is to move from the lab to other settings for research. This improves ecological validity but it raises another variant of the consent issue. The possibility of a subject biasing her or his response is reduced when unobtrusive measures are used in natural settings since subjects are unaware of being observed. Wood (1981) classifies naturalistic studies according to the presence or absence of intervention. Observing where people sit in a movie would not involve intervention, while looking at who helps a simulated heart attack victim would be an intervention study because it involves an intentional environmental manipulation. Nonintervention studies should not produce problems if the behavior of interest is clearly public. If only public behavior is observed, it would be hard to argue for a right to privacy; leaving your home obviously reduces your claim to this right. The sole contact the experimenter has involves observing public behavior, and this intrusion on privacy is routine in public places. Individuals are not identified except in terms of gross demographic characteristics (e.g., sex or age). Only a radical interpretation of consent would raise ethical issues with this kind of study. To the extent that the behaviors are private (or people expect or desire privacy) the issue of consent is raised. Studies that take place in settings such as jury rooms or bathrooms are cases in point. As Koocher (1977) points out, "Though one could claim that the college lavatory is a public place, it is a non-sequitur to suggest that one does not expect a degree of privacy there" (p. 121). Consent is more important as settings become more private. Technological advances make the possibility of observing private behavior more likely. There is clear recognition of the inappropriateness of using concealed devices. In addition to producing ethical concerns, it is, of course, illegal. The taping of jury deliberations, without the awareness of the jury participants, is an example of potential abuses of these devices. Since people normally assume that they would not be observed in this setting, some form of consent would seem to be required. In psychological research one-way mirrors have been used to observe subjects without their knowledge. Many social psychology experiments have been conducted while subjects were in what they believed to be the waiting room. While one-way mirrors are effective with children, most adults are familiar with their use and most researchers openly disclose and discuss their use.

Intervention studies require better justification than nonintervention studies since researchers are not only observing but also producing systematic changes in the environment. The degree of the invasion of privacy of the intervention is the primary dimension needing assessment. Not all levels of intervention are objectionable; for example, the lost-letter technique involves leaving stamped letters addressed to various organizations near mailboxes and the number mailed is used to infer attitudes about these organizations. This technique involves intervention but the cost or risks are so minimal that it does not raise serious ethical issues. However, bystander studies where a confederate fakes a heart attack clearly present problems. The potential for stressful reactions on the part of the unknowing subject does exist in this type of study. If an unsuspecting subject actually had a heart attack when an apparent car accident victim came to her door to ask to use the phone, this would be an unacceptable level of risk, and exposure to this type of risk without consent is inappropriate. Unfortunately in a case such as this, the unacceptable level of risk can only be known after the fact, but informed consent in this case would not yield valid results.

Intrusion into private thoughts using psychological technology has been suggested as a potential problem area. Examples might include using projective devices such as the Rorschach, hypnosis, or even the use of lie detectors. If the technology were as powerful as critics assume, these concerns would be more meaningful. Fortunately, or unfortunately, current procedures do not have the power attributed to them by nonpsychologists. Lie detector use does present ethical problems for psychologists employed by law enforcement and business since they utilize this instrument even though interpretation is questionable. In research applications the potential for invasion of privacy beyond that contracted for by the subject is minimal.

Invasion of privacy is a more frequent difficulty in research than breaches of confidentiality. Researchers usually guarantee confidentiality and this is an area where problems are the exception rather than the rule. Dickson et al. (1977) distinguish confidentiality from anonymity: "A confidential response is made by a respondent whose identity is known but kept secret, whereas an anonymous response is made by an unidentifiable respondent" (p. 100). In some cases anonymity is promised but only confidentiality is delivered. Dickson et al. (1977) discuss problems associated with using invisible ink to code questionnaires to identify the respondents. This clearly unethical practice involves all of the problems associated with deception and none of the protection offered by debriefing. The primary justification for using invisible ink is to acquire knowledge about the respondent, which saves money; claims of methodological advantage are diminished since subjects are probably suspicious about the claim of anonymity. Psychologists have used a similar procedure to investigate cheating. Tests were returned for self-grading after the answer sheets were photographed and the number of items changed was the measure of cheating. In this case although confidentiality is preserved, anonymity is not.

Is the promise of confidentiality reaosnable? How much protection can be offered to subjects? A court case involving research confidentiality indicates that there is some legal precedent for researchers to refuse to disclose names or information about subjects (Culliton, 1976). This case dealt with a political economics professor who refused to disclose his sources when subpoenaed. The nature of his research was such that he had access to information about individuals and practices that were relevant to a court case. This case was settled out of court but the judge's opinion supported the researcher's refusal to testify.

Breach of confidence is unusual in research. It is hard to imagine the purpose of or potential profit from disclosing confidential research information. Studies of illegal behavior might be of interest to law enforcement but researchers and subjects would probably act to prevent access. Few subjects would report illegal behavior and then sign their names. The possibility of leakage from data banks has caused some concern. This is a current problem for our society in general, as more information becomes computerized, rather than for psychology in particular. Names are not critical for data storage unless subjects need to be contacted in the future. Longitudinal and clinical follow-up studies would require this information but Siegal (1979) reviews practical options for preventing unauthorized access. These options usually separate identifying information from the data and provide for the security of the identifying information. Accidental disclosure always represents a remote possibility and researchers are responsible for appropriate data storage and destruction procedures. The issue of access to records has been debated with regard to therapy notes but has not been considered in the area of research. Most researchers would willingly release research data to subjects unless there were compelling reasons not to release the information. For example, release would be inappropriate if the scores came from unvalidated instruments that were still in the process of development.

RESEARCH WITH ANIMALS

Not all research conducted by psychologists includes human subjects; psychologists also use animals as subjects. The ethical issues and problems that arise in research on animals are quite different from those that arise with human subjects. Animals cannot be informed of risks and hence cannot give their consent. Precisely because of the fact that animals are at the mercy of researchers requires that special precautions be taken against misuse of animals.

We do not believe it is necessary to give an argument for the claim that animals have feelings. As Solomon (1982) points out,

> Contemporary neurological studies have demonstrated a clear continuity between animal and human brain structures and functions that makes it utterly unreasonable to deny animals at least some of the psychological feelings that we ascribe to ourselves. (p. 36)*

For this reason researchers have a duty not to cause suffering to the animals they use.

Singer (1975) notes that researchers face a dilemma that is especially acute in psychology:

---

*Reprinted with permission from R. Solomon, "Has not an animal organs, dimensions, senses, affections, passions?" *Psychology Today*, 16:3 (March, 1982), pp. 36-45. Copyright © 1982 Ziff-Davis Publishing Co.

either the animal is not like us, in which case there is no reason for performing the experiment, or else the animal is like us, in which case we ought not to perform the experiment on the animal which would be considered outrageous if performed on one of us. (p. 47)

Thus if it is assumed that animals have no feelings, animal research in psychology would make little sense. If animal behavior in fact tells us something about human behavior, it is only because animals and humans are alike in relevantly similar ways.

It is often acknowledged that researchers should not cause *unnecessary* suffering, but what is considered unnecessary depends on the researcher. Principle 10.d says that "A procedure subjecting animals to pain, stress, or privation is used only when an alternative procedure is unavailable and the goal is justified by its prospective scientific, educational, or applied value." As we indicated earlier, researchers tend to focus on benefits, real or imagined, whereas subjects tend to focus on risks. Because researchers are likely to see some value in their own research whether there is any or not, and because it may be too much trouble to find an alternative, painless procedure, causing pain to an animal may be rationalized by the researcher as necessary. But there are alternatives to using animals in research. Bowd (1980) suggests the use of computer models and, for teaching purposes, the use of films and videotapes instead of repetitive experiments that do nothing to advance knowledge.

Causing pain to a sentient individual is justifiable by utilitarian standards only if the amount of good produced by doing so outweighs the amount of pain. It is questionable whether many of the painful experiments performed by psychologists on animals can be justified on these grounds. There have been reports that most findings involving animal research in psychology are not published and "research which remains unpublished has in all likelihood been judged insignificant by the experimenter's peers . . . " (Bowd, 1980, p. 207). Of those that are published, according to Bowd (1980), "An indifferent examination of the literature involving painful animal experimentation reveals that a significant proportion of published research is repetitive or deals with problems to which the answers are self-evident" (p. 207).

While psychologists have become quite concerned over issues involving human subjects, there has been relatively little concern shown regarding the ethical issues surrounding their treatment of animals. This is reflected in the fact that IRBs do not review research proposals in which the subjects are animals. Special precautions are taken with human beings who are not competent to give their consent to participate in research. Thus the level of a human being's intelligence does not determine whether conducting research on him or her is morally permissible. In fact, the clearest cases of morally permissible research are those where the subject is intelligent enough to give informed consent. So why is it that the same protection given to human beings who cannot give their consent to be research subjects because of limited intelligence is not afforded to animals? Why is it that in the case of human subjects there has been great concern about exposing them to harm but when animals who can be equally harmed are involved,

CASE STUDY 6.2

A new teacher at a small liberal arts college decided to replicate one of the early studies on the "voo doo" death phenomenon. This phenomenon is so called because the cause of death is uncertain and may relate to loss of hope. The teacher planned to use the same methodology used by previous researchers. This method employed an underwater maze through which rats were forced to swim. The maze was filled to the brim with water and covered with plexiglass. At the goal box the rats could surface and start to breathe again. While some rats do learn their way through the maze, others experience a panic attack and die, which may relate to loss of hope.

The aim of the study was simply to replicate a former study in order to determine, to the researcher's satisfaction, if the phenomenon does actually occur. The researcher sent the proposal to the Human Subjects Review Committee even though he did not feel compelled to do so since the research only involved lower animals. The Committee was very critical of the planned study since it did not seem to promise any advancement of knowledge.

Because the researcher viewed the review as an optional courtesy, he decided to go ahead with the study. The study was quietly conducted and the results of the earlier study were replicated. No concerns were voiced until the researcher presented a report of this research to the Departmental Personnel Committee as evidence of "creative scholarly endeavor." The Committe seriously questioned the new teacher's judgment.

there has been so little concern? When the subjects of research are human, their protection is not simply dependent upon the researcher's own conscience but is reviewed by a board. But this is not the case for animals. In fact, Principle 10 states just that: "an animal's immediate protection depends upon the scientist's own conscience." We indicated earlier that poorly designed studies that do not advance knowledge should be subject to strict review. Animals cannot speak for themselves and that fact would seem to require that there be stringent regulations regarding their use in research.

Bowd (1980) points to several reasons why research psychologists have been insensitive to their treatment of animals. One is the language used, such as referring to starvation as deprivation, to the animal as the organism ["for no particularly scientific reason" (p. 205)], and describing the subjects as being sacrificed rather than killed (though Principle 10.e refers to terminating an animal's life). He points out that

> the overall customary linguistic practice in the scientific literature is to maintain an *unscientific* distinction between the human species and others. When combined with the prevailing philosophical assumptions about animals, experiments involving severe pain to nonhumans may be carried out and discussed dispassionately in the almost complete absence of reasoned consideration of the ethical issues involved. (p. 205)

Another reason he cites for insensitive attitudes toward animals is peer pressure—to react sensitively to animals is seen as being sentimental and unscientific. An emotional reaction to the suffering of animal subjects is considered irrational, but to suppress these emotions is not.

Psychologists who do not concern themselves with the ethical issues surrounding the use of animals in their work and who are insensitive to the fact that animals do suffer as humans do are acting irresponsibly, both from a moral and a professional point of view.

PROFESSIONAL PRACTICE

While the focus of research ethics has been on the (human) subject-researcher contract, the interaction between professionals themselves raises other issues. Today's researcher must actively struggle with conflicting values and responsibilities. On the one hand, being a psychologist implies a commitment to advancing knowledge, a value that can conflict with the responsibility for insuring the ethical treatment of subjects. On the other hand, as Haywood (1976) says, "Psychologists may also be guilty of unethical conduct if they fail to conduct important research" (p. 311). Some psychologists can solve this dilemma by giving up research activities, especially if they work in one of the areas where complete compliance is difficult. This is an infrequent response and most psychologists are actively struggling to find creative methodological solutions which respect subjects' rights. Reiss (1977) interprets this conflict in a slightly different way, suggesting that overregulation affects the relation between researcher and subject, turning it into an adversary relationship. This is an abstract conflict and the practical or concrete conflicts are probably more important. Researchers are assumed to be honest, unbiased, and accurate. There are, however, situations where integrity is threatened if not compromised. Fabricating or faking research results was considered improbable until the debate about Sir Cyril Burt's research surfaced. He conducted a series of studies aimed at estimating the proportional contributions of heredity and environment in the determination of intelligence. Gillie (1977) contends that he fabricated co-authors, reported IQ scores that were subjective estimates rather than measures, and reported identical correlations emerging from different sets of data. The latter is commonly called "dry-labbing." Though being found out is unusual, we assume that this practice is not infrequent, considering the professional and financial advantages associated with good data. While we are not in a position to verify or discount these claims, the amount of smoke suggests the possibility of fire. Recent cases in cancer research verify some clear cases of data manipulation in medicine. The motivations for these abuses are not hard to understand (professional advancement, grants, or publications). Since there is no formal replication requirement in psychological research, the door is left open for these kinds of problems. Replication does take place but it is usually after publication. Jensen (1977) and Eysenck (1977) both provide weak defenses for Burt, claiming that his work was more theoretical than empirical, that using data over and over does not constitute fraud, and that Burt was merely careless with his data. If Burt were working in a nonprovocative area, these violations might be acceptable. But he was working in an area where theoretical knowledge has tremendous social implications. The social implications of research are important and to claim that science is value-free is absurd. Since the theoretical question of heritability of intelligence has strong implications for black/white performance differences on intelligence tests, this is a socio-political question.

Practically speaking, the involvement in research for other agencies presents a real threat to integrity. Foreign affairs research (Walsh, 1966) is one area where constraints are operable. Findings or methods that compromise or threaten national security are likely to produce sanctions or censorship. As Campbell (1969) indicates, psychologists often have difficulties when they are required to evaluate social reforms or programs. Even though these reforms are experimental, vested interests in program continuation on the part of administrators often infringe on freedom of inquiry. These programs are usually based on strong assumptions that they are (or will be) meaningful and successful and evidence to the contrary will not be tolerated. Institutional pressure to look only at certain outcomes or to use weak designs compromise the psychologist's integrity. Professional bias, on an individual or collective basis, presents similar problems. Student protests in the late 1960s (Nikelly, 1971) generated considerable interest and many articles. Authors writing about this phenomenon demonstrated clear biases, which were not about to be abandoned. In this case biases were strong and rigid on both sides. At times psychologists' professional organizations have confused objectivity and advocacy. Health care reimbursement for psychologists (Brayfield, 1967) involves this kind of conflict. Requests for information about costs and effectiveness required objectivity while representation of the professionals required advocacy.

Publication credit and other related matters have been identified as ethical issues. Professional standards address this problem and relate credit assignment to the importance of the contribution. Seashore (1978) documents some unusual cases where, for example, a journal article appears verbatim in another journal under another author's name. However, Spiegel and Keith-Spiegel (1970) surveyed psychologists using a set of cases dealing with credit assignment and concluded that there is substantial agreement on authorship and footnote citation.

The content and intent of the *Ethical Principles* dealing with research ethics have been fully debated but enforcement issues are frequently ignored. The responsibility for enforcement is diffuse, involving the researcher, state and national organizations, and IRBs. The *Ethical Principles* focus on the researcher as having primary responsibility. This approach assumes a knowledgeable, objective, and ethically sophisticated researcher. Baldick (1980) raises questions about these assumptions. He questioned predoctoral interns in clinical and counseling psychology about their training and ability to recognize ethical issues. He reports that only 24 percent of the sample had a formal course in professional ethics and that 17 percent of the interns reported no exposure to ethics. Since he found that the ability to identify issues was related to training, most likely it is the case that practitioners miss many of the critical issues when they appear even though they are becoming more aware of ethical issues. Recent recommendations for training do include ethics as part of the core content for doctoral students but programs have been slow to respond. While Baldick's survey involved applied specialties, we suspect that the situation is as bad in research specialties. A second line of defense is provided by APA's Committee on Scientific and Professional Ethics and Conduct. This resource is infrequently used and little known to subjects. Sanders (1979) summarizes the cases considered by this committee from 1977 to 1979 and most of the complaints involved therapy and training. State and local organizations and licensing boards have some power to enforce the principles but this is an even more infrequent occurrence.

The federal government has supported the development of local IRBs. The purpose of these boards is to approve and monitor the treatment of human subjects. Gray, Cooke and Tannenbaum (1978) provide an excellent comprehensive review based on empirical data of the functioning of IRBs. Two problems associated with the review board's functions are that (1) approval rather than monitoring is the norm, and (2) some institutions review only funded projects. Gray et al. (1978) found that a majority of the boards have follow-up procedures that can be used and that a majority of the boards will review nonfunded research. The cases without review or follow-up still present enforcement issues. Serious questions exist about the legal and ethical consequences of psychology departments reviewing their own proposals. In-house reviews are probably biased favoring the researcher and his or her interests. The most frequently ignored resource for enforcement is the subject. A subject who knows her or his rights and what actions to follow if they are violated is the best protection against abuse.

If it appears that this discussion of the ethical problems arising in research is inconclusive, the reason is that research ethics has and will continue to be an area where ethical problems resist neat solutions.

Chapter 7

Special Populations

Special populations require special protection, and ethical considerations are involved with most of the psychologist's interactions with these individuals. The term "special population" is defined in various ways, including references to characteristics of the individual and/or his or her placement within an institution. For our purpose we will use the term "special population" to refer to individuals who are incapable of making autonomous decisions or providing valid consent due to cognitive or coercive envionmental factors. This definition is more inclusive than the legal concepts of competence and incompetence. Even though many mentally handicapped individuals have difficulty with autonomous decision making, only a small percentage of these individuals have been found to be legally incompetent. Most exist in highly supervised environments (homes, institutions, or other state facilities) but they continue to possess all basic rights. Cognitive limitations may be permanent, as with the developmentally delayed individual, or they may be temporary. At a given point in time, for example, a child or mentally ill adult may be incapable of rational thinking but may later develop or recover this capacity. Coercive environments exist within many total institutions (prisons or mental hospitals), and at times less restrictive settings such as the military or schools include some coercive elements.

Pettifor (1979) has a more inclusive concept of special populations for he includes not only prisoners, mentally ill and mentally handicapped individuals, and children, but also physically handicapped persons, women, minorities, and culturally or economically deprived individuals as examples of special populations and he points out that membership in these populations is not voluntary. Lasagna (1969) expands this list to include the elderly, patients in general, students, and members of the military. Employees, group therapy participants, and families might be added to this list. However, in this chapter we will focus on the populations most frequently affected by psychologists: children, institutionalized individuals, and prisoners.

CHILDREN

Many clients of psychologists are children, yet they seldom initiate therapy or other psychological contacts. Children come to therapy through the actions of adults, usually parents, school officials, or other agents of the state. Anyone who has worked with children has experienced conflict with regard to expectations and roles. It is often difficult to determine who is the appropriate client—the child or the person who refers the child—or what the problem is.

Most contacts with children contain some elements of dual relationships that produce this role confusion. With adults, therapists can avoid this client definition problem by assuming that the person who comes to see them is the client. The person who comes to a psychologist with concerns about a neighbor or relative who is displaying strange, annoying, even pathological behaviors is still the client. Unless the "other person" is dangerous, psychologists need to restrict their services to the person who requests help. But with children, the appraoch to resolving the client definition issue varies primarily as a function of therapist orientation. Behavior therapists often work with only the parents on a consulting basis, psychoanalysts work only with the child in therapy, while family therapists insist that the whole family or system participate in therapy. Rigid adherence to a particular model of therapy that results in not considering "who is the client" is a serious problem in child therapy. Each therapy model also encounters predictable problems which therapists need to anticipate. A behavior therapist using parent training will need to be a child's advocate to ensure that the changes will help the child and not just make the parents life more convenient or less stressful. Psychoanalysts will need to communicate with parents without violating the child's confidentiality. Family therapists have to recognize that their ideal therapeutic approach (i.e., the whole family) may conflict with the other family members' right to choose regarding participation. If these approaches were selectively applied, depending on the particular circumstances of each case, then few problems would occur. If the mode of treatment was selected because of its efficiency for that particular problem, these predictable difficulties become costs that need to be compared to the expected benefits. In practice, most therapists operate using a single mode of treatment regardless of the presenting problem. Perhaps this is an infrequent concern in group practice where therapists with diverse skills are available since clients can be referred to the most appropriate model for treatment. Even though this is an unlikely practical solution in private practice, since referrals result in lost income for the therapist, it nevertheless is the ethical responsibility of the therapist to make a referral when indicated.

Similar difficulties are evident with goal selection since the therapist is often required to mediate between the needs and desires of the child, parents, and other agents. In some instances, where self-destructive, violent, or illegal behaviors are involved, there may be no disagreement concerning appropriate goals but in most cases the solution is not that simple. Meyerson and Hayes (1979) indicate that many factors influence the selection of goals or target behaviors. The statistical uniqueness, adaptiveness, amount of threat to society, pain or duress experienced by the individual, and intrusiveness of the behavior are basic factors which shape goal selection. With adults, problems can be avoided by relying on the client to be the primary agent in this process. But when the client is a child, the parents, society, and the therapist all represent potential sources of influence. The central issue here is paternalism versus autonomy and the changing nature of children's cognitive abilities. For young children we would expect and respect the parent's paternalistic interests. Since young children cannot be expected to act in their own best interest, the parents have primary responsibility for ensuring the best interest of their child. If the advocacy orientation of the parents is questionable, the state shares a similar responsibility and is empowered to take over to ensure that the child's best interest is served. Unless the state has acted to diminish parental responsibility, the parents of young children would be the primary agent in goal selection. This does not suggest that therapists simply accept any parent-specified goal without considering the appropriateness of such goals. For example, the fact that parents are annoyed by the activity level of a two-year-old does not necessarily make changing this behavior an appropriate goal. To suggest that the therapist can function as a value-free agent in this process ignores the reality of the situation. Most child therapists recognize their influence, attempt to understand their own values, and assume an advocacy orientation when decisions that impact the child are being considered.

While autonomy is not to be expected from young children, the situation is less clear as children grow older. As children approach adulthood, the paternalistic solution effective with young children becomes less satisfactory. Older adolescents usually have the cognitive capacity to make decisions or set goals for themselves but their legal rights are limited. Conflicts exist when the adolescent's wishes differ drastically from the parents. Anticipating this conflict, therapists who work regularly with this age group will attempt to settle the issue before it becomes a problem. The original contract will usually specify the therapist's position on this dual relationship. Gender disturbances in children provide a provocative example of this problem. Parents are usually very disturbed when behaviors that are not sex appropriate occur, but the adolescent may or may not be interested in changing. Does an older child have the right to refuse treatment or can paternalistic interests be enforced and the child be required to receive therapy? Therapist orientation would also enter into this decision. Psychoanalysts (Rekers et al., 1977) would tend to provide therapy while behavior therapists (Davison and Wilson, 1973) would not necessarily treat this problem. Since the effectiveness of therapy with a coerced adolescent would be limited, experimental therapists usually involve advanced adolescents in the goal selection process. The inverse of this problem occurs when the child desires therapy but the parents oppose the child's entering therapy. Similar problems occur in medicine and the issue of access of the underaged to medical treatment without parental consent has been debated in relation to problems resulting from sexual activity (e.g., birth control, venereal disease clinics, and access to abortion). It is difficult to make general ethical recommendations because these problems defy neat solutions or rules and there are many factors to consider in each particular case.

The means used to realize therapeutic goals is another area that requires consideration. As we have already discussed, behavioral approaches have often been criticized for using intrusive means. Much of this debate has been caused by semantic confusion between behavior control and behavior modification, which will be discussed later. Early practitioners of behavior modification emphasized effectiveness as the primary consideration in selecting a therapeutic approach. While current practice still can involve intrusive means, behavior therapists now evaluate intrusiveness using a cost/benefit analysis. When intrusive (or aversive) techniques are used, the justification of effectiveness is acceptable if there has been careful consideration of other, less intrusive techniques. If other techniques are eliminated from consideration because they are ineffective (not just inconvenient), some intrusiveness is acceptable. This clearly places some demands on therapists in terms of competence; eliminating techniques because they are ineffective assumes knowledge of research findings and probably some clinical experience with the technique. If other therapeutic approaches have been tried and found ineffective, then some intrusiveness is tolerable, at least in situations where the behavior in question is physically harmful or life-threatening. Self-mutilation or other forms of self-destructive behavior would seem to be good examples. The psychologist's responsibility in such cases is increased and dealing with such cases requires not just basic competence but also special expertise and knowledge about the particular disorder. Therapists who recommend an intrusive program today because of lack of knowledge about current practice would expose themselves to the possibility of ethical as well as legal sanctions.

Confidentiality has always been a problem for therapists who work with children and certain types of therapy aggravate the situation. Family therapy is perhaps the best example. The responsibility for confidentiality does not rest solely with the therapist but is shared by all group members. We can expect psychologists to be cautious concerning their professional training or role but other members of the system may not be as responsible and may use or disclose information outside of therapy. While some of the most obvious issues related to confidentiality arise in family therapy, confidentiality presents problems in all forms of therapy with children. When a child is seen in individual therapy, does his or her communication have the same level of privacy as an adult's would? Since children lack some basic abilities (e.g., the ability to provide valid consent and to make decisions regarding their best interest), we assume that the right to confidentiality is also limited or compromised. Even though children may lack a legal claim to privacy, special rules are usually established by therapists who work with children to provide for confidentiality. This would seem essential if therapy is to be effective. If the child thought that all of his or her disclosures would be shared with the parents or other agents, then the child would limit his or her disclosures. As Graham (1981) points out,

> In individual therapy with children it is common practice for material disclosed by the child to be kept secret from the parents on the grounds that the child will not produce this material once he knows his parents will be informed. This exclusion raises anxiety in them, and it is arguable whether therapy of this type should be undertaken unless concommitant discussion occurs with parents and they are fully agreeable. (p. 243)

Since the parents are likely to be a focus, if not the focus, of a child's discussion, they are likely to exert pressure to find out what is going on. Since the parents are paying for the services, they would seem to be entitled to some information (at least about what progress is being made). These issues need to be settled as part of the original consent agreement to prevent disputes once therapy has commenced. The rules for disclosure of material shared in therapy would otherwise be the same as with adults.

CASE STUDY 7.1

A fifteen-year-old high school student was brought by his mother to a psychologist in private practice. The problem presented by the mother was a recently developing obsessive-compulsive reaction. The mother reported that the boy had been a typical adolescent up until his fourteenth birthday. While he had always been a little nervous he had developed some strange behaviors in the last year. By her report his life was ruled by a series of rituals and if any of these were disrupted, he responded with fierce anger and resentment. Her response had been to indulge him but she had grown tired of respecting his "silly quirks." The boy seemed to insist on some type of arbitrary order and sequence in the aspects of his life that he was in charge of (his room, his schedule, his food, his schoolwork, etc.).

The psychologist treated him in individual therapy for six weeks and was beginning to develop a positive relationship with him and get a clearer understanding of the problem. The boy has been angry and fearful since his parents separated eighteen months ago. He blames his mother for the breakup since she always overwhelmed and overpowered his father. In trying to share his feelings with his mother he has been routinely rebuffed. He has had no contact with his father since the separation. He also has serious concerns about his sexual/social adjustment. Right after the separation he had a traumatic sexual experience with a 22-year-old neighbor for whom he occasionally worked. When she approached him sexually he had a panic attack which lasted for two hours. Since this incident took place he has become increasingly socially isolated. These difficult disclosures took place in the initial sessions and were only brought forth after he had asked about the confidentiality of his communications. The therapist reassured him that he would not share his disclosures with anyone. At the end of the sixth session the therapist was concerned that the boy might be experiencing his first psychotic break and felt that hospitalization might be needed.

The mother came in the day after this session and was concerned about the worsening of the boy's symptoms. She also asked about what the boy had talked so that she could better understand his problem. When the therapist began to discuss the confidential nature of therapy, the mother blew up and threatened the therapist. Her claims were that her son was a minor in her care and that since she was paying for the therapy she had a right to know what was going on. The argument ended with the mother forbidding the therapist to continue seeing her son and threatening legal action if there were any subsequent contact.

The boy appears the next day at the therapist's office in a clearly disorganized state and asks the therapist to help him get into a hospital before it's too late.

The school involvement of children is an area where conflict between parents, society, and a child's needs can occur. In their contact with agencies such as the school, children can be exposed to therapy or treatment through teachers' implemented programs without parental knowledge or consent. A psychologist may work with a teacher to develop a treatment program to control a child's classroom behavior. Children might ask to see a counselor or a psychologist in the school system without parental approval. Even though these activities would normally be labeled as "therapy," institutional agents would construe the activities as something other than therapy. Concerns over ethics in the last decade have led to the development of guidelines and regulations which require increased parental involvement in decisions concerning a child's evaluative and therapeutic contacts with psychologists.

Placement decisions concerning children in schools where psychologists make recommendations have serious implications for children's lives. Special class placement, program placement, or even the use of "ability grouping" can have a negative impact on the child. While these decisions are usually made by a committee, the psychologist's test results and opinions are often the basis for these decisions. Few problems would occur if these decisions were always based on what is best for the child, but since psychologists are employees of the school system, other factors are often considered. As with any kind of dual relationships, psychologists need to understand their multiple responsibilities and make sure that they are free to operate in the best interest of the child.

Research involvement of children has always been a problem area. Ramsey (1976) distinguishes between two types of research, therapeutic and nontherapeutic. With nontherapeutic research there is no clear expectation that the individual child who participates will receive any benefit. Therapeutic or clinical research usually deals with treatment of specific problems, and individuals who participate can anticipate direct or indirect benefits as a function of participation. There is no guarantee that the methods investigated will be found to be effective but if they are, participants would anticipate some improvement. There is general agreement concerning children's participation in therapeutic research, for to forbid their involvement would deprive them of opportunities which might improve their health or functioning. The issue of consent can be dealt with by using parental or proxy consent as a substitute for the child's consent. With this approach the child's wishes or preferences are not considered important. This approach may be acceptable for very young children but the practice becomes more questionable with older children. While the child's consent is not necessary (perhaps not even possible) from a legal standpoint, it is desirable from an ethical perspective, at least with older children. Proxy consent allows for a full explanation of the details of a study, so one of the components of informed consent can be fully realized. Proxy consent assumes that the parents are operating without coercion, which is questionable if they have a child with severe problems. The promise of help or an irrational hope for cure may introduce coercive elements into their decisions and the experimenter is responsible for managing such expectation.

The justification for therapeutic research with children would have to meet more stringent safeguards than similar research with adults. Other, less experimental techniques would have to be explored and found ineffective before exposure to new therapeutic experimental procedures. Poorly planned and unfocused studies would, of course, be precluded. Exposure to risk may be tolerated with adult studies but with children the risks would need to be minimal or nonexistent. If an adult makes a decision that the potential benefits exceed the promised risks, then he or she shares some responsibility for negative consequences. With children this decision is being made by another person who will not be affected in the way the child would be if risks turn into harm. Some deviation from this no-risk principle may be acceptable if the behaviors are life threatening (suicide or self-destructive behavior, for example). The promise of benefit must be reasonable based on current knowledge and it should possess the potential for helping the individual participant rather than just advancing knowledge of the disorder. The temporary delay of these benefits for children who participate in control groups is something that needs to be part of the original contract. This delay is assumed to be temporary since all participants should be able to anticipate exposure to the most effective procedure once it is known. Longitudinal clinical research, which involves leaving some children untreated, may encounter difficulties meeting this requirement if there is some critical period for intervention. Since parents and researchers are likely to be positively biased toward the experiment, the involvement of Institutional Review Boards (IRB) or another uninvolved agency is desirable.

Children's participation in nontherapeutic research has been debated from practical, ethical, and legal perspectives. The original concerns expressed were about pediatric research but similar problems exist with psychological research. Ramsey (1976) takes a radical position and argues against the involvement of children in any type of nontherapeutic research. He claims that since children cannot give consent, research *uses* children even when the parents consent for the child. There is no need to consider risks, he argues, since without consent there should never be any research. McCormick (1976) argues against this position by suggesting that many children would consent (if they could), and allowing them to participate provides them with an opportunity to be helpful to society. Bartholome (1976) avoids this debate and offers some practical suggestions for evaluation of specific projects when the research involves children. These suggestions include: (1) careful review and supervision, (2) high potential benefit, (3) a need to use children as subjects, (4) normal risk levels, (5) adequate pretesting with adults, and (6) consent and continued involvement of parents. Despite arguments to the contrary, risks would seem to be the critical dimension requiring evaluation. For example, a study of physiological responses to various stressful stimuli (physical pain versus negative criticism) would seem unacceptable with children since the validity of their consent is questionable and harm is a possible outcome of participation.

Studies which do not include risk factors are probably going to continue. Psychologists have been using a procedure involving proxy and parallel consent for basic research which does not involve risk. This procedure involves obtaining consent from parents and then obtaining consent from the child regardless of her or his age. The parents are given full and complete information concerning the study and the focus of the child's consent is that his or her participation is voluntary. If children are asked to take a test, for example, they are told that they don't have to take the test and that after they start they can stop for *any* reason. It has been found that children are very willing participants as long as the tasks are not exceptionally dull and they are treated well by the experimenter.

INSTITUTIONALIZED INDIVIDUALS

The term "special population" is often equated with residence in a total institution. Outpatients are consumers; they can express their dissatisfaction by taking their business elsewhere. But institutionalized individuals lack the power to exercise this option. Our discussion will be limited to mentally ill and handicapped individuals. Prisoners are frequently included in studies with these two groups but incarceration differs from simple institutionalization in that it involves the loss of some basic rights. The mentally handicapped and ill are two groups that have frequent and varied contacts with psychologists. The issues raised with these populations are also relevant for individuals living in less restrictive envionments (rest homes, group homes, orphanages, etc.).

Critics of institutional treatment often generate strong provocative attacks without developing practical alternatives that would improve the functioning of these facilities. Szasz (1978) has been an outspoken critic, labeling mental hospitals as "snake pits," but he fails to provide solutions to the practical problems that exist. His critique suggests that institutionalization is a political act that is based on a medical or disease model of mental illness. The solution of deinstitutionalization of all but the truly violent seems to be an ideal one until one discovers that those who are released often live equally isolated, alienated, and restricted lives in the community. To ignore the problems that do exist within the institutions would be foolish since institutions provide important services. The basic functions include sanctuary or protection, treatment, and rehabilitation.

Two recent trends, deinstitutionalization and a recognition of patients' rights, have increased public awareness and established strong legal precedents. As Friedman (1975) indicates, in the past, the issue of patients' rights focused on problems associated with admission and release, whereas the issue now also includes treatment in the institution and what happens after release. The trend toward reducing patient populations has introduced new concerns. Since many individuals are now living in the community, patients' rights are an important area of concern for community agencies. Day treatment centers, rest homes, sheltered workshops, halfway houses, and group homes share concerns similar to those of total institutions and exhibit some complex variants of traditional issues as well. While they are less confining than residential institutions, they do restrict behavior. Most institutional residents have not been involuntarily committed or declared incompetent so they retain the full range of basic rights. Children and mentally handicapped adults do not usually volunteer themselves for admission but their guardians have provided proxy consent and it is assumed that their basic rights remain intact.

The right to treatment has already been discussed and is similar to the right to education possessed by exceptional children. School systems once excluded severely handicapped children because they required special treatment. Current interpretation of Public Law 94-142, which states that all handicapped children have a right to education, recognizes handicapping conditions as requiring special and specified educational placement and procedures in a school setting.

CASE STUDY 7.2

A seven-year-old mentally handicapped boy was brought into a children's clinic at a major medical center. The child had a history of severe hyperactivity that did not seem to respond to setting environmental limits. His activity was tolerable in the morning and at its worst from lunch to about 4 PM. He generally started to slow down after dinner. If uncontrolled he would eventually be unable to inhibit his activity. While the parents had at one time tried to set firm limits for his behavior, they quickly gave up and now just tolerate his excessive activity level. When he is in one of his active phases, he is frequently destructive in his play and aggressive toward his playmates.

After an initial multidisciplinary evaluation, the pediatric neurologist prescribed psychostimulant medication on a trial basis. The psychologist on the team was to provide follow-up consultation with the parents and the boy's teachers to determine if the medication was effective. The child's response was stupendous. His teachers reported that he was a different child and they had no problems in managing his behavior. They found him to be more responsive to social praise and punishment. At home the story was similar. His play activity was constructive rather than destructive. There were no further problems with aggression. The initial follow-up was so successful that the case was closed with the provision for one more follow-up visit after three months.

When the psychologist visited the school three months later the teachers reported that the child had maintained progress for two months but then suddenly regressed about four weeks before. They suspected that the parents had discontinued the medication. The principal indicated that he was dealing with the problem using one of the techniques the psychologist had discussed in a previous workshop, namely time out. When the psychologist inquired about details he was informed that the child was being locked in a supply closet that contained potentially dangerous items such as janitorial supplies, paper cutters, and duplicating fluid. The principal said that the child's behavior was so bad one day that he had to stay in the closet all day.

When the psychologist checked with the parents they said that they had discontinued the medication because they had read an article in a popular magazine which was critical of utilizing medication with children. The parents were so emotional in the discussion that attempts to reason with them were unsuccessful.

Patients who have voluntarily admitted themselves to institutions would usually be able to provide consent for treatment; in fact, the act of entering an institution implies a request for treatment. The cognitive limitations of children or the mentally handicapped usually result in the involvement of parents or guardians in consent procedures. This does not suggest that the underaged patient's wishes can be ignored, especially where older children are concerned. Nor can the wishes of mildly handicapped adults be overlooked. The right to refuse treatment for voluntary clients has certain implications. A client who refuses all forms of treatment would be requesting the institution to provide only sanctuary services. This may be the case with long-term residents who are comfortable with institutional life and responsibilities. Generally, the state would be unable to require therapy but institutions would not seem to be required to provide room and board indefinitely. The coercive aspects of consent procedures with involuntary clients are greatly diminished with voluntary clients. Because voluntary clients always have the right to discontinue their stay in the institution, it is difficult to view their consent for therapy as being seriously coerced. Coercive situations are possible (e.g., an alcoholic may lose a job if she refuses treatment) but the institution is not in this case the coercive agent.

Since therapy participation is voluntary for most mental patients, we can and should expect patient involvement in goal selection. Institutional awareness of these rights has increased in recent years and most institutions now involve patients in treatment team meetings and planning sessions. The ideal situation, where the client and the psychologist meet and decide what is best for the client, is compromised in practice. The typical mental patient is usually overwhelmed when confronted with a committee of professionals. Interests of the family, the institution, and the state often shape this goal selection process. To the extent that interests other than the client's are considered in goal selection, the psychologist is involved in a dual relationship and thus clarification of his or her role is necessary. Psychologists need to be cautious when goals are selected that improve a patient's manageability (within the institution or family) but do not necessarily improve his or her independent functioning and/or mental health. Complying with requests of authority figures might be an example of such a goal and while it may indirectly improve functioning it is unlikely that clients would select or seek this type of goal. Client involvement in goal selection would also be important from an effectiveness perspective.

The issue of the method of treatment is the second broad area where ethical problems surface. The use of behavior modification with institutionalized individuals has resulted in legal regulation of treatment in general. Much of the debate over behavior modification in institutions has confused it with the issue of behavior *control*, which includes such intrusive techniques as drug therapy, electro-convulsive thereapy (ECT) and psychosurgery. For our purposes, behavior *modification* involves the systematic application of the principles of learning to human problems. Many of the early criticisms of behavior therapy (Rogers and Skinner, 1956) were a reaction to the implications of learning theory as a model of human behavior and as a potential form of control. The image of persons being controlled by environmental contingencies threatened the notion of free will. The paranoia over the issue of societal control was due to misunderstandings concerning the potency of these procedures. It has been said that "the new ethical considerations arise from the very strength of the technique as demonstrated or promised in the near future" (Holland, 1973, p. 393). However, this strength as promised has yet to be demonstrated. For example, a child who does not use language can be taught to label common objects but such a program would require a trained therapist/educator and many hours of therapy. Those appropriate verbalizations will require further resource expenditure if the behavior is to be maintained outside of therapy. To suggest that these techniques could be used to control the masses ignores the fact that behavior modification is not cost-effective, especially when compared to other means of control (for example, the use of drugs).

The issue of intrusiveness is not as easily dismissed since programs that are intrusive have been used. Concerns over intrusiveness are not restricted to behavioral treatment programs but refer to all treatments. Legal and ethical standards require that treatments decisions be evaluated from a "least intrusive means" perspective. Here again, the precedent was developed around involuntary clients but applies equally well to voluntary patients. There is more flexibility with voluntary clients since they can consent to therapeutic approaches that are intrusive. The use of aversive techniques and token economies are treatments that induce concerns about intrusiveness and restrictiveness. Aversive techniques have been used to punish excessive behaviors (e.g., using shock to punish self-abuse) and to attempt to recondition emotional reactions (e.g., using shock to decrease sexual arousal to homosexual stimuli). (We should point out that the examples used here have been largely discontinued.) Punishment programs have usually been aimed at reducing behaviors such as self-abuse, and the justification for using an intrusive treatment program is in terms of effectiveness. Goldfried and Davison (1976) go beyond a simple right to treatment and suggest that clients have a right to "the *most effective* validated treatment" (p. 275). While exposure to a shock program is intrusive, it can be considerably less restrictive than long-term restraint, to which it is an alternative. Unfortunately, these cost/benefit comparisons are made on the basis of current knowledge but new developments often change what is considered effective. There is nothing in this type of analysis to suggest that any means is acceptable if it produces a good end. The means as well as the ends require evaluation. Aversive conditioning of emotions was expected to be a powerful technology for reconditioning deviant sexual responses, antisocial behaviors, and excessive behaviors (alcoholism or drug addiction). Such techniques have been used with institutionalized individuals but there is currently less interest in such approaches because they have not been shown to be effective. While these techniques produce powerful systematic changes in controlled environments, behavioral changes do not generalize well to uncontrolled environments. If these procedures were more effective, the regulation of their use would be more difficult. The misapplication of these procedures is basically a competence issue.

Token economies represent the behavioral approach to group treatment. Early programs tended to employ deprivation to enhance the effectiveness of the rewards. Legal standards now distinguish between basic rights and contingent privileges, and these standards have helped to clarify the issue of what can be used as reinforcers. Food, communication with family and friends, reasonable sleeping quarters, private property, and access to religious services are basic rights which cannot be made contingent on behavior. Access to a color TV or special foods are not basic rights and can be used contingently. As the definition of basic rights broadens, the privileges used in these programs should become less questionable. Token systems usually focus on adjustment to the institution as the criterion for earning privileges. Institutional work assignments may be therapeutic or rehabilitative but they are not necessarily either. Safier and Barnum (1975) review federal fair labor standards as they relate to this issue. Clients must be paid proportionately based on their production compared with "normal" workers and the work must have a rehabilitative component rather than being merely custodial. Abuses of this practice take place when institutions rely on patient labor (which pays less than the minimum wage) rather than regular employees.

We have discussed client input concerning goals but the role of client preferences for treatment presents some unique problems. Do clients have the right to select or request certain forms of treatment? For outpatients, requests for certain treatments are usually respected if the requested treatment is within the competence of the therapist. Requests for ineffective forms of treatment are usually settled by discussion between client and therapist as part of the regular process of therapy. In hospital settings patient requests are probably respected to the extent that resources are available. A request for individual or group therapy would not be a problem in most institutions whereas a request for bioenergetic therapy would because it includes physical as well as mental procedures and few bioenergetic therapists are available. Institutions have a responsibility to provide effective therapy, but they are not responsible for responding to every request. Voluntary clients always retain the right to seek treatment in other settings, and legal standards protect the rights of the committed patient.

Issues related to research are similar to those discussed in relation to children. Competent patients can give consent, so therapeutic and nontherapeutic research is permissible. Incompetent patients require special protection, usually in the form of proxy consent. As with children, therapeutic research is more easily justified than nontherapeutic research. As Haywood (1976) points out, most of the nontherapeutic research conducted with mental patients and the mentally handicapped is quite meaningless. Studies that demonstrate that those who are institutionalized differ from normal people are particularly unenlightening. The specifics of a given study need to be evaluated to determine if the research is appropriate. The most easily justified studies are those that promise benefits to the residents.

Deinstitutionalization has caused the community to share some of the problems formerly faced by institutions. Patient rights have broader implications when the individual is in the community. Psychologists often become advocates when clients confront the system. Access to voting and driving privileges are sometimes denied and the ability to engage in financial transactions are limited. Advocacy in this type of case becomes a legal matter. While participation in community programs involves client consent, coercion (from family or state agencies) is frequently evident. The most beneficial goals from a "normalization" perspective (independent living, dating, etc.) are often actively opposed by families and/or the community, and it is usually the psychologist who must attempt to resolve this issue.

Even though outpatient homes are less restrictive than typical institutions, they are more restrictive than simple outpatient treatment. Protection of the rights of individuals in such settings is beginning to develop. Since individuals who work in such settings often lack professional credentials, supervision and training of these individuals becomes the responsibility of the professional in charge.

PRISONERS

Prisoners clearly represent a special population but there is considerable doubt about the special protection appropriate for this group. In entering the criminal justice system, individuals experience a loss of certain rights (freedom), and others are compromised (privacy) because of practical difficulties within the system. In the criminal justice system psychologists are asked to fulfill several, often conflicting, roles. Psychologists function as therapists, researchers, evaluators, administrators, and consultants on matters of control within the institution. In addition, they are involved before and after incarceration as expert witnesses on such matters as parole, competence, sentencing, and dangerousness. They also are involved with police selection, training, and therapy. With the expanding use of psychologists in this system the frequency of role conflict is probably going to increase. Resolving role conflicts is difficult since the institutions themselves are unclear about their own role. Gaylin and Blatte (1975) indicate that the roles of the prisons have included punishment, rehabilitation, deterrence, and protection through detention. As Reveron (1982) suggests, the practical problems associated with overcrowding have diminshed the importance of the rehabilitative functions, which is one of the primary areas of activity for psychologists. If the system itself were able to establish a unitary goal or even prioritize the goals, then psychologists' task of establishing their role would be simplified. While recognizing the multiple obligations of the institution, psychologists need to understand specific responsibilities and expectations so that those interacting with them will be so informed. For example, if confidentiality in therapy in a prison setting is compromised, the prisoners need to understand what type of information would be disclosed.

Critical issues for therapeutic practice include confidentiality, effectiveness, goal selection, and method selection. The issue of effectiveness is a general one that reflects concern about how well the system as a whole works. Unfortunately, there is little evidence for the effectiveness of prisons. Models emphasizing deterrence, punishment, or rehabilitation would all predict a decrease in the probability of criminal activity after incarceration. There is little evidence for the general effectiveness of the prison system, and the issue of therapeutic effectiveness with prisoners is more complicated than it is with outpatients since many of the participants are not volunteers.

The Task Force on the role of psychology in the criminal justice system (APA, 1978) studied the ethical issues of psychologists who work within the system. They focus on confidentiality as one of the central issues, and suggest that "confidentiality of therapeutic services in criminal justice settings should be the same as the level of confidentiality that exists in voluntary noninstitutional settings" (APA, 1978, p. 1102).

It is easy to imagine that threats to confidentiality would be more frequent in the prison setting. Even if prison psychologists operate as freely as psychologists in noninstitutional settings, knowledge of dangerous acts is more probable in prison therapy. In actuality prison psychologists do not have the freedom available in outpatient work. As management level employees they are often expected to contribute to the maintenance of order within the facility. As Reveron (1982) indicates,

> corrections officials have sought to use psychologists to control—not necessarily help—prisoners. Prison staff have been known to ask mental health care personnel to get troublemakers committed or given medication. . . . And psychologists have been "obliged" to honor such requests in order to keep their jobs. (p. 9)

Even when the pressures are not overt, subtle pressures probably operate to suggest that institutional control and less than full disclosure are part of the psychologist's responsibility. Many of the psychologist's clients are the more severely disturbed prisoners who are required to receive therapy as part of disciplinary action. These actions often require some report of progress to institutional agents and such drastic confidentiality compromises need to be shared as part of the original contract. Therapy with the volunteer prisoner is difficult enough but a majority of a prison psychologist's clients are probably not truly voluntary. Encouragement of voluntary therapy was one of the Task Force recommendations since it avoids basic ethical difficulties and probably enhances therapeutic effectiveness. We assume that the experienced prison psychologist is much more explicit than the average psychologist in explaining the extent and limits of confidentiality.

Consent for therapy and goal selection raise concerns about basic rights of prisoners. While mental patients have a right to treatment when they are involuntarily committed, only a rehabilitation model would suggest a similar right for prisoners. This issue is complicated since many inmates are also mentally ill. While only a small number are classified as being criminally insane, the incidence of psychopathology is significantly higher in prison populations. Claims to a right to treatment for prisoners on legal or moral grounds are weak unless one adopts a completely rehabilitative model. But on a practical basis there is at least a strong need for treatment. Can the state require therapy participation from a prisoner? Violation of prisoners' right to decide for themselves is justified on a legal basis when compelling state interest is at stake. Within institutions the state is allowed to impose sanctions for safety or control. Solitary confinement is a predictable consequence of certain actions in prisons. Which compelling state interest would be protected by requiring therapy is unclear, since therapy has not been effective in reducing recidivism. The fact that the prison has a right to control behavior does not indicate that is has a right to control beliefs (Gaylon & Blattee, 1975).

In some cases, involvement of prisoners in therapy is based on a voluntary contract. Prisoners retain the right to refuse treatment although coercive factors may make it impractical or difficult to exercise this option fully. If therapy is voluntary, then goal selection should take place with client input as .it does in other settings. Most requests for therapy probably deal with adjustment problems within the prison or other mental difficulties rather than requests to reduce criminal tendencies. Conflicts would arise when the client's goals are unacceptable in terms of their impact on individuals, society, or perhaps even on the institution. Since therapy is more likely to be coerced in prison settings, psychologists need to be aware of this influence in the goal-setting process. Actions on the part of psychologists that enhance the voluntary quality of therapy in prison settings are helpful in terms of effectiveness and are required from a moral point of view. Some contacts with prisoners will continue without voluntary consent. Psychological evaluations before and after sentencing are viewed as a required part of incarceration and a client's right to refuse is limited. However, there are at least some safeguards since evaluations require some degree of cooperation. Participation in institution-wide group programs may involve required participation.

Selection of treatment means is another area of general concern and the abuses that have taken place in the prison setting are shocking. There has been much concern over the means used with group programs, especially when they become excessively depriving. In individual therapy, client preferences or wishes can be respected up to the limits of a professional's competence. But in group programs individual clients are usually in a poor position to influence the structure of the program. Group programs usually involve a behavioral approach exemplified by tier systems where prisoners earn privileges by moving to less restrictive settings. As with mental patients, legal regulations have clarified the distinction between basic rights and contingent privileges. While psychologists may want to divorce themselves from intrusive treatment techniques such as ECT or psychosurgery, they have been involved with some other classical examples of intrusiveness involving aversive conditioning. Despite decreasing interest in these specific techniques among psychologists because of limited effectiveness, all of the methods used for treatment need to be evaluated in terms of intrusiveness and effectiveness.

The criminally insane present special problems for the criminal justice system. Experimental institutions often operate on a medical model that suggests that criminal acts are symptoms of pathology. Criminally insane individuals are kept in institutions until adequate therapeutic progress makes their release safe. As Meister (1975) points out, these institutions can involve "preventive detention disguised as psychotherapy" (p. 38). Since release is contingent on therapy, participation is coerced.

Psychologists working within the criminal justice system are expected to have special competence not expected of other psychologists. Prison psychologists need to have some legal expertise so that they will be sophisticated enough to recognize when a client needs to be referred for additional professional legal services and will therefore avoid giving legal advice. Individuals trained in forensic psychology probably receive some direct instruction in law which most psychologists lack.

While one of the goals of psychology is prediction, the predictions expected of psychologists working with criminals have serious implications. Decisions regarding sentencing, treatment, and parole are often based on psychologists' recommendations. When asked to predict dangerousness, probability of a repeat offense, or responsiveness to treatment, psychologists face a difficult dilemma. Because current knowledge does not allow psychologists to predict with any great degree of accuracy, there is a natural reluctance when confronted with these tasks. Often the psychologist will be operating on personal impressions rather than on firm empirical evidence. It is doubtful that psychologists will stop making these kinds of predictions so it is important to specify what is being predicted, for what length of time, and on what basis. To the extent that psychological expertise adds to simple actuarial predictions, these activities are part of competent practice. If predictability is not increased, the whole system needs evaluation.

The coercive nature of prisons has led to many questions concerning research in this setting. While we can usually assume the "rationality" of prisoners, being incarcerated results in situational coercion. This issue has been left up to the state since most facilities are state operated. Legal regulations vary from state to state with some states continuing to forbid prisoner participation in research. The coercive elements, which introduce questions concerning the quality of a prisoners' informed consent, include money, increased chance of parole, better medical care, and access to better environments. These incentives would not be coercive for a free individual but the depriving nature of prisons makes these incentives more compelling or attractive. Prisoners themselves tend to support prison research because of the practical advantages and they claim to see it as an opportunity to be helpful or constructive. Even if one questions the altruistic reasons cited by the prisoners, to forbid all involvement in research seems excessively restricting if the coercive aspects of consent can be minimized. Most research with prisoners has been medical research involving disease processes, drug effects and their side effects. Prisoners make excellent subjects, especially when full sample follow-up is part of the research design. Since prisoners are coerced (or at least excessively tempted), the federal government has acted to reduce the risks to which prisoners can be exposed. If coerced they would be more likely to participate in excessively risky procedures than other individuals. In medical research they can no longer be used for initial clinical trials but only to demonstrate the generality of effect. As with children, there is more concern about nontherapeutic research. The primary reasons for using prisoners for nontherapeutic research are economic. Paid volunteers usually expect rewards commensurate with risks and inconvenience. Prisoners are typically paid about 10 percent of what a paid volunteer would receive. Researchers argue that prisoners would really be coerced if they were offered the full fee, for earning money is more difficult in prisons and financial resources are used to make life more comfortable and tolerable.

Psychologists are involved with both therapeutic and nontherapeutic research with prisoners. They might, for example, want to use prison volunteers to validate a personality test measuring sociopathy. Even though most of their research is risk-free, it is nevertheless subject to controls regarding intrusive medical procedures. If all incentives were eliminated and participation became truly voluntary, most types of research (without risk) would be acceptable. The lines between research and application can easily be blurred in prison settings. A research project may start out without reference to application (predicting parole violations on the basis of a personality test) but then become applied (when these scores are reported to boards considering parole). Participants in this type of study might want to know about this kind of risk, no matter how remote. And it would be the duty of the psychologist to inform participants if their consent is to be morally adequate.

Chapter 8

Teaching, Testing, and Consulting

The remaining activities in which psychologists may engage are teaching, testing, and consulting. The fact that a discussion of these activities appears as the final chapter does not mean they are the least important. For in teaching, testing, or consulting, as in doing therapy or research, psychologists are affecting the lives of others. As teachers, psychologists are acquainting students with the nature of psychology or are training future psychologists. On the basis of tests given to an individual, the psychologist may make recommendations regarding that person's future. And the same holds for psychologists who act as consultants for some agency. The ethical issues that arise in these areas are sometimes obvious and sometimes subtle. The more subtle issues can be easy to overlook, and it is especially important to bring attention to them.

TEACHING

More than half of the members of the American Psychological Association (APA) are teachers of psychology. While psychology teachers may have to deal with unique ethical issues, we will first discuss those ethical concerns common to all teachers.

Among concerns common to all teachers are competency in subject area, competency in developing new courses, objectivity in testing materials, and certain constraints on confidentiality regarding student information. These areas overlap and influence such issues as policies toward make-up examinations, attendance, class participation, etc. All teachers should be able to define the limits of their competency, should strive to be fair and objective in dealing with students, and should recognize that students have the right to privacy. When problems arise in these areas, consultation is often helpful.

Objectivity of the material presented is another concern of teachers in general and this issue has been addressed in the teaching of Introductory Psychology by Hogan and Schroeder (1981). These authors claim that most of the textbooks they surveyed were biased. For example, psychodynamic psychology tends to be ignored in favor of behaviorist principles, narrow research designs are presented, and other approaches such as personality theories are sometimes called prescientific or unscientific. Limited space is devoted to moral development with attention being given almost totally to one theory. They claim that the most widely used textbooks in Introductory Psychology have a tendency to be biased in favor of behavioristic psychology, which in turn leads to narrowly defined goals.

> Why do these tendencies persist? There are at least two good answers. The first has to do with the failure of graduate education in America. Education properly conceived and conducted would include making students aware of their values and theoretical presuppositions. But in America we do graduate training, not education: graduate school is more like barber college than like Plato's Symposium. Students are taught how to do research (in the approved manner); the focus is almost exclusively on professional training rather than on a careful examination of theoretical premises. Biases persist in part because they are unexamined (Hogan & Schroeder, 1981, p. 14).*

The *Ethical Principles* specifically note that "as teachers, psychologists are aware of the fact that their personal values may affect the selection and presentation of instructional materials" (Principle 2.a). Thus in order to eliminate biases in textbooks and the presentation of material, psychologists as teachers must examine their own biases and values just as therapists must do.

The concept of academic freedom presupposes the competence of the teacher and recognizes the teacher's autonomy. Occasionally there may be institutional or cultural pressures that threaten to impinge on a teacher's academic freedom. For example, suppose a teacher wants to use a film illustrating alternative sexual preferences. Most likely there will be some students who object to such a film. The student's right not to attend should be respected. As Principle 3.a states, psychologists "recognize and respect the diverse attitudes that students may have toward such materials." However, the institution would have no right to forbid the use of such a film.

Dual relationships present frequent problems and sexual interaction with students is probably the most provocative example. Though the *Ethical Principles* address the issue, there is no principle dealing with *voluntary* sex between teacher and student. Principle 7.d says that psychologists do not exploit their professional relationship with students nor do they "condone or engage in sexual harassment," which is defined as "deliberate or repeated comments, gestures, or physical contacts of a sexual nature that are *unwanted* by the recipient" (emphasis added). While the issue of sex between students and faculty is not peculiar to psychology faculty, the *Ethical Principles* deal with all the various areas in which psychologists work, and thus address this issue.

Because in psychology, as in other fields, teachers sometimes supervise student research, they should be careful to give proper credit for research. As Principle 7.f says, "Acknowledgement through specific citations is made for unpublished as well as published material that has directly influenced the research or writing. . . . All contributions are to be acknowledged and named." This should include work done by students. If the student is the major contributor to a project, the students' name should be listed first when

---

*Reprinted with permission from R. Hogan and D. Schroeder, "Seven Biases in Psychology," *Psychology Today* (July, 1981), pp. 8-14. Copyright © 1981 Ziff-Davis Publishing Co.

there is joint authorship (Principle 7.f). Again, this follows from the more general principle that psychologists as teachers do not exploit their professional relationship with students.

Most psychology teachers have at least some acquaintance with counseling or therapeutic techniques. This places them in a position different from teachers in most other fields. Someone who teaches physics or history is less apt to have students come to him or her with personal problems because counseling is not part of the field. But because therapy is part of the field of psychology, a question that arises for psychologists *qua* teachers is whether they have more responsibility to help students with problems than do teachers in other fields. The problem is not a difficult one for those who teach in universities with a counseling or psychological services center. The student can be referred and, in fact, some universities require that a student be referred if the problem cannot be solved in one session. The apparent assumption of these institutions is that a full-time teacher does not have the time to prepare for classes, teach, *and* do involved psychotherapy. In most of these schools, released time from teaching is provided so that some psychologists may do therapy with university students.

The real problem arises if there is no center at the college or university to help students deal with their personal problems. It would be insensitive to tell the student that no help can be provided. The psychology teacher should at least listen to a student who comes to him or her with a problem. However, the psychologist is not morally obligated to engage in an extended therapeutic process with the student because it may interfere with other responsibilities. The primary responsibility of psychologist *qua* teachers is, according to the *Ethical Principles of Psychologists*, "to help others acquire knowledge and skill" (Principle 1.3), not to engage in psychotherapy.

Because psychology teachers may do research with human subjects, their students are a source of research subjects. It thus becomes possible to use the teaching position to get students to participate in experiments. That in itself is not an ethical issue, but the *manner* in which a psychology teacher gets students to participate is. In Chapter 3 we made a distinction between tempting and coercing: the latter is morally objectionable but the former is not. Thus to offer extra credit for consenting to be a research subject may be only to tempt the student, because he or she may refuse without any untoward consequences (though in Chapter 6 we indicated that such a practice may be ethically questionable). However, to make participation in research part of the grade of the student would be coercion, because the students would have no choice but to participate without suffering unfair consequences. The role of the psychology teacher as researcher must be carefully weighed. Students have less freedom to choose than do nonstudents. The advancement of knowledge must be put in the context of the overall good of the students.

Conducting an experiment within the classroom also raises ethical problems, perhaps even more so than asking students to be subjects outside the classroom, for in that case students have the opportunity to consent or refuse. In the classroom, however, there is no opportunity to consent. For example, a psychology teacher may have a stranger walk into the classroom and then some time later ask the students to describe the person in order to test accuracy of perception. While there is no danger to the students in this case and the results may well be enlightening to the students, there is still no opportunity to consent or refuse. However, some in-class experiments could have devastating effects. For example, having a confederate pretend to shoot the teacher during an examination could result in negative reactions although some professors might justify such a demonstration on the basis of academic freedom. One might want to question, in light of this example, whether or not academic freedom would extend to a case such as this. Psychology teachers, in the role of researchers, should be careful not to take unfair advantage of students.

Another issue is the use of demonstration to acquaint students with a particular therapeutic technique. For example, as a pedagogical device a teacher may have students engage in psychodrama (e.g., having students switch roles). But this can be intrusive and devastating to participants. Before using this method, the classroom situation should be analyzed carefully.

Psychology teachers who also do therapy have access to examples from their therapeutic activities to illustrate certain problems. At the undergraduate level the psychologist can modify and embellish the examples to ensure confidentiality. But in teaching graduate students it may be that details relevant to the case that are necessary to illustrate a point could identify the client. Where this is so the teacher must make the students aware of their responsibility to maintain confidentiality.

Psychology teachers may have the opportunity of doing consultation with other agencies and thus arises a problem of dual relationships. Does the outside work interfere with the primary responsibilities of teaching? How much time should be allotted to this type of activity and who should regulate the amount of time? The *Ethical Principles* give no guidelines specifically relating to this type of dual relationship. It seems that the primary employer (in this case a university) must formulate its own regulations. And if the psychologist's primary employer is the university, his or her first responsibilities are to students, not to some agency. However, there might be a time when the urgency of working with a client of the outside agency could take precedence over *prima facie* obligations to the university. Suppose, for example, that a psychologist agrees to work only one day a week off campus. She is informed one day while working at an agency that it is urgent for her to come back that same week to do some counseling with a given client. To do so in this one case would not interfere with her teaching responsibilities. Hence the benefit to the client in this case outweighs the *prima facie* obligation she has to the university. However, should the counseling interfere with teaching responsibilities, it would not be justifiable for the psychologist to put those aside since the primary obligation of a psychologist *qua* teacher is to the students. It should be pointed out that limited professional activity outside the classroom may lead to professional growth that will enhance the psychologist's teaching activities.

Constructing a doctoral degree program and supervising graduate students are important activities for graduate school faculty in psychology. The Council for the National Register of Health Service Providers in Psychology has provided "Guidelines for Defining 'Doctoral Degree in Psychology' "

(1977). Programs have to be accredited by the American Psychological Association or meet nine general criteria as defined by the APA. Included in these criteria is a comprehensive program

> including a minimum of three or more graduate semester hours (5 or more graduate quarter hours) in each of these 4 substantive content areas:
>
> a) Biological bases of behavior: Physiological psychology, comparative psychology, neuropsychology, sensation and perception, psychopharmacology.
> b) Cognitive-affective bases of behavior: Learning, thinking, motivation, emotion.
> c) Social bases of behavior: Social psychology, group processes, organizational and systems theory.
> d) Individual differences: Personality, human development, abnormal psychology. (1981, p. 1/81)

In addition, these guidelines require instruction in scientific and professional ethics.

Two important areas of supervision are research and psychotherapy. In both areas the supervisor is responsible for the quality of the work done by the trainee. In both research and therapy psychologists often rely on the accuracy of students' self-report to monitor the quality of services or interaction. Since students are often being evaluated in conjunction with their self-report, the pressures to bias their self-report, ignoring the negative aspects of their activities, can be great. Students in research classes may pressure other students into participating in their studies to obtain an adequate sample size. While quality control of funded faculty research (and sometimes unfunded research) is augmented through the use of Institutional Review Boards (IRB), student research is evaluated on an ethical basis only informally.

Supervision of graduate student research often involves a subject pool of students in Introductory Psychology. Many students have a preconceived idea that psychological research is painful or dangerous. Britton (1979) found that this expectation of harm can be minimized by having the subjects rate the experimenter on politeness and reporting "on the personal comfort of the subject after the experiment" (p. 196). Britton left unanswered the question of whether experimenters are normally polite or whether "experimenters who know they are about to be evaluated by subjects will take special pains to treat them well" (p. 197). An answer to this question seems to require further investigation. Even when the experimenters were told that they were going to be evaluated, 4 percent of the subjects still felt discomfort at the end of the experiments. Britton says, "Ethical and practical concerns dictate that further research be directed toward the identification of the reasons for their discomfort, and altering procedures in subject pool systems to reduce the likelihood of such reactions" (p. 198). Psychologists who supervise student research are responsible not only for the quality of the research but also for the quality in interactions. Since politeness would seem to be a prerequisite for minimizing presupposed negative outcomes, supervisors should try to ensure that their supervisees are polite. As Britton suggests, one way to do this is to tell them that they will be rated on politeness, though this does not guarantee that discomfort will be totally eliminated for *all* subjects.

In therapy the ratio of supervision varies considerably, from one-to-one direct observation to one-hour supervision to ten hours of therapy. If considerable care were exercised in determining the appropriate ratio for an individual student (based on his or her skills), this variability would be easily justified. In practice, supervisors are often overloaded and provide less supervision than they should. The ideal would involve frequent direct supervision with beginning students that becomes less frequent or direct as the supervisor develops confidence in the student.

Faculty supervision of students who are learning psychotherapeutic techniques can pose problems. Not informing the client of the supervision (for example, when one-way mirrors are used) violates the principles of confidentiality and consent. But to inform the client may generate anxiety or inhibit the therapeutic process. Cavenar, Rhodes, and Sullivan (1980) discuss this issue and propose a partial solution—informing the client that there *may* be some supervision. However, this does not solve the problem because in such a setting there *will* be supervision. Therefore, the most that can be said is that the judgment of a competent psychologist, i.e., the supervisor, is crucial regarding what to tell which client.

Specific discussion of confidentiality with students who are trainees in psychotherapy seems necessary because while students may be aware that information obtained in therapy is confidential, they may not know that such information cannot be shared with spouses either. Spouses may inadvertently put pressure on their mate to tell them what they are doing in their work, and lack of experience may make it tempting to share client information.

A more touchy problem that could arise pertains to allowing a student to graduate from a clinical or counseling program when personal characteristics of the student would seem to be detrimental to the field of professional psychology. For example, suppose a student meets the academic requirements for a degree in clinical psychology but that his attitudes are obviously racist, sexist, and rigidly authoritarian. The student's committee has good reason to believe that he will not be an effective therapist yet there are no academic grounds on which he can be denied a degree. The *Principles* give no clear guidelines on this problem and Principle 2 on competence seems to emphasize academic credentials. From this it would seem unacceptable to deny a student a degree merely on the basis of his or her attitudes, even though the student is clearly not competent to do professional therapy. This indicates that the *Principles* need expansion to emphasize not only academic credentials but also the ability to work effectively with clients. Nonacademic criteria could become part of the selection process and a part of the formal evaluation process. If this plan were adopted, it would become essential to notify the unqualified student as early as possible in his or her graduate career so that the student could seek another area of study. We might point out that in some situations this problem will probably take care of itself. If the client-

CASE STUDY 8.1

Undergraduates in psychology classes were encouraged to go to the Psychological Services Center to volunteer to be interviewed by beginning graduate students. When the class announcements were made, students were told that they would not be analyzed and were in fact helping these beginning graduate students to develop their skills. A female undergraduate was interviewed by one of the graduate students even though his supervisor was unavailable at the time. The session focused on the undergraduate's concerns about her planned marriage, which was to take place in two months. While her parents endorsed the marriage plans the young woman was confused about what she wanted. Her fiancé was very conservative and there were clear disagreements over women's roles and sexual variations within the relationship. The graduate student focused on her sexual needs and desires to the point where she became embarrassed. The graduate student indicated that she needed therapy and offered to see her on a regular basis. At the time she declined and the interview was terminated at that point. A week later she sought out the graduate student at the psychology department and indicated that the session had helped—she planned to break off the relationship. Several sessions were held in the graduate student's office (he was a teaching assistant) even though it was clear that she was becoming fascinated with him. The graduate student focused these discussions on her sex life and suggested that she had sexual difficulties, primarily being too inhibited. After their fourth meeting he invited her to his apartment for dinner and she accepted. Sexual intimacy quickly followed. This same sequence was repeated four times over the next two weeks until the graduate student became uncomfortable with the dependency needs of the young woman. He told her that his professional responsibility would not allow him to continue with the relationship and that her problems were not all that bad. The undergraduate student experienced a two-day episode characterized by confusion and depression. She sought counsel from a campus minister who complained about the graduate student's behavior to both the chair of the Psychology Department and the Psychological Services Center, and arranged for a therapist in private practice in town to work with the young woman.

therapist relationship is voluntary, a consumer would probably not engage the help of such a therapist once the client discovered the therapist's attitudes. However, the problem becomes acute if such a therapist is employed in an institutional setting where the client has no choice of therapist. Thus psychology teachers who are on a graduate program admissions committee have the responsibility to screen very carefully on the basis of recommendations and personal interviews those persons they select for a clinical or counseling program.

One final point needs to be made regarding the teaching of psychology, and that has to do with the place of ethics in a graduate psychology program. The "Report on the Task Force on the Role of Psychology in the Criminal Justice System" (APA, 1978) recommends that *"The American Psychological Association should strongly encourage graduate and continuing education in the applied ethics of psychological intervention and research"* (p. 1111). Psychology teachers have an obligation to their students to make them aware of the ethical problems that arise in psychology. Only recently have psychologists themselves become more keenly aware of ethical issues arising in their various professional activities and it would seem appropriate that some attention be given to applied ethics in psychology courses. Perhaps an entire course at the graduate level should be devoted to a discussion of moral problems that arise in the profession. Unless potential practicing psychologists are made aware of the ethical issues in their field, they will either not see many of them as ethical in nature or will not be able to deal with them systematically and adequately. Baldick (1980) found that "interns who have completed formal training in ethics score significantly higher on the Ethical Discrimination Inventory than interns who have received no formal training in ethics" (p. 276). This is surely an argument for formalized training in ethics in all graduate programs in psychology.

TESTING

Psychological evaluation is a major activity for many psychologists and testing activities are one of the most frequent areas of successful malpractice suits because they create a permanent record that can be independently evaluated.

Many agencies require a battery of psychological tests before providing services. The administration and interpretation of test scores can pose a number of ethical problems. One basic reason ethical issues arise in testing is that it can be seen as an invasion of privacy and hence informed consent is crucial. As Petzelt and Craddick (1978) point out,

> Psychological testing, by its nature, can often be viewed as an invasion of privacy of the individual client. In this respect it is no different from psychotherapy, behavioral manipulations, or psychological research. Obtaining informed consent is one important way to maintain the integrity of the client. (p. 587)

They go on to point out that "some argue that it is impossible for the client to give fully informed consent to psychological testing because of the very nature of the assessment process" (p. 587). Just as we argued that in psychoanalysis informed consent of the client is impossible because of the nature of the process, so in testing neither the client nor the psychologist knows what the results will be and hence it is impossible to know ahead of time what one is consenting to in terms of test results. The client can only consent to the test itself. However, this is not to say that there is no "informed" aspect to consent in the evaluation process. As Principle 8.a states

> In using assessment techniques, psychologists respect the right of clients to have full explanations of the nature and purpose of the techniques in language the clients can understand, unless an explicit exception to this right has been agreed upon in advance. When the explanations are to be provided by others, psychologists establish procedures for ensuring the adequacy of these explanations.

Informed consent is an inherent problem of the evaluation process but once a psychologist has evaluated a client, the question arises regarding the client's right to know the test results. The *Ethical Principles* repeatedly refer to the welfare of the client and here there is a possible conflict: on the one hand, it would seem that the client has the right to know what conclusions the psychologist has reached about him or her based on the test results, but on the other, such knowledge on the part of the client may be detrimental to his or her welfare. For example, if a client perceives her intelligence to be in the gifted range and the intelligence test shows a score in the high normal range, sharing this information with the client could possibly have devastating effects. In such a case, it might be that the welfare of the client takes precedent over the client's right to know. However, Smith (1978) points out that

> under most legal circumstances, psychological test reports are included in what are referred to as "medical records" and courts seem increasingly inclined to grant patients access to their medical records during or after treatment. Despite the erosion of privileged communication in many states, most state laws still do not require professionals to give reports to patients except in specified circumstances. The federal Buckley-Pell amendment, for example, which allows students over eighteen and parents of minor children access to any records maintained by an educational institution, clearly distinguishes clinical records from educational ones by stating that "educational records" do not include records "created or maintained by a physician, psychiatrist, or psychologist." (p. 151)

Nevertheless, from a moral point of view, if doing so would not adversely affect the client's well-being, then the client does have the right to know. And even if the psychologist may have reason to believe that client knowledge of test results or a diagnosis might be detrimental, to refuse to share this knowledge with the client when the client insists may be unjustified paternalism. There may be rare cases where denying a client access to his or her records would be justified paternalism. Unfortunately, this can be known only after the fact. Though the following case does not deal directly with testing, it does illustrate the potential problem of sharing information with a client: a middle-aged woman was hospitalized by her internist because of bizarre complaints. The internist asked a psychiatrist to see her since she was withdrawn and overly preoccupied with herself. The psychiatrist diagnosed her as psychotic and treated her successfully with medication. However, she experienced two recurring psychotic episodes within the next couple of years. When medication did not prove successful, because of her severe state, and as a last resort, the psychiatrist recommended electroconvulsive therapy (ECT). With her and her husband's consent, he treated her with ECT and each time the results were remarkably successful. Some months later she made an appointment with the psychiatrist. She accused him of mistreating her and demanded to see her hospital records. Though he did not believe it was in her best interest, he reluctantly agreed if she would let him go over the records with her. The records were released to her without the benefit of his presence. She then accused him of writing lies about her and continued to call him, repeating the accusation. Seeing the records apparently enhanced her paranoid thinking. In this case the client's right to know had to be weighed against possible harmful effects on the client. Though clinical judgment implied that client access to her records would be deleterious, there was no way of knowing what the exact outcome would be.

Another client's rights question concerns whether the client should have a say in the selection of what tests are to be used. For example, suppose a client requests that the psychologist give her the Minnesota Multiphasic Personality Inventory (MMPI). If the psychologist is competent in the administration and interpretation of that test, there may be no ethical issue unless a client has a misunderstanding of what the test measures. In this case, the first step would be to try to clarify the misunderstanding. Then if there are no other ethical issues, e.g., a suspicion that knowledge of the test results could be damaging to the client, the psychologist should probably do what the client wants because, after all, the client is paying for the service and has a right to know. While a psychologist is not always obligated to do what the client wishes, if the client is an agency and, for example, a rehabilitation counselor of the agency requests a certain test for his own client, according to Principle 7 the psychologist should respect the competencies of the other professional if the request is appropriate. The psychologist should assume that the other professional knows best what information is needed about the agency's client. The major exception to this is when the psychologist is not competent to administer the required test.

An additional issue of client's rights in testing is whether it is justifiable to test an individual against his or her will. For example, suppose a person wants vocational rehabilitation assistance and the agency sends her to a psychologist for evaluation. But she refuses to be tested. The psychologist knows that without evaluation the client will not receive aid. The psychologist could try to coerce her into being tested on the grounds that unless she consents she will not receive aid but chances are the results would be invalid because there would be no way to force truthful answers. Even if that were not the case, it does not seem justifiable to coerce the client because that is a denial of the person's autonomy in the sense that the person's choice is not respected. The client should be given the opportunity to decide for herself what will be done.

Another important fact is that the testee does have a right to decline, although he or she is not always notified of this right. For example, during orientation freshmen are often told to report to a certain room at some specified hour where they are administered a battery of tests. Few, if any, of these students have been informed that they have a right to decline certain types of evaluations, e.g., personality assessment. A clear contract between individual and institution could eliminate many potential problems.

Psychologists should be aware that psychological evaluation procedures can be extremely stressful to some individuals, for example, a standardized achievement test for low achievers or memory tests for brain-injured adults. A conscientious psychologist must be aware of these anxiety-provoking situations and must do everything possible to minimize this anxiety.

Also important is the right of the testee to have the best test setting possible. Ideal testing areas are not always available but it is the duty of the psychologist to provide the best setting possible. Rapport involves more than a mere relationship. It also involves consideration of the rights of the client.

In discussing client rights in testing, we raised the question of the client's right to know the test results. Because psychological evaluation often leads to assignment of a diagnostic label, one must also consider whether the client has a right to know what diagnostic label has been assigned. Just as knowledge of specific test results could have harmful effects on a client, so also might labeling. For example, if an individual were to be labeled "educable mentally handicapped" by a psychologist and informed of this label, it could lead to a self-fulfilling prophecy. And if such a label is revealed to the individual's parents and teachers, the result could be low expectation on their part (parents and teachers frequently see IQs as a fixed index of the individual's potential). However, many agencies cannot or will not provide services without a label, such as "educable mentally handicapped," "emotionally handicapped," "learning disabled," "schizophrenic" "inadequate personality," etc. The *Ethical Principles* do not deal with the issue of labeling, but several Principles deal with the welfare of the individual. For example, Principle 1.f says, "As practitioners, psychologists know that they bear a heavy social responsibility because their recommendations and professional actions may alter the lives of others." And Principle 3.c states, "In their professional roles, psychologists avoid any action that will violate or diminish the legal and civil rights of their clients or others who may be affected by their actions." Thus psychologists have to weigh the beneficial consequences to the client against the possible harmful consequences of labeling. If the label is shared with the client, it becomes important to investigate the client's understanding of the label and to clarify any misconceptions.

Often, evaluation of an individual is done for an institution or agency and, as we mentioned, these institutions and agencies require labeling according to the Diagnostic and Statistics Manual of the American Psychiatric Association III (DSM III) before services will be given. When the agency or insurance company requires a nosological label (one which refers to disease) such as those included in DMS III, the testee is often uninformed about the "mental illness" label or, sometimes, is told that knowing the diagnosis could be harmful to the individual. Smith (1981) points out that

> psychologists remain virtually silent on their clients' rights to be informed regarding nosological labeling and coding, particularly in the procurement of third-party payments. Nor are clients informed that when they sign confidential information release forms they are often giving blind consent to the release of secret diagnostic data. Psychologists are sacrificing both their philosophical integrity and the dignity of their clients for economic gain. (p. 22)

Smith suggests that the testee has a right to know that these diagnostic labels are being used and has a right to choose whether or not to be coded. Even though Principle 8.a says that there may be an exception to this right if agreed upon in advance, it does not address the issue of what kind of informed consent contract clients or parents are signing. It may be blanket consent to do testing but not explicit consent for the results to be shared.

CASE STUDY 8.2

A psychologist has evaluated a child with results indicating that the child is functioning in the mildly mentally handicapped range. While the psychologist is comfortable with the validity of her test results, the magnitude of the academic delays suggests a secondary diagnosis of learning disabled. Based on her knowledge of the school system, she believes that the child will receive adequate services through the resource room program.

The mother of the child has requested to see the psychologist's report. After reading the tests results and the label used by the psychologist, she calls the psychologist and insists that her child be labeled as learning disabled instead of mentally handicapped. She implies that she will not consent to any services for her child if the current label is used. The psychologist is aware that many parents have a false impression about educational opportunities offered to mentally handicapped children. She explains carefully to the mother that the current procedure is to set up conditions so that no stigma is attached to the child by other children. The mother says that she is aware of the current educational practice but that a psychologist who previously tested the child at the school had informed her that mentally handicapped children will always be slow learners and that the child's major problem has come from her expecting too much from the child. The current psychologist tells her that with proper help and motivation handicapped children can progress beyond academic levels as projected by test scores. The mother still insists that she will not consent to having her child put in a program with the mentally handicapped. She says, "I am a university professor and it would be a disgrace to place my child in a class with retards."

One way to correct this problem is to offer a consent form that specifies evaluation for what, by whom, with what, etc.

In writing reports psychologists should be especially careful not to include anything damning about the client and to word their evaluations carefully so that nothing in the report will be misinterpreted. It is pointed out in the "Code of Ethics for a Community Mental Health Program" (1976) that

> records kept for clinical purposes should contain no unnecessary reference to antisocial or socially embarrassing behavior. Personal values and judgments are not appropriate in clinical records. It is important to describe specific aspects of problematic behavior without personal value judgments about this behavior. (Principle 1.d)

While this seems to imply that the reason for omitting value judgments is that they are simply personal and hence subjective opinions, even if they are not, the psychologist's job is not that of a moral evaluator. The psychologist must recognize the client's choice of and responsibility for his or her behavior even if it is immoral.

If the psychologist is doing evaluations for an institution or agency, it has to be assumed that the test results will be shared with the paying party. But this raises the question of who the client is. Is the client the individual being tested or the paying party? Because the psychologist's contract is with the agency, the agency is the direct client, but psychologists assume that agencies take into account the best interests of their client and that an agency would not do something that would be detrimental to the individual. Because psychologists employed by agencies are ultimately concerned with the welfare of the agency's clients, indirectly they are also the psychologist's clients. In general, there is no conflict of interest between the hiring agency and the testee. If in some rare case there were, it would be the duty of the psychologist to inform the agency that he or she could not do something that would harm the individual. Suppose, for example, an agency is having budget problems and cannot provide service for all its clients. The agency wants some label placed on an individual which would result in his being institutionalized instead of obtaining help from that agency. The psychological evaluation reveals schizoid processes but not full-blown schizophrenia. The psychologist should diagnose at the minimum level though the agency wants the stronger label. The agency should be informed that the welfare of the individual takes precedence over the contractual agreement with the agency.

Related to this is the problem of whether recommendations should be made on the basis of available services or ideal services. To recommend strictly on the basis of available services could lead agencies or institutions to remain static and not try to expand services. To recommend on the basis of ideal services could have the effect of limiting services. This is probably a situation where utilitarian considerations will help guide the psychologist's decision. For example, the psychologist may want to recommend further evaluation, such as neurological testing, which is expensive for the employing agency. Some institutions may resist this added expense and consequently pressure the psychologist to refrain from making this type of recommendation. The psychologist must then weigh the benefits to the client in terms of utilizing available services, and hence succumbing to the institution's pressure against the possible long-term benefits to clients by insisting on ideal services which may result in the agency expanding its services. This kind of problem could probably be avoided if an explicit contract is drawn up when the psychologist is hired by the employing agency. Not enough attention has been paid to contracts for testing.

Another example where a psychologist is not wholly obligated to an agency or institution, even though it is the paying party, is if the psychological evaluation is not being put to any meaningful use for those being tested. The "Report of the Task Force on the Role of Psychology in the Criminal Justice System" (1978) points out that "a substantial number of psychologists . . . were dismayed by their assignment to administer endless batteries of tests to prisoners to assess their suitability for treatment programs, when in fact no treatment programs existed nor were likely to" (p. 1104). The Report says that such "assessment-without-disposition functions, when not done for legitimate research purposes . . . (are) an unethical intrusion into the lives of offenders and an unprofessional squandering of limited resources and limited public funds" (pp. 1104–5). It further states that the administration of these tests may help create an illusion that psychological services are being given when in actuality they are not. By refusing to participate in this sham the psychologist may effect needed reform. Ethical Principle 3.d states in part that when Federal, state, provincial, organizational, or institutional laws, regulations, or practices are in conflict with Association standards and guidelines, psychologists make known that commitment to Association standards and guidelines and, whenever possible, work toward a resolution of the conflict.

Thus a psychologist who is required to do unnecessary testing should work to change the situation.

The *Ethical Principles* also stress the importance of competence, including competence in testing. Principle 2.e states, "Psychologists responsible for decisions involving individuals or policies based on test results have an understanding of psychological or educational measurement, validation problems, and test research." There are several possible problems arising in this area. One is the many new instruments that are developed and published each year. A psychologist who has been in practice for several years may be unfamiliar with these new instruments or the procedures involved. Recommended steps to develop competence with a new instrument might include: (1) *basic* knowledge of test development, validity, reliability, statistics, and other psychometrics, (2) practice with nonclinical individuals, (3) supervision by psychologists who are knowledgeable about the instrument and (4) continued supervision in initial clinical cases regarding administration, scoring, and interpretation.

Another problem that could arise in violation of Principle 2.e is the use of a previous psychologist's test results and interpretation. Despite the fact that this practice is clearly unethical and unprofessional, it is not uncommon.

Still another issue raised by that principle is test validity.[1] Test validity can pose ethical problems in psychological assessment. Vollmer (1970) states,

> In medicine, a particular drug is not considered acceptable unless its reaction can be predicted with a probability error at less than .001. Psychology attempts to follow a medical model. I personally have never heard of a psychological test that ever came anywhere near approaching this probability. (p. 514)

Many have argued the inappropriateness of using the medical model in psychology. Even if this level of accuracy were reached (which is highly improbable), the psychologist must be aware that the criteria against which the tests are compared can change. For example, in industrial/organizational evaluation the test is frequently validated against job performance. Standards in job performance are constantly changing and hence the test must be continually changed to meet the new standards for job performance. (However, job performance is probably more objective than some other things psychologists try to measure, e.g., achievement motivation, anxiety, depression, etc.) Petzelt and Craddick (1978) say that

> when test discrimination charges have been brought to court, the burden of proof that a test was related to measuring job capability was placed on the tester....Again, it appears that ultimate responsibility rests on the individual psychologist and his/her ethical values. (p. 587)

From a legal point of view, Lerner (1978) notes that in the past several years the supreme court has been depending much more on the "Standards of Educational and Psychological Tests" (APA, 1974) in making decisions regarding validity in the context of discrimination. The court is increasingly looking at the ethical standards of professional organizations before reaching a legal decision.

CONSULTING

The ethical issues and problems in consulting overlap with many other areas covered in this book. For example, consulting can involve evaluation, counseling, and research. The usual problems of consent, confidentiality, and validation occur here as in other areas of psychology. And consulting can and sometimes does involve the issues of dual relationships.

One area of psychology that has received little attention so far in this book is industrial/organizational (I/O) psychology. Many teachers of psychology serve as part-time consultants to industry or to organizations such as hospitals, service organizations, the military, or even to professional athletes. Other psychologists are full-time employees of these organizations. Division 14 (I/O psychology) is one of the fastest growing divisions of the APA. I/O psychologists participate in such activities as selection and placement of employees, recruitment, job analysis and evaluation, training and development of employees, screening, improving employee motivation, and appraisal of performance. All of these areas can involve discrimination.

If an I/O psychologist is working full-time for an organization, he or she is one part of the management team and is therefore legally responsible for nondiscriminatory employment practices. Even if the psychologist is only serving as a consultant, he or she is still legally responsible for the work performed and services provided because of the federal Uniform Guidelines on Employee Selection Procedures to be discussed shortly. In addition, he or she is morally responsible according to the *Specialty Guidelines for the Delivery of Services by Industrial/Organizational Psychologists* (APA, 1981).

I/O psychologists are probably more subject to litigation than most other types of psychologists because industries have been taken to court more often on discrimination charges than have clinical psychologists on malpractice charges. Unethical and illegal behavior on the part of psychologists may be harder to hide in the I/O area than in the clinical field because I/O psychologists, when performing their work, must constantly be aware of the federal guidelines, and they may have to appear in court to explain and justify procedures used to develop a test, validate an existing test, etc. Clinicians do not necessarily operate under this type of constraint except in the case of a malpractice suit. For that reason we will focus on the major legal precedents that are relevant to the work of I/O psychologists. As Cascio (1978) says,

> Sweeping civil rights legislation enacted by the federal government during the 1960s and early 1970s, combined with increased motivation on the part of individuals to rectify unfair employment practices, makes the legal aspects of employment perhaps the most dominant issue in personnel management today. (p. 11)

Even though I/O psychologists have legitimate concerns about the legal aspects of their work, they also should be aware that morality, at times, supercedes legality. Ethically speaking, they should be more concerned with trying to ensure fair treatment of those whom they may affect than with what is merely legal. Morality may require going beyond what is merely legally acceptable. And because of the strong emphasis on legality in the I/O area, it may be even more important that psychologists who work in that field be aware of ethical issues. For when legality is overemphasized, ethics tend to be ignored.

In recent years all three branches of the federal government—legislative, executive, and judicial—have been actively involved in equal opportunity (Cascio, 1978). In order to understand the legal framework of current civil rights legislation, Cascio suggests that I/O psychologists must know the major legal principles embedded in the following:

1. The United States Constitution
2. The Civil Rights Act of 1866 and 1871
3. The Equal Pay Act of 1963
4. The Civil Rights Act of 1964 (as amended by the Equal Employment Act of 1972)
5. The Age Discrimination in Employment Act of 1967
6. Executive Orders 11246, 11375, and 11478. (p. 13)

Not only I/O psychologists but also any psychologist who offers consultation services should be aware of the legal implications of his or her work. We will summarize the legislative, executive, and judicial decisions that affect consulting psychologists and center this section around those decisions.

When discussing the work and responsibilities of I/O psychologists, it is important to mention the federal Uniform Guidelines on Employee Selection Procedures. The history of the Guidelines dates back to 1966 when the first set, called "Testing Guidelines," was issued by the Equal Employment Opportunity Commission (EEOC). Between 1968 and 1976 a number of testing orders and guidelines were issued not only by the EEOC but also by the Office of Federal Contract Compliance (OFCC) and the Civil Service Commission. In 1976, three federal agencies (Department of Labor, Civil Service Commission, and Justice Department) issued their own guidelines, and the EEOC republished its own. Needless to say, all these different versions caused much confusion for I/O psychologists trying to comply with the provisions as set forth by the various agencies. Finally in 1978, the four agencies got together and published the current version of the Guidelines.

The 1978 version of the Uniform Guidelines may be considered one of the main sources to which I/O psychologists refer when performing any work in the employment area. The Guidelines are very broad in scope, covering the following areas: employment decisions related to hiring, retention, promotion, transfer, demotion, dismissal, and referral. Specific types of procedures covered by the Guidelines include: interviews, minimum qualifications, training and experience requirements, application blanks, work samples or performance tests, paper-and-pencil tests, as well as performance in training programs or during a probationary period. In their publication, which discusses the Guidelines in great detail, the Ad Hoc Group on the Guidelnes (Day, Erwin, & Koral, 1981) make the following statement:*

> The Uniform Guidelines on Employee Selection Procedures represent a significant attempt by the federal equal employment opportunity (EEO) agencies to achieve consistency in interpreting the requirement of equal employment opportunity laws as such laws impact on employer personnel practices. Some provisions are pragmatic and helpful and, if properly interpreted, should discourage unwarranted litigation while encouraging employers to use selection procedures that are job-related and consistent with sound equal employment opportunity objectives. The Guidelines leave many questions unanswered, however, and some crucial terms are professionally and legally unsound, or both. (p. 5)

This last statement refers to certain aspects of the Guidelines that are in conflict with professional opinions. For example, the concept of fairness as discussed in the Guidelines has been debated. The Ad Hoc Group has the following to say about the inclusion of the fairness concept in the Guidelines:

> The "fairness" concept assumes that if a selection procedure does not produce results that reflect "parity" for group membership in the test population, there is reason to study the "fairness" of the procedure for each group to see if the procedure is equally predictive for each. The agencies' inclusion of the "fairness" concept in the Guidelines is legally indefensible and professionally unsupported. Parity is not required by Title VII, and a selection procedure valid under professional standards is sufficient to meet any legally required showing of job-relatedness in most circumstances. The "fairness" concept is closely linked to the professionally discredited statistical concept of "differential validity."[2] There is no professionally agreed-upon model for evaluating "fairness." (1981, p. 69)

From this quotation it is evident that at least one objection to the inclusion of a discussion of fairness in the Guidelines is legalistic and the other objections are slanted toward legality insofar as there is no indication that the Ad Hoc Group is concerned with morality. However, it is important to realize, as we indicated earlier, that just because an I/O psychologist's work is within legal bounds, his or her *moral* responsibility does not end there. Even though the professional opinion is that the concept of fairness should be eliminated from the Guidelines and is "legally indefensible," I/O psychologists are not morally exempt from trying to ensure fairness in their work.

Regarding the practical significance of the Guidelines, the Ad Hoc Group goes on to say:

> The Guidelines are not definitive statements of the law. . . . Only the courts can produce definitive interpretations and the Guidelines are merely administrative interpretations of what the law requires. The courts may reject a particular

---

*Reprinted from A Professional and Legal Analysis of the Uniform Guidelines on Employee Selection Procedures, copyright the American Society for Personnel Administration, 30 Park Drive, Berea, OH 44107, July 1981.

Guideline requirement, as a number of courts, including the Supreme Court, did with some provisions of the 1970 EEOC Guidelines. But the Guidelines are likely to be accorded great weight by the court, especially since they constitute a unanimous and recent expression of agency interpretation. It remains to be seen whether the fact that some major Guideline provisions are inconsistent with professional opinion or are legally dubious will be taken into account by the courts. (p. 8)

The Uniform Guidelines incorporate a "bottom line" concept. This means that an employer does not have to demonstrate the validity of his or her testing procedure unless there is evidence of adverse impact. If a testing process does show adverse impact, the employer has four alternatives: (1) demonstrate the job-relatedness of the procedures; (2) modify the procedure so the adverse impact is eliminated; (3) use a different procedure which has no adverse impact; or (4) justify the procedure according to the law, such as a showing of "business necessity." If the employer decides to show the job-relatedness, then a validation study must be conducted as set forth in the Guidelines. We should note, however, that whenever the Supreme Court rules on a case involving I/O, psychologists who work in that area should be aware of the decision handed down because this provides a definitive interpretation of the Guidelines.

These Uniform Guidelines are outgrowths of earlier federal guarantees of rights. The Fifth and Fourteenth Amendments to the Constitution have been referred to as the due process amendments. In part, the Fifth Amendment states that "No person shall . . . be deprived of life, liberty, or property, without due process of law. . . . " This amendment protects a person's right to due process at the federal level and the Fourteenth Amendment extends this protection at the state level. The due process amendments are relevant to I/O psychologists' work because sometimes a person's job is considered one's "property" and emphasis has been placed on due process in this regard. (These amendments are also related to the requirement that a person receive a fair hearing before being involuntarily committed to a mental institution. Thus even though a psychologist may judge that a person should be committed to a mental institution rather than be in prison, he or she would have no legal or ethical right to take it upon himself or herself to transport the individual to a mental institution.)

Any constitutional guarantee of civil rights dictates anti-discrimination policies. Therefore, a psychologist who is part of a company's personnel department and who condones that company's practice of hiring new employees on the recommendation of present employees who all happen to be white males would be in violation of these amendments; such a practice only serves to perpetuate discrimination. The psychologist *is* legally responsible for such practices because chances are he or she will be aware of the importance of an affirmative action plan.

The idea behind all federal legislation on employment testing is "*intent* to discriminate." That is, the legal aspects of the I/O area stem from the federal government's desire to prevent employers from *willfully* and *purposely* discriminating against minorities in employment practices. The only way intent can be determined is to look at the actual methods used by an employer when

CASE STUDY 8.3

An industrial psychologist was hired by a city to be an expert witness in a discrimination suit filed by a black police officer against the city. The officer claimed that racial discrimination was evident in the department's promotional process in an assessment center where complex testing procedures were used.

The officer's suit listed several factors that allegedly contributed to his charge of racial discrimination. One of these was the use of prejudiced assessors who were members of other police departments within the state and who rated the individuals participating in the assessment center (the candidates). Another charge claimed that the white candidates had better knowledge about an assessment center (and therefore were better able to perform in it) than did the blacks because some of the whites had participated in classes where material on assessment centers had been taught.

During the court proceedings, the black police officer attempted to show evidence of discrimination for each point listed in the suit. But apparently not enough satisfactory evidence was presented and the judge ruled in favor of the city.

The psychologist was in somewhat of a dilemma during his entire involvement in the case. He had been hired as an expert witness by the city because he had had extensive experience in the development and operation of assessment centers. In preparation for the case, he reviewed all of the assessors' notes and evaluations of all candidates who participated in the assessment center in question. During his review he observed, much to his consternation, that the assessors had not done a very good job in some of the more technical areas of their role as assessors, such as taking adequate notes on each candidate's performance. He also found out from the city's personnel director that the assessors had not been properly trained because they were simply assumed to be experienced assessors. In short, the psychologist came to the conclusion that the assessment center had been very sloppily and hurriedly assembled and administered. It was his opinion that the entire conduct of the assessment center would have received no more than a 3 on a 10-point scale of level of acceptability. Had he been asked to testify regarding his professional opinion of the quality of the assessment center in question, he would have had to state his discoveries and conclusions about the assessment center. This would obviously have placed the city's position in jeopardy because a poorly run assessment center could conceivably contribute to a failure in identifying the most qualified candidate for promotion. The psychologist did not believe that the city was guilty of *intentional* discrimination; nevertheless he thought it was inexcusable that the assessment center was handled so poorly.

The psychologist had not been asked by the judge to testify. However, during the presentation of the plaintiff's case he became aware of the fact that if the plaintiff and his attorney had had access to the information he had gathered about the assessment center, the plaintiff would have had a much better case (even though it would not necessarily have been related to intentional racial discrimination). But he felt he could not give this information to the plaintiff since he had been hired by the city.

making employment decisions. For example, even if an employer does not discriminate against blacks "on purpose," but a selection test used shows adverse impact against blacks, this would be evidence of discrimination and in violation of EEO laws. Thus even if an employer does not intentionally discriminate against a minority group but the result of the employment practices is discrimination, then those practices would have to be changed in order to be in accord with EEO laws and the federal Uniform Guidelines.

Principle 3.b of the *Ethical Principles* notes that psychologists do not condone discriminatory practices. This implies that if a psychologist is employed by a company which does not try to rectify such practices, whether they be intentional or unintentional, he or she has the moral obligation to try to do so. Suppose a company in the aerospace industry needs to hire someone in nuclear physics. The only minimum qualification set is a degree in nuclear physics. All applicants are given a job knowledge test. The applicants consist of ten whites and five blacks. Of these 15, only three pass the test—all three are white. This would be evidence of adverse impact against blacks but validity could be demonstrated by a content validity approach (i.e., by showing that all items are directly related to important or critical aspects of the job) or by a criterion-related study (i.e., by showing that scores on the test are highly correlated with a criterion such as actual job performance). The test results imply that only one-fifth of the applicants are qualified for the job, and the qualified applicants all happen to be white. Because the test is valid, the focus of emphasis shifts from the test to the company's recruitment program. If it could be shown that the company had no affirmative action program, the government could further examine this issue. But because the implementation of an affirmative action program is considered voluntary by the government, the company is probably on safe legal grounds. Here is a case where the requirements of morality go beyond legal requirements. Even though the psychologist developed a valid test, he or she should investigate the company's recruitment program and find ways to recruit qualified blacks. Principle 3.d in part says that

> when . . . organizational . . . regulations or practices are in conflict with Association standards and guidelines, psychologists make known their commitment to Association standards and guidelines and, wherever possible, work toward a resolution of the conflict.

Civil rights legislation gained momentum during the 1960s. The Equal Pay Act of 1963 was passed as an amendment to the Fair Labor Standards Act (FLSA) of 1938. This Act reads in part:

> No employer having employees subject to any provisions of this section shall discriminate, within any establishment in which such employees are employed, between employees on the basis of sex by paying wages to employees in such establishments at a rate less than the rate which he pays wages to employees of the opposite sex in such establishments for equal work on jobs the performance of which requires equal skill, effort, and responsibility, and which are performed under similar working conditions, except where such payment is made pursuant to (i) a seniority system; (ii) a merit system; (iii) a system which measures earnings by quantity or quality of production; or (iv) a differential based on any other factor other than sex: *Provided*, that an employer who is paying a wage rate different in violation of this subsection shall not, in order to comply with the provisions of this subsection, reduce the wage rate of any employee.[3]

The Equal Pay Act is relevant to I/O psychologists when they are involved in the development of job evaluation systems. A job evaluation system is one that determines the relative worth of jobs and forms the basis for the salary level of each job. When a job evaluation system is set up, it is important that the system be based on a thorough analysis of the major duties and responsibilities associated with each job, including the knowledge and abilities required to perform the job duties. This information must be available before the worth of a job can be fairly determined.

Not to be confused with job evaluations is job performance evaluation, or performance appraisal. Performance evaluation is the process whereby the performance of an employee is rated according to how successfully the employee is fulfilling the requirements of the job. As with job evaluation, it is important that a performance appraisal system be based on a thorough job analysis, and that the factors upon which the employee is rated are job-related. The job-relatedness is especially significant since the federal Guidelines consider performance evaluations to be tests, as we shall see, and so they must be validated just as a test is.

Though discrimination can surface when evaluating the performance of a person in a job, discriminatory practices are more likely to appear during the job evaluation process where they are not as obvious. For example, suppose a company is setting up two management positions and salary levels are being set. One position is overseeing clerical workers who are mostly women and the other is overseeing maintenance people who are mostly men. The number of those to be supervised in each type of job is the same. The company has decided to fill the former management position with a female and the latter with a male because it is believed that this would be most effective. Even if in actuality the jobs involve similar duties, responsibilities, knowledge, and abilities, the company could easily manipulate the situation to ensure a higher salary for the male manager because it could be mistakenly assumed that that job would be more difficult due to the type of employees being supervised. This is a type of assumption made by organizations that could lead to discrimination in salary, though a thorough analysis of each position would show that the jobs are comparable in relevant aspects.

The Civil Rights Act of 1964 is composed of several titles or sections. Each title deals with discrimination in differing areas, e.g., public education, voting rights, etc. Of particular interest to I/O psychologists is Title VII (referred to earlier in a quotation by the Ad Hoc Group on the Guidelines), especially as amended by the Equal Employment Opportunity Act of 1972. The EEOC is an outgrowth of the Civil Rights Act and this agency has done more to enforce fair employment in the United States than any other agency of the federal government.

Section 703(a) of Title VII is of major importance because it specifically deals with unlawful discriminatory practices.

One function of I/O psychologists where a possible violation of this particular section of Title VII could occur is the interview process. Interviewing must be considered an assessment technique; in fact, the federal Guidelines cover interviews as well as tests. Objective standards must be established by interviewers to meet both legal and ethical requirements, otherwise subjective biases may enter into the interview. For example, firmness of a handshake, the weight of an individual, or even an individual's surname may unconsciously and subjectively bias the interviewer. One way of reducing subjective bias is to have interviewers of different races, sexes, etc., conduct joint interviews. Other ways to reduce subjectivity in the interview process is to have a set of well-defined areas of interest based on job analysis, to use a structured interview, which allows for more standardization of the interview process, and to focus on applicants' observable behaviors rather than make inferences based on behavior.

Section 703(b) extends this antidiscrimination policy to apprenticeship programs. Section 704(a) covers individuals who have opposed unlawful employment practices and Section 704(b) makes it unlawful for advertisements to include discriminatory clauses. The Equal Employment Opportunity Act of 1972 extended the rights of employees to public employers including state and local governments and private and public educational institutions if such agencies have 15 or more employees. But we should point out that regardless of the fact that an agency with less than 15 employees is not bound by this act, I/O psychologists who work with such agencies still have a moral obligation to correct any discriminatory practices.

The intent of Title VII also seems to imply that reverse discrimination is equally unacceptable. For example, someone with seniority could not be terminated in order to fill the position with a minority person. Because I/O psychologists may be part of the management team, they should be aware that they cannot condone any discriminatory practice. In fact, competent I/O psychologists will not consider such practices acceptable if they know the federal Guidelines and decisions of relevant court cases. While psychologists support affirmative action, any quota system an organization may have is likely to result in some discriminatory practice. (In some situations, however, an organization may be operating under a court-mandated quota system in order to deal with the effects of past discriminatory practices in which job opportunities may have been denied to members of certain minority groups. Moral considerations also may require this in some cases.)

Thus Title VII makes it illegal to discriminate in any of the evaluation procedures used in advertising, screening, testing, placing, or discharging employees. These are some of the major activities of I/O psychologists. Not only is discrimination based on irrelevant factors illegal, it goes without saying that it is also unethical. This is specifically recognized in Principle 3.b which states in part that "As employees or employers, psychologists do not engage or condone practices that are inhumane or that result in illegal or unjustifiable actions." This Principle is reinforced by the Guidelines for I/O psychologists. Guideline 2.1 states, "I/O psychological practice supports the legal and civil rights of the user." Guideline 2.3 says, "All providers within an I/O psychological service unit are familiar with relevant statutes, regulations, and legal precedents established by federal, state, and local governmental groups." And Guideline 3.2 states, "There are periodic, systematic, and effective evaluations of psychological services" (APA, 1981). This last Guideline means that no job can remain static because working conditions change; requirements may be continually changing and to ensure nondiscriminatory practices, these systems must be periodically reevaluated. Besides, if a job evaluation program is discriminatory and salary levels are not based on job requirements, it is automatically invalid.

Here we should point out that validity coefficients are never perfect and are usually far less than perfect. And even if the correlations were a perfect + 1.0, there would be no assurance that humanistic factors were being considered. It is quite conceivable that validity, a mathematical and hence an ethically neutral concept, could include practices that are not in the interests of justice. Though Title VII also seems to reject reverse discrimination as legally acceptable, under some circumstances it may be morally acceptable or even required. If this should be the case, requirements beyond validity requirements may be necessary from a moral point of view. What this points to is the fact that legality does not necessarily ensure moral practices.

Another issue of special interest to I/O psychologists concerns testing. Relevant to this topic is paragraph 703(h) of the Civil Rights Act of 1964 which states that it is not

> an unlawful employment practice for an employer to give and to act upon the results of any professionally developed ability test provided that such test, its administration, or action upon the results is not designed, intended or used to discriminate because of race, color, religion, sex, or national origin.

Although this statement refers specifically to "any professionally developed ability test," it should not be construed to mean tests only in the common sense of the word. In fact, in addition to interviews as we mentioned earlier, the federal Guidelines include as tests such things as review of experience and education from an application, physical requirements, and the application blank itself because they are all used to make employment decisions. From this it can be seen that the federal government recognizes that discrimination can occur at many levels, and as early in the process as initial screening. Rusmore (1967) found, in a survey of 39 organizations in the San Francisco area, that most receptionists were unaware of any rules or regulations governing the initial screening of applicants. Since the employers had not made the rules clear, the receptionists developed their own standards. This means that if I/O psychologists, as part of the management team, overlook this possible discriminatory agent, they, as well as the organization, would be held accountable. Though, technically speaking, receptionists are not part of the interviewing process and hence are not legally accountable, I/O psychologists have the obligation to ensure fairness at all levels even if they are not legally responsible for the whole selection process.

We should point out that it would be difficult but not impossible for I/O psychologists to engage in unethical testing practices that on the surface appear to be valid but may not really be so. The whole area of I/O is ambiguous and there is no "one right way" to conduct a validation study or job analysis. People are constantly looking for new methods that are less time-consuming, less expensive, etc. A psychologist could develop a new test that is shorter and easier to administer than existing tests and demonstrate the alleged validity through a criterion-related study in which the criterion scores were manipulated to come out a certain way. Such a test would most likely be used because it is shorter and easier to administer. The psychologist would probably not get into any legal trouble unless the study were replicated. But until this is done, the psychologist can claim to have developed a better test which has "proven" validity. Though this could possibly be justified by utilitarian standards if it could be shown to promote more happiness than unhappiness for the majority of those involved, it is clearly unethical from the point of view of justice.

The emphasis up to this point in this section has been on the legislative branch of the government as its actions affect the work of I/O psychologists. The executive branch has also been active in equal employment opportunity. Since Franklin D. Roosevelt issued Executive Order 8802 in 1941 outlawing discrimination in defense industries, the executive branch has been concerned with antidiscrimination. Of special interest are Executive Orders 11246, 11375, and 11478.

President Lyndon B. Johnson issued Executive Order 11246 in 1965. This order affecting federal agencies, contractors, and subcontractors prohibited discrimination on the basis of race, color, religion, or national origin. In 1967, Johnson issued Executive Order 11375, which prohibited discrimination on the basis of sex. President Richard Nixon issued Executive Order 11478 in 1969, which superseded Order 11246. In addition to discrimination in employment, this Order covers "upgrading, demotion, or transfer; recruitment or recruitment in advertising; layoff or termination; rates of pay or other forms of compensation; and selection for training, including apprenticeship. . . . " These Executive Orders are under the jurisdiction of the Civil Service Commission. Order 11478 added to Title VII by setting up a federal agency which was responsible for enforcing equal opportunity. In addition, these orders require employers to advertise as "equal opportunity employers." Since 1965, enforcement has been the responsibility of the OFCC. The OFCC can and does refer to other agencies, e.g., EEOC or the Department of Justice, according to the suspected type of violation. Most discrimination complaints are handled by the EEOC.

A case involving possible violation of the federal Uniform Guidelines by an I/O psychologist would be the use of IQ in the placement of a skilled worker. Beyond a minimum level of intelligence, there is little correlation between IQ and most skilled labor jobs. In *Griggs v. Duke Power Co.* (1971), the Supreme Court ruled that unlawful discrimination occurred against blacks by requiring a high school diploma or scoring above a cutoff point on an intelligence test since those factors were irrelevant to the job skill. Thus using irrelevant factors in hiring procedures is not only illegal but unethical. A competent psychologist would develop only a job-related procedure.

Some complaints referred to EEOC become court cases. Thus the judicial branch of the government can and does get involved in discrimination litigation. As mentioned earlier in this chapter, Lerner (1978) has pointed out that the Court is turning more and more to professional standards and principles for guidelines. This is especially true when testing is involved. Section 703(h) of the 1964 Civil Rights Act, as previously discussed, exempts "professionally developed ability test(s)" from the provisions of Title VII as long as these tests do not lead to discrimination. But what are the standards for a "professionally developed test"? Lerner (1978) addresses this question as follows:

> At this point in time, what the Court needs—and seems to want—as circumstances force it to venture deeper and deeper into this unfamiliar and highly specialized area, is the psychometric equivalent of *Gray's Anatomy*: a dispassionate, lucid, and practical set of technical-scientific standards, based upon but also limited by the best research evidence currently available and, as a consequence, capable of commanding clear majority support from recognized experts in the field of psychometrics regardless of their views on what additional steps might or might not be desirable on the basis of special policy preferences. (p. 916)

Because the courts are looking to psychologists more and more to ensure nondiscriminatory practices, psychologists have the responsibility to continually evaluate the validation procedures and to improve them. This trend of the Court to turn to professional standards for validation of any evaluation procedure, especially testing, has been increasing steadily through the 1970s. Lerner (1978) points out that in *Griggs v. Duke Power Co.* (1971) the court refers only to EEOC guidelines and claimed that whether or not there was intent to discriminate was irrelevant. There is no mention of standards of test validation established by the American Psychological Association (p. 917). By the time the *Washington v. Davis* (1976) case was heard, the APA Standards seemed to be "approaching preeminence" over the federal Guidelines (p. 918). In this case a black policeman charged that the verbal ability test used by the District of Columbia screened out more blacks than whites. The employer claimed that the test was job-related. Expert witnesses were called in to help the Court understand how the standards were set up, thus showing that a test could be discriminatory but valid. The Court then ruled that success in a job-related test is a legitimate criterion for validation of an employment test. Because of this, the Court held that there was no *intent* to discriminate and thereby reversed the intent clause of *Griggs*.

Again the Court turned to professional standards of the APA to determine that the test in question for hiring teachers, which was challenged by the National Education Association in *National Education Association v. State of South Carolina* (1978), was not discriminatory and met all EEOC guidelines. What these later court cases indicate is that ethical and legal responsibility for nondiscriminatory practices is now being placed on psychologists who develop material for the purpose of recruitment, hiring, promoting, and initial screening (including application forms and interviews). Hence consulting psychologists are an integral part of not only any affirmative action program but the entire employment process. The following quotation from Schaeffer (1973) indicates that even if psychologists who serve as personnel managers are not concerned with their moral obligation to ensure nondiscriminatory practices, they had better be concerned with their legal obligations:

> After watching the bored response of a group of middle managers to a discussion of the nondiscrimination laws, the general consel of one very large organization stopped the meeting. He suddenly gained their rapt attention by saying:

"Gentlemen, including back pay awards, this company has already spent hundreds of thousands of dollars preparing, defending, and *losing* nondiscrimination cases in the Federal Courts. We do not intend to continue doing so.

"This meeting was called to tell you what the laws require. The attorneys on the other side are likely to be very able. And we now know that the courts intend to enforce these laws fully.

"If *you* do not expect to comply with all the nondiscrimination laws, consider this to be a fair warning. You will be fired."

A written summary of that meeting was prepared; senior company executives say it is being avidly read and discussed. (p. 3)

Although in this section we have focused on the legal role of consulting psychologists in general and I/O psychologists in particular, we should emphasize that even though there are laws to ensure fair and just practices in organizations that employ psychologists as consultants, they nevertheless have the *moral* obligation to protect the well-being of those whom they may affect in their professional role.

Ethical Principles of Psychologists

PREAMBLE

Psychologists respect the dignity and worth of the individual and strive for the preservation and protection of fundamental human rights. They are committed to increasing knowledge of human behavior and of people's understanding of themselves and others and to the utilization of such knowledge for the promotion of human welfare. While pursuing these objectives, they make every effort to protect the welfare of those who seek their services and of the research participants that may be the object of study. They use their skills only for purposes consistent with these values and do not knowingly permit their misuse by others. While demanding for themselves freedom of inquiry and communication, psychologists accept the responsibility this freedom requires: competence, objectivity in the application of skills, and concern for the best interests of clients, colleagues, students, research participants, and society. In the pursuit of these ideals, psychologists subscribe to principles in the following areas: 1. Responsibility, 2. Competence, 3. Moral and Legal Standards, 4. Public Statements, 5. Confidentiality, 6. Welfare of the Consumer, 7. Professional Relationships, 8. Assessment Techniques, 9. Research With Human Participants, and 10. Care and Use of Animals.

Acceptance of membership in the American Psychological Association commits the member to adherence to these principles.

Psychologists cooperate with duly constituted committees of the American Psychological Association, in particular, the Committee on Scientific and Professional Ethics and Conduct, by responding to inquiries promptly and completely. Members also respond promptly and completely to inquiries from duly constituted state association ethics committees and professional standards review committees.

This version of the Ethical Principles of Psychologists (formerly entitled Ethical Standards of Psychologists) was adopted by the American Psychological Association's Council of Representatives on January 24, 1981. The revised Ethical Principles contain both substantive and grammatical changes in each of the nine ethical principles constituting the Ethical Standards of Psychologists previously adopted by the council of Representatives in 1979, plus a new tenth principle entitled Care and Use of Animals. Inquiries concerning the Ethical Principles of Psychologists should be addressed to the Administrative Officer for Ethics, American Psychological Association, 1200 Seventeenth Street, N.W., Washington, D.C. 20036.

These revised Ethical Principles apply to psychologists, to students of psychology, and to others who do work of a psychological nature under the supervision of a psychologist. They are also intended for the guidance of nonmembers of the Association who are engaged in psychological research or practice.

Any complaints of unethical conduct filed after January 24, 1981, shall be governed by this 1981 revision. However, conduct (a) complained about after January 24, 1981, but which occurred prior to that date, and (b) not considered unethical under the 1981 revision, shall not be deemed a violation of ethical principles. Any complaints pending as of January 24, 1981, shall be governed either by the 1979 or by the 1981 version of the Ethical Principles, at the sound discretion of the Committee on Scientific and Professional Ethics and Conduct.

Principle 1

RESPONSIBILITY

In providing services, psychologists maintain the highest standards of their profession. They accept responsibility for the consequences of their acts and make every effort to ensure that their services are used appropriately.

a. As scientists, psychologists accept responsibility for the selection of their research topics and the methods used in investigation, analysis, and reporting. They plan their research in ways to minimize the possibility that their findings will be misleading. They provide thorough discussion of the limitations of their data, especially where their work touches on social policy or might be construed to the detriment of persons in specific age, sex, ethnic, socioeconomic, or other social groups. In publishing reports of their work, they never suppress disconfirming data, and they acknowledge the existence of alternative hypotheses and explanations of their findings. Psychologists take credit only for work they have actually done.

b. Psychologists clarify in advance with all appropriate persons and agencies the expectations for sharing and utilizing research data. They avoid relationships that may limit their objectivity or create a conflict of interest. Interference with the milieu in which data are collected is kept to a minimum.

c. Psychologists have the responsibility to attempt to prevent distortion, misuse, or suppression of psychological findings by the institution or agency of which they are employees.

d. As members of governmental or other organizational bodies, psychologists remain accountable as individuals to the highest standards of their profession.

e. As teachers, psychologists recognize their primary obligation to help others acquire knowledge and skill. They maintain high standards of scholarship by presenting psychological information objectively, fully, and accurately.

f. As practitioners, psychologists know that they bear a heavy social responsibility because their recommendations and professional actions may alter the lives of others. They are alert to personal, social, organizational, financial, or political situations and pressures that might lead to misuse of their influence.

Principle 2

COMPETENCE

The maintenance of high standards of competence is a responsibility shared by all psychologists in the interest of the public and the profession as a whole. Psychologists recognize the boundaries of their competence and the limitations of their techniques. They only provide services and only use techniques for which they are qualified by training and experience. In those areas in which recognized standards do not yet exist, psychologists take whatever precautions are necessary to protect the welfare of their clients. They maintain knowledge of current scientific and professional information related to the services they render.

a. Psychologists accurately represent their competence, education, training, and experience. They claim as evidence of educational qualifications only those degrees obtained from institutions acceptable under the Bylaws and Rules of Council of the American Psychological Association.

b. As teachers, psychologists perform their duties on the basis of careful preparation so that their instruction is accurate, current, and scholarly.

c. Psychologists recognize the need for continuing education and are open to new procedures and changes in expectations and values over time.

d. Psychologists recognize differences among people, such as those that may be associated with age, sex, socioeconomic, and ethnic backgrounds. When necessary, they obtain training, experience, and counsel to assure competent service or research relating to such persons.

e. Psychologists responsible for decisions involving individuals or policies based on test results have an understanding of psychological or educational measurement, validation problems, and test research.

f. Psychologists recognize that personal problems and conflicts may interfere with professional effectiveness. Accordingly, they refrain from undertaking any activity in which their personal problems are likely to lead to inadequate performance or harm to a client, colleague, student, or research participant. If engaged in such activity when they become aware of their personal problems, they seek competent professional assistance to determine whether they should suspend, terminate, or limit the scope of their professional and/or scientific activities.

Principle 3

MORAL AND LEGAL STANDARDS

Psychologists' moral and ethical standards of behavior are a personal matter to the same degree as they are for any other citizen, except as these may compromise the fulfillment of their professional responsibilities or reduce the public trust in psychology and psychologists. Regarding their own behavior, psychologists are sensitive to prevailing community standards and to the possible impact that conformity to or deviation from these standards may have upon the quality of their performance as psychologists. Psychologists are also aware of the possible impact of their public behavior upon the ability of colleagues to perform their professional duties.

a. As teachers, psychologists are aware of the fact that their personal values may affect the selection and presentation of instructional materials. When dealing with topics that may give offense, they recognize and respect the diverse attitudes that students may have toward such materials.

b. As employees or employers, psychologists do not engage in or condone practices that are inhumane or that result in illegal or unjustifiable actions. Such practices include, but are not limited to, those based on considerations of race, handicap, age, gender, sexual preference, religion, or national origin in hiring, promotion, or training.

c. In their professional roles, psychologists avoid any action that will violate or diminish the legal and civil rights of clients or of others who may be affected by their actions.

d. As practitioners and researchers, psychologists act in accord with Association standards and guidelines related to practice and to the conduct of research with human beings and animals. In the ordinary course of events, psychologists adhere to relevant governmental laws and institutional regulations. When federal, state, provincial, organizational, or institutional laws, regulations, or practices are in conflict with Association standards and guidelines, psychologists make known their commitment to Association standards and guidelines and, wherever possible, work toward a resolution of the conflict. Both practitioners and researchers are concerned with the development of such legal and quasi-legal regulations as best serve the public interest, and they work toward changing existing regulations that are not beneficial to the public interest.

Principle 4

PUBLIC STATEMENTS

Public statements, announcements of services, advertising, and promotional activities of psychologists serve the purpose of helping the public make informed judgments and choices. Psychologists represent accurately and objectively their professional qualifications, affiliations, and functions, as well as those of the institutions or organizations with which they or the statements may be associated. In public statements providing psychological information or professional opinions or providing information about the availability of psychological products, publications, and services, psychologists base their statements on scientifically acceptable psychological findings and techniques with full recognition of the limits and uncertainties of such evidence.

   a. When announcing or advertising professional services, psychologists may list the following information to describe the provider and services provided: name, highest relevant academic degree earned from a regionally accredited institution, date, type, and level of certification or licensure, diplomate status, APA membership status, address, telephone number, office hours, a brief listing of the type of psychological services offered, an appropriate presentation of fee information, foreign languages spoken, and policy with regard to third-party payments. Additional relevant or important consumer information may be included if not prohibited by other sections of these Ethical Principles.

   b. In announcing or advertising the availability of psychological products, publications, or services, psychologists do not present their affiliation with any organization in a manner that falsely implies sponsorship or certification by that organization. In particular and for example, psychologists do not state APA membership or fellow status in a way to suggest that such status implies specialized professional competence or qualifications. Public statements include, but are not limited to, communication by means of periodical, book, list, directory, television, radio, or motion picture. They do not contain (i) a false, fraudulent, misleading, deceptive, or unfair statement; (ii) a misinterpretation of fact or a statement likely to mislead or deceive because in context it makes only a partial disclosure of relevant facts; (iii) a testimonial from a patient regarding the quality of a psychologists' services or products; (iv) a statement intended or likely to create false or unjustified expectations of favorable results; (v) a statement implying unusual, unique, or one-of-a-kind abilities; (vi) a statement intended or likely to appeal to a client's fears, anxieties, or emotions concerning the possible results of failure to obtain the offered services; (vii) a statement concerning the comparative desirability of offered services; (viii) a statement of direct solicitation of individual clients.

   c. Psychologists do not compensate or give anything of value to a representative of the press, radio, television, or other communication medium in anticipation of or in return for professional publicity in a news item. A paid advertisement must be identified as such, unless it is apparent from the context that it is a paid advertisement. If communicated to the public by use of radio or television, an advertisement is prerecorded and approved for broadcast by the psychologist, and a recording of the actual transmission is retained by the psychologist.

d. Announcements or advertisements of "personal growth groups," clinics, and agencies give a clear statement of purpose and a clear description of the experiences to be provided. The education, training, and experience of the staff members are appropriately specified.

e. Psychologists associated with the development or promotion of psychological devices, books, or other products offered for commercial sale make reasonable efforts to ensure that announcements and advertisements are presented in a professional, scientifically acceptable, and factually informative manner.

f. Psychologists do not participate for personal gain in commercial announcements or advertisements recommending to the public the purchase or use of proprietary or single-source products or services when that participation is based solely upon their identifications as psychologists.

g. Psychologists present the science of psychology and offer their services, products, and publications fairly and accurately, avoiding misrepresentation through sensationalism, exaggeration, or superficiality. Psychologists are guided by the primary obligation to aid the public in developing informed judgments, opinions, and choices.

h. As teachers, psychologists ensure that statements in catalogs and course outlines are accurate and not misleading, particularly in terms of subject matter to be covered, bases for evaluating progress, and the nature of course experiences. Announcements, brochures, or advertisements describing workshops, seminars, or other educational programs accurately describe the audience for which the program is intended as well as eligibility requirements, educational objectives, and nature of the materials to be covered. These announcements also accurately represent the education, training, and experience of the psychologists presenting the programs and any fees involved.

i. Public announcements or advertisements soliciting research participants in which clinical services or other professional services are offered as an inducement make clear the nature of the services as well as the costs and other obligations to be accepted by participants in the research.

j. A psychologist accepts the obligation to correct others who represent the psychologist's professional qualifications, or associations with products or services, in a manner incompatible with these guidelines.

k. Individual diagnostic and therapeutic services are provided only in the context of a professional psychological relationship. When personal advice is given by means of public lectures or demonstrations, newspaper or magazine articles, radio or television programs, mail, or similar media, the psychologist utilizes the most current relevant data and exercises the highest level of professional judgment.

l. Products that are described or presented by means of public lectures or demonstrations, newspaper or magazine articles, radio or television programs, or similar media meet the same recognized standards as exist for products used in the context of a professional relationship.

Principle 5

CONFIDENTIALITY

Psychologists have a primary obligation to respect the confidentiality of information obtained from persons in the course of their work as psychologists. They reveal such information to others only with the consent of the person or the person's legal representative, except in those unusual circumstances in which not to do so would result in clear danger to the person or to others. Where appropriate, psychologists inform their clients of the legal limits of confidentiality.

a. Information obtained in clinical or consulting relationships, or evaluative data concerning children, students, employees, and others, is discussed only for professional purposes and only with persons clearly concerned with the case. Written and oral reports present only data germane to the purposes of the evaluation, and every effort is made to avoid undue invasion of privacy.

b. Psychologists who present personal information obtained during the course of professional work in writings, lectures, or other public forums either obtain adequate prior consent to do so or adequately disguise all identifying information.

c. Psychologists make provisions for maintaining confidentiality in the storage and disposal of records.

d. When working with minors or other persons who are unable to give voluntary, informed consent, psychologists take special care to protect these persons' best interests.

Principle 6

WELFARE OF THE CONSUMER

Psychologists respect the integrity and protect the welfare of the people and groups with whom they work. When conflicts of interest arise between clients and psychologists' employing institutions, psychologists clarify the nature and direction of their loyalties and responsibilities and keep all parties informed of their commitments. Psychologists fully inform consumers as to the purpose and nature of an evaluative, treatment, educational, or training procedure, and they freely acknowledge that clients, students, or participants in research have freedom of choice with regard to participation.

a. Psychologists are continually cognizant of their own needs and of their potentially influential position vis-à-vis persons such as clients, students, and subordinates. They avoid exploiting the trust and dependency of such persons. Psychologists make every effort to avoid dual relationships that could impair their professional judgment or increase the risk of exploitation. Examples of such dual relationships include, but are not limited to, research with and treatment of employees, students, supervisees, close friends, or relatives. Sexual intimacies with clients are unethical.

b. When a psychologist agrees to provide services to a client at the request of a third party, the psychologist assumes the responsibility of clarifying the nature of the relationships to all parties concerned.

c. Where the demands of an organization require psychologists to violate these Ethical Principles, psychologists clarify the nature of the conflict between the demands and these principles. They inform all parties of psychologists' ethical responsibilities and take appropriate action.

d. Psychologists make advance financial arrangements that safeguard the best interests of and are clearly understood by their clients. They neither give nor receive any remuneration for referring clients for professional services. They contribute a portion of their services to work for which they receive little or no financial return.

e.   Psychologists terminate a clinical or consulting relationship when it is reasonably clear that the consumer is not benefiting from it. They offer to help the consumer locate alternative sources of assistance.

Principle 7

PROFESSIONAL RELATIONSHIPS

Psychologists act with due regard for the needs, special competencies, and obligations of their colleagues in psychology and other professions. They respect the prerogatives and obligations of the institutions or organizations with which these other colleagues are associated.

a.   Psychologists understand the areas of competence of related professions. They make full use of all the professional, technical, and administrative resources that serve the best interests of consumers. The absence of formal relationships with other professional workers does not relieve psychologists of the responsibility of securing for their clients the best possible professional service, nor does it relieve them of the obligation to exercise foresight, diligence, and tact in obtaining the complementary or alternative assistance needed by clients.

b.   Psychologists know and take into account the traditions and practices of other professional groups with whom they work and cooperate fully with such groups. If a person is receiving similar services from another professional, psychologists do not offer their own services directly to such a person. If a psychologist is contacted by a person who is already receiving similar services from another professional, the psychologist carefully considers that professional relationship and proceeds with caution and sensitivity to the therapeutic issues as well as the client's welfare. The psychologist discusses these issues with the client so as to minimize the risk of confusion and conflict.

c.   Psychologists who employ or supervise other professionals or professionals in training accept the obligation to facilitate the further professional development of these individuals. They provide appropriate working conditions, timely evaluations, constructive consultation, and experience opportunities.

d.   Psychologists do not exploit their professional relationships with clients, supervisees, students, employees, or research participants sexually or otherwise. Psychologists do not condone or engage in sexual harassment. Sexual harassment is defined as deliberate or repeated comments, gestures, or physical contacts of a sexual nature that are unwanted by the recipient.

e.   In conducting research in institutions or organizations, psychologists secure appropriate authorization to conduct such research. They are aware of their obligations to future research workers and ensure that host institutions receive adequate information about the research and proper acknowledgment of their contributions.

f.   Publication credit is assigned to those who have contributed to a publication in proportion to their professional contributions. Major contributions of a professional character made by several persons to a common project are recognized by joint authorship, with the individual who made the principal contribution listed first. Minor contributions of a professional character and extensive clerical or similar nonprofessional assistance may be acknowledged in footnotes or in an introductory statement. Acknowledgment through specific citations is made for unpublished as well as published material that has directly influenced the research or writing. Psychologists who compile and edit material of others for publication publish the material in the name of the originating group, if appropriate, with their own name appearing as chairperson and editor. All contributors are to be acknowledged and named.

g. When psychologists know of an ethical violation by another psychologist, and it seems appropriate, they informally attempt to resolve the issue by bringing the behavior to the attention of the psychologist. If the misconduct is of a minor nature and/or appears to be due to lack of sensitivity, knowledge, or experience, such an informal solution is usually appropriate. Such informal corrective efforts are made with sensitivity to any rights to confidentiality involved. If the violation does not seem amenable to an informal solution, or is of a more serious nature, psychologists bring it to the attention of the appropriate local, state, and/or national committee on professional ethics and conduct.

Principle 8

ASSESSMENT TECHNIQUES

In the development, publication, and utilization of psychological assessment techniques, psychologists make every effort to promote the welfare and best interests of the client. They guard against the misuse of assessment results. They respect the client's right to know the results, the interpretations made, and the bases for their conclusions and recommendations. Psychologists make every effort to maintain the security of tests and other assessment techniques within limits of legal mandates. They strive to ensure the appropriate use of assessment techniques by others.

a. In using assessment techniques, psychologists respect the right of clients to have full explanations of the nature and purpose of the techniques in language the clients can understand, unless an explicit exception to this right has been agreed upon in advance. When the explanations are to be provided by others, psychologists establish procedures for ensuring the adequacy of these explanations.

b. Psychologists responsible for the development and standardization of psychological tests and other assessment techniques utilize established scientific procedures and observe the relevant APA standards.

c. In reporting assessment results, psychologists indicate any reservations that exist regarding validity or reliability because of the circumstances of the assessment or the inappropriateness of the norms for the person tested. Psychologists strive to ensure that the results of assessments and their interpretations are not misused by others.

d. Psychologists recognize that assessment results may become obsolete. They make every effort to avoid and prevent the misuse of obsolete measures.

e. Psychologists offering scoring and interpretation services are able to produce appropriate evidence for the validity of the programs and procedures used in arriving at interpretations. The public offering of an automated interpretation service is considered a professional-to-professional consultation. Psychologists make every effort to avoid misuse of assessment reports.

f. Psychologists do not encourage or promote the use of psychological assessment techniques by inappropriately trained or otherwise unqualified persons through teaching, sponsorship, or supervision.

Principle 9

RESEARCH WITH HUMAN PARTICIPANTS

The decision to undertake research rests upon a considered judgment by the individual psychologist about how best to contribute to psychological science and human welfare. Having made the decision to conduct research, the psychologist considers alternative directions in which research energies and resources might be invested. On the basis of this consideration, the psychologist carries out the investigation with respect and concern for the dignity and welfare of the people who participate and with cognizance of federal and state regulations and professional standards governing the conduct of research with human participants.

a. In planning a study, the investigator has the responsibility to make a careful evaluation of its ethical acceptability. To the extent that the weighing of scientific and human values suggests a compromise of any principle, the investigator incurs a correspondingly serious obligation to seek ethical advice and to observe stringent safeguards to protect the rights of human participants.

b. Considering whether a participant in a planned study will be a "subject at risk" or a "subject at minimal risk," according to recognized standards, is of primary ethical concern to the investigator.

c. The investigator always retains the responsibility for ensuring ethical practice in research. The investigator is also responsible for the ethical treatment of research participants by collaborators, assistants, students, and employees, all of whom, however, incur similar obligations.

d. Except in minimal-risk research, the investigator establishes a clear and fair agreement with research participants, prior to their participation, that clarifies the obligations and responsibilities of each. The investigator has the obligation to honor all promises and commitments included in that agreement. The investigator informs the participants of all aspects of the research that might reasonably be expected to influence willingness to participate and explains all other aspects of the research about which the participants inquire. Failure to make full disclosure prior to obtaining informed consent requires additional safeguards to protect the welfare and dignity of the research participants. Research with children or with participants who have impairments that would limit understanding and/or communication requires special safeguarding procedures.

e. Methodological requirements of a study may make the use of concealment or deception necessary. Before conducting such a study, the investigator has a special responsibility to (i) determine whether the use of such techniques is justified by the study's prospective scientific, educational, or applied value; (ii) determine whether alternative procedures are available that do not use concealment or deception; and (iii) ensure that the participants are provided with sufficient explanation as soon as possible.

f. The investigator respects the individual's freedom to decline to participate in or to withdraw from the research at any time. The obligation to protect this freedom requires careful thought and consideration when the investigator is in a position of authority or influence over the participant. Such positions of authority include, but are not limited to, situations in which research participation is required as part of employment or in which the participant is a student, client, or employee of the investigator.

g. The investigator protects the participant from physical and mental discomfort, harm, and danger that may arise from research procedures. If risks of such consequences exist, the investigator informs the participant of that fact. Research procedures likely to cause serious or lasting harm to a participant are not used unless the failure to use these procedures might expose the participant to risk of greater harm, or unless the research has great potential benefit and fully informed and voluntary consent is obtained from each participant. The participant should be informed of procedures for contacting the investigator within a reasonable time period following participation should stress, potential harm, or related questions or concerns arise.

h. After the data are collected, the investigator provides the participant with information about the nature of the study and attempts to remove any misconceptions that may have arisen. Where scientific or humane values justify delaying or withholding this information, the investigator incurs a special responsibility to monitor the research and to ensure that there are no damaging consequences for the participant.

i. Where research procedures result in undesirable consequences for the individual participant, the investigator has the responsibility to detect and remove or correct these consequences, including long-term effects.

j. Information obtained about a research participant during the course of an investigation is confidential unless otherwise agreed upon in advance. When the possibility exists that others may obtain access to such information, this possibility, together with the plans for protecting confidentiality, is explained to the participant as part of the procedure for obtaining informed consent.

Principle 10

CARE AND USE OF ANIMALS

An investigator of animal behavior strives to advance understanding of basic behavioral principles and/or to contribute to the improvement of human health and welfare. In seeking these ends, the investigator ensures the welfare of animals and treats them humanely. Laws and regulations notwithstanding, an animal's immediate protection depends upon the scientist's own conscience.

a. The acquisition, care, use, and disposal of all animals are in compliance with current federal, state or provincial, and local laws and regulations.

b. A psychologist trained in research methods and experienced in the care of laboratory animals closely supervises all procedures involving animals and is responsible for ensuring appropriate consideration of their comfort, health, and humane treatment.

c. Psychologists ensure that all individuals using animals under their supervision have received explicit instruction in experimental methods and in the care, maintenance, and handling of the species being used. Responsibilities and activities of individuals participating in a research project are consistent with their respective competencies.

d. Psychologists make every effort to minimize discomfort, illness, and pain of animals. A procedure subjecting animals to pain, stress, or privation is used only when an alternative procedure is unavailable and the goal is justified by its prospective scientific, educational, or applied value. Surgical procedures are performed under appropriate anesthesia; techniques to avoid infection and minimize pain are followed during and after surgery.

e. When it is appropriate that the animal's life be terminated, it is done rapidly and painlessly.

References

American Psychiatric Association. Position statement on guidelines for psychiatrists:Problems in confidentiality. *American Journal of Psychiatry*, 126:10 (April 1970), 187–93.

American Psychological Association. Guidelines for psychologists conducting growth groups. *American Psychologist*, 28:10 (1973), 933.

American Psychological Association. *Standards for educational and psychological tests*. Washington, D.C.: 1974.

American Psychological Association. *Standards for providers of psychological services*. Washington, D.C.: 1977.

American Psychological Association. Report of the task force on the role of psychology in the criminal justice system. *American Psychologist*. 33:12 (December 1978), 1099–1113.

American Psychological Association. *Ethical principles of psychologists*. Washington, D.C.: 1981.

American Psychological Association. Specialty guidelines for delivery of services by industrial/organizational psychologists. *American Psychologist*, 36:6 (June, 1981), 664–69.

Ayer, A. J. *Language, truth and logic*. New York: Dover, 1946.

Baldick, T. L. Ethical discrimination ability of intern psychologists: A function of training in ethics. *Professional Psychology*, 11 (April, 1980), 276–81.

Bartholome, W. G. Parents, children and the moral benefits of research. *Hastings Center Report*, 6:6 (December, 1976), 44–45.

Benn, S. I. Freedom and persuasion. In *Self-Determination in Social Work*. London: Routledge and Kegan Paul, 1975, 224–40.

Berscheid, E., Baron, R. S., Dermer, M., & Libman, M. Anticipatory informed consent. *American Psychologist*, 28:10 (1973), 913–25.

Bindrim, P. Group therapy: Protecting privacy. *Psychology Today*, 24 (July, 1980), 27–28.

Birnbaum, M. The right to treatment. *American Bar Association Journal*, 46 (May, 1960), 499–505.

Blackstone, W. T. The APA code of ethics for research involving human participants: An appraisal. *Southern Journal of Philosophy*, 13 (1975), 407–18.

Boehm, V. R. Negro-white differences in validity of employment and training selection procedure: Summary of research evidence. *Journal of Applied Psychology*, 56 (1972), 33–39.

Bowd, A. Ethical reservations about psychological research with animals. *Psychological Record*, 30 (1980), 201–10.

Brayfield, A. H. Psychology and public affairs. *American Psychologist*, 22:3 (1967), 182–86.

Breggin, P. Psychotherapy as applied ethics. *Psychiatry*. 34 (February, 1971), 59–74.

Britton, B. K. Ethical and educational aspects of participating as a subject in psychology experiments. *Teaching of Psychology*, 6:4 (December, 1979), 195–98.

Broverman, I., Broverman, D., and Clarkson, F. Sex-role stereotypes and clinical judgments of mental health. *Journal of Consulting and Clinical Psychology*, 34:1 (1970), 1–7.

Butler, S. and Zelen, S. Sexual intimacies between therapists and patients. *Psychotherapy: Theory, Research and Practice*, 14 (1977), 139–45.

Campbell, D. T. Reforms as experiments. *American Psychologist*, 24 (1969), 409–29.

Cascio, W. F. *Applied psychology in personnel management*. Reston, Va.: Reston Publishing Co., 1978.

Cavenar, J. O., Rhodes, E. J., & Sullivan, J. L. Ethical and legal aspects of supervision. *Bulletin of the Menninger Clinic*, 44:1 (1980), 15–22.

Code of ethics for a community mental health program. *Hospital and Community Psychiatry*, 57:1 (January, 1976), 29–32.

Council for the National Register of Health Service Providers in Psychology, "Guidelines for defining 'doctoral degree in psychology'," in *List of Designated Doctoral Programs in Psychology*, 1981.

Culliton, B. J. Confidentiality: Court declares researcher can protect sources. *Science*, 193 (1976), 467–69.

Davison, G. C. Homosexuality: The ethical challenge. *Journal of Consulting and Clinical Psychology*, 44:2 (1976), 157–62.

Davison, G. C. & Stuart, R. B. Behavior therapy and civil liberties. *American Psychologist* (July, 1975), 755–63.

Davison, G. C. & Wilson, G. T. Attitudes of behavior therapists toward homosexuality. *Behavior Therapy*, 4 (1973), 686–96.

Day, V., Erwin, F., & Koral, A., eds. *A professional and legal analysis of the uniform guidelines on employee selection procedures*. Berea, Ohio: The American Society for Personnel Administration, 1981.

Dickson, J. P., Casey, M., Wyckoff, D., & Wynd, W. Invisible coding of survey questionnaires. *Public Opinion Quarterly* 41:1 (1977), 100–106.

Diener, E. & Crandall, R. *Ethics in social and behavioral research*. Chicago: The University of Chicago Press, 1978.

Dworkin, G. Paternalism. In J. Feinberg and H. Gross, eds., *Philosophy of Law*, Belmont, Calif.: Dickenson, 1975, 174–84.

Dworkin, G. Autonomy and behavior control. *Hastings Center Report*, 6:1 (February, 1976), 23–28.

Ellis, A. *Reason and emotion in psychotherapy*. New York: Lyle Stuart, 1962.

Ellis, A. Humanistic psychotherapy: A revolutionary approach. *The Humanist*, 32:1 (Jan./Feb., 1972), 24–28.

Ellis, A. Rational-emotive therapy. In Corsini, R., ed., *Current psychotherapies*. Itasca, Ill.: Peacock, 1973, 167–206.

Ellis, A. Rational-emotive therapy. In Corsini, R., ed., *Current psychotherapies*. 2d ed.; Itasca, Ill.: Peacock, 1979, 185–229.

Ellis, A. & Harper, R. A. *A guide to rational living*. Englewood Cliffs, N.J.: Prentice-Hall, 1961. (Paperback edition, Hollywood: Wilshire Books, 1971.)

Ellsworth, P. C. From abstract ideas to concrete instances. *American Psychologist*, 32:8 (1977), 604–15.

Engelhardt, H. T., Jr. Psychotherapy as meta-ethics. *Psychiatry*, 36 (November, 1973), 440–45.

Ennis, B. & Litwack, T. R. Psychiatry and the presumption of expertise: Flipping coins in the courtroom. *California Law Review*, 62 (1974), 693–752.

Ennis, B. & Siegel, L. *The rights of mental patients*. New York: Avon Books, 1973.

Erwin, E. *Behavior therapy: Scientific, philosophical, and moral foundations*. New York: Cambridge University Press, 1978.

Eysenck, H. J. The case of Sir Cyril Burt. *Encounter*, 48 (1977), 19–24.

Faden, R. & Beauchamp, T. Philosophical and psychological issues about informed consent. Presented at Southern Society for Philosophy and Psychology, Louisville, 1981.

Farr, J. L. & Seaver, W. B. Stress and discomfort in psychological research. *American Psychologist*, 30:7 (1975), 770–73.

Feinberg, J. The nature and value of rights. *Journal of Value Inquiry*, 4:4 (Winter, 1970), 243–57.

Festinger, L. *A theory of cognitive dissonance*. Stanford, Calif.: Stanford University Press, 1957.

Fine, R. The age of awareness. *Psychoanalytic Review*, 59:1 (1972), 55–71.

Fine, R. Psychoanalysis. In Corsini, R., ed., *Current psychotherapies*. Itasca, Ill.: Peacock, 1973, 1–33.

Fletcher, J. *Situation ethics*. Philadelphia: Westminster, 1966.

Freedman, B. A moral theory of informed consent. *Hastings Center Report*, 5:4 (August, 1975), 32–39.

Friedman, P. R. Legal regulation of applied behavior analysis in mental institutions and prisons. *Arizona Law Review*, 17 (1975), 39–104.

Gaylin, W. & Blatte, H. Behavior modification in prisons. *American Criminal Law Review*, 13:11 (1975), 11–35.

Gillie, O. Did Sir Cyril Burt fake his research on heritability of intelligence? Part 1. *Phi Delta Kappan* (February, 1977), 469–71.

Goldfried, M. R. & Davison, G. C. *Clinical behavior therapy*. New York: Holt, Rinehart and Winston, 1976.

Goldstein, A. Behavior therapy. In Corsini, R., ed., *Current psychotherapies*. Itasca, Ill.: Peacock, 1973, 207–49.

Graham, P. Ethics in child psychiatry. In Bloch, S. and Chodoff, P., eds., *Psychiatric ethics*. New York: Oxford University Press, 1981, 235–54.

Gray, B. H., Cooke, R. H., & Tannenbaum, A. S. Research involving human subjects. *Science*, 201:4361 (1978), 1094–1101.

Griggs v. Duke Power Co., 401 U.S. 424 (1971).

Gross, S. J. The myth of professional licensing. *American Psychologist*, 33:11 (1978), 1009–1016.

Hare-Mustin, R. & Hall, J. Procedures for responding to ethics complaints against psychologists. *American Psychologist*, 36:12 (1981), 1494–1505.

Hartmann, H. *Psychoanalysis and moral values*. New York: International Universities Press, 1960.

Hartshorne, H. & May, M. A. *Studies in the nature of character*. Vol. 1. New York: Macmillan, 1928.

Haywood, H. C. The ethics of doing research and of not doing it. *American Journal of Mental Deficiency*, 81:4 (1976), 311–17.

Hogan, R. & Schroeder, D. Seven biases in psychology. *Psychology Today* (July, 1981), 8–14.

Holland, J. G. Ethical considerations in behavior modification. In Shore, M. F. and Golann, S. E., eds. *Current ethical issues in mental health*. DHEW Publication No. (HSM) 73-9029 1973, 24–30.

Holmes, D. S. Debriefing after psychological experiments. I. Effectiveness of post-experimental dehoaxing. *American Psychologist* 31:12 (1976a), 858–67.

Holmes, D. S. Debriefing after psychological experiments. II. Effectiveness of post-experimental desensitizing. *American Psychologist*, 31 (1976b), 868–75.

Holroyd, J. and Brodsky, A. Psychologists' attitudes and practices regarding erotic and nonerotic physical contact with patients. *American Psychologist*, 32:10 (1977), 834–49.

Horn, J. Is informed deceit the answer to informed consent? *Psychology Today*, (May, 1978), 36–37.

Jensen, A. R. Did Sir Cyril Burt fake his research on heritability of intelligence? Part II. *Phi Delta Kappan* (February, 1977), 471–92.

Kant, I. *Groundwork of the metaphysic of morals*. Trans. H. J. Paton. New York: Harper and Row, 1964. (1785)

Karasu, T. B. The ethics of psychotherapy. *American Journal of Psychiatry*, 137:12 (1980), 1502–12.

Katz, J. The right to treatment—An enchanting legal fiction? *University of Chicago Law Review*, 36 (1969), 755–83.

Kelman, H. C. Manipulation of human behavior: An ethical dilemma for the social scientist. *Journal of Social Issues*, 21 (1965), 31–46.

Kelman, H. C. Human use of human subjects: The problem of deception in social psychological experiments. *Psychological Bulletin*, 67:1 (1967), 1–11.

Kelman, H. C. The rights of the subject in social research: An analysis in terms of relative power and legitimacy. *American Psychologist*, 27 (1972), 989–1016. Koocher, G. P. Bathroom behavior and human dignity. *Journal of Personality and Social Psychology*, 35:2 (1977), 120–21.

Lasagna, L. Special subjects in human experimentation. In Freund, P., ed., *Experimentation with human subjects*. New York: George Braziller, 1969, 262–75.

Lazarus, A. A. *Behavior therapy and beyond*. New York: McGraw-Hill, 1971.

Lessard v. Schmidt. 349 F. Supp. 1078 (1972).

Lerner, B. The Supreme Court and the APA, AERA, NCME test standards. *American Psychologist* 33:10 (1978), 915–19.

Levine, M. *Psychiatry and ethics*. New York: George Braziller, 1972.

Livermore, J. M., Malmquist, C. P., & Meehl, P. E. On the justification for civil commitment. In Gorovitz, S. et al., eds., *Moral problems in medicine*. Englewood Cliffs, N.J.: Prentice-Hall, 1976, 168–81.

London, P. *Behavior control*. New York: Harper & Row, 1969.

Martarella v. Kelley. 373 F. Supp. 487 (1974).

McCormick, R. H. Experimentation on children: Sharing in sociality. *Hastings Center Report*, 6 (December, 1976), 41–46.

Meador, B. & Rogers, C. Person-centered therapy. In Corsini, R., ed., *Current psychotherapies*, 2d ed. Itasca, Ill.: Peacock, 1979, 131–84.

Meister, J. S. "Participation is voluntary . . . " *Hastings Center Report*, 5:2 (April, 1975), 37–38.

Melden, A. I. Utility and moral reason. In DeGeorge, R. T., ed., *Ethics and society*. New York: Doubleday, 1966, 173–96.

Meyerson, W. A. & Hayes, S. C. Controlling the clinician for the client's benefit. In Krapfl, J. E. and Vargas, E. A., eds., *Behaviorism and ethics*. Kalamazoo, Mich.: Behaviordelia, 1979, 243–64.

Michaels, T. F. & Oetting, E. R. The informed consent dilemma: An empirical approach. *Journal of Social Psychology*, 109 (1979), 223–30.

Milgram, S. Behavioral study of obedience. *Journal of Abnormal and Social Psychology*, 67 (1963), 371–78.

Milgram, S. *Obedience to authority*. New York: Harper and Row, 1974.

Mill, J. S. *On liberty*. New York: Crofts Classics, 1947. (1859)

Mill, J. S. *Utilitarianism*. New York: Bobbs-Merrill, 1957. (1861)

Miller, A. G. Role playing: An alternative to deception? A review of the evidence. *American Psychologist*, 27:7 (1972), 623–36.

Mixon, D. Instead of deception. *Journal of the Theory of Social Behavior*, 2 (1972), 147–77.

Mixon, D. Why pretend to deceive? *Personality and Social Psychology Bulletin*, 3:4 (1977), 647–53.

Morgenstern, K. and Tevlin, H. Behavioral interviewing. In Hersen, M. and Bellack, A., eds., *Behavioral assessment*, 2nd ed. New York: Pergamon Press, 1981, 71–100.

Murphy, J. Incompetence and paternalism. *Archiv für Rechts und Sozialphilosophie*, 60 (1974), 465–85.

Murphy, J. Total institutions and the possibility of consent to organic therapies. *Human Rights*, 5 (Fall, 1975), 25–45.

National Education Association v. State of South Carolina. 434 U.S. 1026 (1978).

Nikelly, A. G. Ethical issues in research in student protest. *American Psychologist*, 26:5 (1971), 475–78.

O'Connor v. Donaldson, 43 U.S.L.W. 4929 (1975).

Pavlov, I. P. *Conditioned reflexes: An investigation of the physiological activity of the cerebral cortex*. London: Oxford University Press, 1927.

Perlin, M. Rights of the mentally handicapped. *Bulletin of the American Academy of Psychiatry and the Law*, 4:1 (1976a), 77–86.

Perlin, M. The right to refuse treatment in New Jersey. *Psychiatric Annals*, 6 (June, 1976b), 90–96.

Pettifor, J. L. Practice wise: Ethical issues with special populations. *Canadian Psychological Review*, 20:3 (1979), 148–50.

Petzelt, J. T. & Craddick, R. Present meaning of assessment in psychology. *Professional Psychology* (November 1978), 587–91.

Rachels, J. Do animals have the right to liberty? In Regan, T. and Singer, P., eds., *Animal rights and human obligations*. Englewood Cliffs, N.J.: Prentice-Hall, 1976, 205–23.

Ramsey, P. The enforcement of morals: Nontherapeutic research on children. *Hastings Center Report*, 6:4 (August, 1976), 21–29.

Rawls, J. Two concepts of rules. *Philosophical Review*, 64 (1955), 3–13.

Rawls, J. Justice as fairness. In Feinberg, J. and Gross, H., eds., *Philosophy of law*. Belmont, Calif.: Dickenson, 1975, 276–90.

Reiss, D. Freedom of inquiry and subjects rights: An introduction. *American Journal of Psychiatry,* 134:8 (1977), 891–92.

Rekers, G. A., Bentler, P. M., Rosen, A. C., & Lovaas, O. I. Child gender disturbances: A clinical rationale for intervention. *Psychotherapy: Theory, Research and Practice,* 14:1 (1977), 2–11.

Resnick, J. H. & Schwartz, T. Ethical standards as an independent variable in psychological research. *American Psychologist,* 28:2 (1973), 134–39.

Reveron, D. Mentally ill—And behind bars. *A.P.A. Monitor,* 3 (1982), 8–9.

Richards, D. *The moral criticism of law.* Belmont, Calif.: Dickenson, 1977.

Roberts v. State. Ind. 307 N.E. 2d 505 (1974).

Robitscher, J. Courts, state hospitals and the right to treatment. *American Journal of Psychiatry,* 129:3 (1972), 298–304.

Rogers, C. R. *Counseling and psychotherapy: Newer concepts in practice.* Boston: Houghton Mifflin, 1942.

Rogers, C. R. *Client-centered therapy.* Boston: Houghton Mifflin, 1951. Paperback, 1965.

Rogers, C. R. *A way of being.* Boston: Houghton Mifflin, 1980.

Rogers, C. R. & Skinner, B. F. Some issues concerning the control of human behavior. *Science,* 1243231 (1956), 1057–66.

Roos, P. Human rights and behavior modification. *Mental Retardation,* 12:3 (1974), 3–6.

Ross, W. D. *The right and the good.* Oxford: The Clarendon Press, 1930.

Rouse v. Cameron. 373 F. 2d 451 (1966).

Rozecki v. Gaughan. 450 F. 2d 6 (1972).

Ruebhausen, O. M. & Brim, O. G. Privacy and behavioral research. *American Psychologist,* 21:5 (1966), 423–27.

Rusmore, J. T. *Psychological tests and fair employment: A study of employment testing in the San Francisco Bay area.* State of California Fair Employment Practice Commission, 1967.

Russell, B. *The conquest of happiness.* New York: Liveright Publishing Corp., 1930.

Sade, R. M. Medical care as a right: A refutation. In Gorovitz, S. et al., eds., *Moral problems in medicine.* Englewood Cliffs, N.J.: Prentice-Hall, 1976, pp. 480–85.

Safier, D. & Barnum, R. Patient rehabilitation through hospital work under fair labor standards. *Hospital and Community Psychiatry,* 26:5 (1975), 299–302.

Salzman, L. Truth, honesty and the therapeutic process. In Gorovitz, S. et al., eds., *Moral Problems in Medicine.* Englewood Cliffs, N.J.: Prentice Hall, 1976, 99–103.

Sanders, J. R. Complaints against psychologists and adjudicated informally by APA's committee on scientific and professional ethics and conduct. *American Psychologist,* 34:12 (1979), 1139–44.

Schaeffer, R. G. *Nondiscrimination in employment: Changing perspectives, 1963–1972.* New York: The Conference Board, Report No. 589, 1973.

Schutz, W. C. Encounter. In Corsini, R., ed., *Current psychotherapies.* Itasca, Ill.: Peacock, 1973, 401–43.

Seashore, S. E. Plagiarism, credit assignment and ownership of data. *Professional Psychology,* (November, 1978), 719–22.

Scott v. Plante. 532 F. 2d 937 (1976).

Shelton v. Tucker. 349 F. Supp. 1078 (1972).

Siegel, M. Privacy, ethics, and confidentiality. *Professional Psychology* (April, 1979), 249–58.

Singer, P. *Animal liberation*. New York: Avon Books, 1975.

Skinner, B. F. *The behavior of organisms: An experimental analysis*. New York: Appleton-Century, 1938.

Smart, J. J. C. Extreme and restricted utilitarianism. *Philosophical Quarterly*, 6 (1956), 344–54.

Smith, D. Unfinished business with informed consent procedures. *American Psychologist*, 36:1 (1981), 22–26.

Smith, W. H. Ethical, social, and professional issues in patients' access to psychological test reports. *Bulletin of the Menninger Clinic*, 42:2 (1978), 150–55.

Soble, A. *Informed consent and experimental deception*. (1978a) Unpublished manuscript.

Soble, A. Deception in social science research: Is informed consent possible? *Hastings Center Report* (1978b), 40–46.

Solomon, R. Has not an animal organs, dimensions, senses, affections, passions? *Psychology Today*, (March, 1982), 36–45.

Spiegel, D. & Keith-Spiegel, P. Assignment of publication credits: Ethics and practices of psychologists. *American Psychologist*, 25:8 (1970),738–47.

Stace, W. T. *The concept of morals*. New York: Macmillan, 1965. (1937)

Steadman, H. J. & Cocozza, J. J. *Careers of the criminally insane*. Lexington, Mass.: D. C. Heath, 1974.

Stolz, S. *Ethical issues in behavior modification*. San Francisco: Jossey-Bass, 1978.

Sullivan, D. S. & Deiker, T. E. Subject-experimenter perceptions of ethical issues in human research. *American Psychologist*, 28:7 (1973), 587–91.

Szasz, T. S. *The ethics of psychoanalysis*. New York: Basic Books, 1965.

Szasz, T. S. The right to health. In Gorovitz, S. et al., eds., *Moral problems in medicine*. Englewood Cliffs, N.J.: Prentice-Hall, 1976, 470–80.

Szasz, T. S. Behavior therapy: A critical review of the moral dimensions of behavior modification. *Journal of Behavior Therapy and Experimental Psychology*, 9 (1978), 199–203.

Tarasoff v. Regents of University of California. 529 P. 2d 553 (1974).

Tesch, F. E. Debriefing research participants: Though this be method there is madness to it. *Journal of Personality and Social Psychology*, 35:4 (1977), 217–24.

Thorndike, E. L. *Animal intelligence: Experimental studies*. New York: Macmillan, 1911.

Tooley, M. Abortion and infanticide. *Philosophy and Public Affairs*, 2:1 (1972), 37–65.

Turnbull, H. R., ed. *Concept handbook*. Washington, D. C.: American Association of Mental Deficiency, Special Publication #3, 1977.

Tymchuk, A. J. A perspective on ethics in mental retardation. *Mental Retardation* (December, 1976), 44–47.

Uniform guidelines of employee selection procedures. *Federal Register*, 43:166 (August 25, 1978).

Veatch, R. M. Ethical principles in medical experimentation. In Rivlin, A. M. and Timpane, P. M., eds., *Ethical and legal issues of social experimentation*. The Brookings Institute, 1975.

Veatch, R. M. & Sollitto, S. Human experimentation: Ethical questions persist. *Hastings Center Report*. 3:3 (June, 1973), 1–3.

Vollmer, W. B. The ethics of discrimination and probability. *Professional Psychology* (January, 1970), 514.

von Hirsch, A. Prediction of criminal conduct and preventive confinement of convicted persons. *Buffalo Law Review*, 21 (1972), 717–58.

Walsh, J. Foreign affairs research: Review process rises on ruins of Camelot. *American Psychologist*, 21:5 (1966), 438–40.

Washington, v. Davis. 426 U.S. 229 (1976).

Watson, J. B. & Rayner, R. Conditioned emotional reaction. *Journal of Experimental Psychology*, 3:1 (1920), 1–14.

Welsch v. Likins. 349 F. Supp. 575 (1975).

West, S. G. & Gunn, S. P. Some issues of ethics and social psychology. *American Psychologist*, 33:1 (1978), 30–38.

White, M. D. & White, C. A. Involuntary committed patients: Constitutional rights to refuse treatment. *American Psychologist*, 36:9 (1981), 953–62.

Wolberg, L. R. *The technique of psychotherapy*, 3d ed. New York: Grune and Stratton, 1977.

Wolfensberger, W. Ethical issues in research with human subjects. *Science*, 155 (1967), 47–51.

Wolpe, J. *Psychotherapy by reciprocal inhibition.* Stanford, Calif.: Standford University Press, 1958.

Wolpe, J. Behavior therapy versus psychoanalysis: Therapeutic and social implications. *American Psychologist*, 36:2 (1981), 159–64.

Wood, G. *Fundamentals of psychological research.* Boston: Little, Brown & Co., 1981.

Wright, R. Psychologists and professional liability (malpractice) insurance. *American Psychologist*, 36:12 (1981a), 1485–93.

Wright, R. What to do until the malpractice lawyer comes. *American Psychologist*, 36:12 (1981b), 1535–41.

Wyatt v. Stickney. 325 F. Supp. 781 (1971).

Yoell, W., Stewart, D., Wolpe, J., Goldstein, A., & Speirer, G. Marriage, morals and therapeutic goals: A discussion. *Journal of Behavior Therapy and Experimental Psychiatry*, 2 (1971), 127–32.

Notes

CHAPTER 1

1. If one holds the view that a moral judgment is a *statement* about one's feelings, then such a judgment may be true or false depending on whether or not the statement corresponds to how one in fact feels. If one holds the view that such alleged judgments are merely *expressions* of one's feelings, they are neither true nor false but rather are representative or not depending on one's actual feelings (Ayer, 1946). For example, if a psychologist says that it is wrong to break a confidence under any circumstance when he really feels that it is not wrong to do so, what he is doing in effect on the former view is to make a false statement since it does not correspond with his feelings. On the latter view, which has been called the boo-hurrah theory, the psychologist is booing when he should be hurrahing.

2. What makes people happy varies from person to person. Some prefer physical pleasures and others prefer intellectual pleasures. However, Mill (1861, 1957) thought that those who experience both would prefer the latter to the former:

It is better to be a human being dissatisfied than a pig satisfied, better to be a Socrates dissatisfied than a fool satisfied. And if the fool, or the pig, is of different opinion, it is because they only know their own side of the question. The other party to the comparison knows both sides. (p. 14)

   But despite Mill's belief that a lack of mental cultivation is a chief source of unhappiness, he nevertheless held that no one's happiness can be ignored even if that person prefers (in Mill's words) "lower" forms of pleasure to "higher" forms.

3. It should be pointed out that although Kant uses the term "humanity," he is not referring to the biological species but to rational nature.

4. Kant could argue, however, that the parents were using the child as a means to their own happiness and hence the correct ethical decision would be to remove the child from the home.

CHAPTER 2

1. Kant (1785, 1964), for example, claimed that consequences are totally irrelevant to the moral worth of an action, that what matters is whether the agent acted merely for the sake of duty and respect for the moral law. However, be-

cause we believe consequences should enter into moral decision making at least in some cases, we reject that aspect of his theory even though we defended the categorical and the practical imperatives.

2. However, not all psychologists ignore the effects of deceiving subjects and they are not so much concerned with the obligation to be honest but rather with the possible effects of deception. Some argue that if deception is widespread, research subjects will expect to be deceived and that suspicion will alter experimental results. This problem is discussed in detail in Chapter 6.

3. One could view this case from a consequential standpoint if one focuses on consequences to the client whose confidence is broken, but if viewed solely from the point of view of duty one has in this case, the consequences are not the determining factor in the decision but rather the fact that the psychologist is fulfilling an obligation. Of course what this shows is that consequences can never be completely ignored even when thinking primarily about fulfilling an obligation.

4. Of course there is also a conflict of obligations here and the psychologist must determine whether she wants to be in a position where her primary obligation is to the university. And this depends on her ranking of values.

CHAPTER 4

1. It should be noted that a homosexual may feel pressured into having his sex preference changed and hence his choice to do so would not be voluntary (see Davison, 1976).

2. However, it may be that the client gives *prior* consent to the use of restrictive techniques in cases where he or she knows that engaging in uncontrollable behavior is likely and that the use of a restrictive technique is an effective means of controlling the behavior so that a nonrestrictive technique can then be used.

3. Although psychoanalysts prefer to use the term "patient" or "analysand" because they think "client" is too businesslike, for purposes of consistency we will use that term.

4. According to some psychoanalysts, another reason psychoanalysis has escaped moral criticism is that "analysts themselves are so sensitive to ethical issues and have had to look so closely at the workings of their own superego that they seldom violate ethical principles." (Allen Dyer, personal correspondence)

CHAPTER 5

1. However, if it is true of rights in general that they can be waived, then this is not a right since, from a legal point of view, citizens must receive a certain amount of education whether they want it or not. Thus, the right to education is one that people are in some cases coerced into exercising, and that is rather odd to say about a right. The right to education starts looking more like a duty on the part of citizens to be educated, since one may be legitimately coerced into fulfilling one's duty. In arguing for the right to treatment we want to say that treatment must be made available to those who want it but that in many cases it is not something that a person can be coerced into accepting.

2. For a discussion of a basis for this right, see Tooley (1972).

3. There are really two separate questions here; one is a moral question, the other is factual. (1) do persons have a *moral* right to treatment, and (2) do persons have a *legal* right to treatment? The first is a question about what *ought* to be protected by law. The second is a question about what *is* protected.

4. The difference between mental illness and most other illnesses is that the state can deprive a person of liberty if the individual is mentally ill but not when the illness is of a different (but noncontagious) nature. Thus even if people were able to provide for their own health care, if the state had the power to commit an individual involuntarily it would still have the obligation to provide treatment. This point will be developed later.

5. The extent of that (moral) right depends on the therapist's reasons. If the individual is badly in need of psychological services but unable to afford them, and if there is no other available therapist or means to help the person, it is doubtful that in such a case the therapist has a *moral* right to refuse to treat the person. Legally, of course, there is that right, for the law does not always require that we act morally.

6. It should be noted that the court was not concerned in this case with a right to treatment. This case is significant because the U.S. Supreme Court held for the first time that to confine a person involuntarily who is not dangerous to a mental institution is to violate the constitutional right to liberty and that a "finding of 'mental illness' alone cannot justify a State's locking a person up against his will and keeping him indefinately in simple custodial confinement. Assuming that that term can be given a reasonably precise content and that the 'mentally ill' can be identified with reasonable accuracy, there is still no constitutional basis for confining such persons involuntarily if they are dangerous to no one and can live safely in freedom" (p. 4933).

7. From a practical point of view it does not mater whether a right to treatment was created in order to guarantee certain constitutional rights, or whether that right is implicitly contained in various constitutional rights. But it should be noted that the latter viewpoint seems dominant in the courts. (Most rulings in favor of institutionalized patients have been on the grounds of violation of due process.) In *Welsch v. Likins* the court was very specific on this point: "In holding that plaintiffs possess a right under the due process clause to receive adequate treatment, the Court is not undertaking to 'create substantive constitutional rights . . . .' The absence of any explicit or implicit textual right to treatment in the Constitution is not determinative . . . . The contention in this case is that the right is embodied within the concept of due process. Just as a myriad of other 'rights' have been found to have evolved under the due process clause without expressly being proclaimed in the text of the Constitution, . . . so, too, must it embody the principle being asserted here by the plaintiffs. Having determined that 'some process is due,' the Court may hereafter use the flexibility of the concept of due process in determining the scope of the plaintiff's rights" (p. 499). However, in *Rouse v. Cameron* the court spoke of "the intent to establish a broader right to treatment" (pp. 567–68), which seems to imply that a right to treatment is a right which was created perhaps in order to guarantee due process. At any rate, it is clear that at least some states have recognized this right.

8. However, in this passage Mill also states that "each is the proper guardian of his own health, whether bodily, or mental and spiritual." (We assume Mill means in cases where the person is mentally and financially able to do so.) This passage was also quoted in a footnote in *Lessard v. Schmidt* (1972) in which the court stated that "the power of the State to deprive a person of

the fundamental liberty to go unimpeded about his or her own affairs must rest on a consideration that society has a compelling interest in such deprivation" (p. 1084).

9. We shall postpone a discussion of what counts as rational and autonomous until later in the chapter.

10. We say "to oneself" and omit "to others" since paternalism is coercion for the person's own good. Coercion for the good of others is not a paternalistic act even though in the long-run it may turn out to have good consequences for the individual.

11. In commenting on this chapter, Michael Perlin, director of the Division of Mental Health Advocacy of New Jersey, responded to Dworkin's statement as follows: "Sure, but not behind bars."

12. "Of course, only an infinitesimal percentage of state hospital patients have ever been found to be judicially 'incompetent' " (Perlin, 1976b, p. 90).

13. We are concerned here only with treatment and not questions that arise about involuntary commitment in general. Those involve, for example, the issues of privacy and the retention of other civil rights while institutionalized.

CHAPTER 7

1. Validity is a statistical concept referring to correlation between test scores and some outside criterion or criteria. Validity is an indication of whether the test measures what it is supposed to measure. Because it is a probabilistic concept, there are varying degrees of validity.

2. Differential validity occurs when two subgroups differ significantly with regard to validity coefficients or when these coefficients differ significantly from zero in either one or both of the subgroups (Boehm, 1972); in other words, different formulas are used for different subgroups.

3. A major issue regarding this Act has been and may continue to be "equal pay for comparable (not necessarily equal) work."

Index